Caring Management in Health Organizations

Health and Innovation Set

coordinated by
Corinne Grenier

Volume 3

Caring Management in Health Organizations

A Lever for Crisis Management

Edited by
Christelle Bruyère

iSTE

WILEY

First published 2022 in Great Britain and the United States by ISTE Ltd and John Wiley & Sons, Inc.

ISTE Ltd
27-37 St George's Road
London SW19 4EU
UK

www.iste.co.uk

John Wiley & Sons, Inc.
111 River Street
Hoboken, NJ 07030
USA

www.wiley.com

Library of Congress Control Number: 2022941871

British Library Cataloguing-in-Publication Data
A CIP record for this book is available from the British Library
ISBN 978-1-78630-795-8

Contents

Foreword

Caring Management in Health-care Institutions: Oxymoron or Pleonasm?

The question may seem incongruous, so it is important to remember that, in the short-term, the return of care to the forefront has its roots in the crisis of psychosocial risks at the beginning of this century. This crisis, assuming that it has not become chronic, has highlighted the existence of abusive, sometimes malicious, work relationships, embodied in the worst of situations by moral harassment, that is, the harasser and the harassed, the executioner and the victim, trapped in a strictly interpersonal, often reductive, approach to the deterioration of the work relationship. This degradation was raised and documented fairly early on in the care environment, either in a general way through the systemic description of the undesirable effects of the reorganization of a health-care system in search of efficiency, or in an individual way, through the denunciation of the excesses of power of a particular official with regard to their collaborators. It is regrettable that the link between the two is often insufficiently highlighted, with the expression of personal failings, in practice, often made possible by the shortcomings of the organization.

In any case, we started talking about suffering at work, that is, work that *destroys health*, only to remember that if work can cause suffering, it is precisely when it breaks with its purpose to *build health*. As a result, for a long time, we thought that we had lost control over work, that we no longer had any room for maneuver, that we were condemned to experience a deterioration in professional relations that was made inescapable, sometimes by the transformations at work, sometimes by archaisms. Then we gradually sought to emancipate ourselves from a mortifying vision and to identify what in some circles was protective. The logic of the evaluation of *constraints* was counterbalanced by that of the mobilization of *resources*, and the logic of the evaluation of *psychosocial risks* (PSR) was counterbalanced by that of *quality of life at work* (QLW). Many people have seen this as nothing more than semantics, while others have perceived a possible paradigm shift. This change, beyond an ideological opposition between the two poles of a duality, testifies to the search for a new balance between an approach to work seen exclusively as a factor of exposure to risks and a more anthropological and developmental approach. The health sector is well placed to know the difference between a curative approach and a health promotion approach. The two approaches do not use the same resources, nor do they act on the same levers or in the same timeframe. Above all, the two approaches are not in opposition, but rather articulated in an iterative manner.

Also, just as the prevention of psychosocial risks echoes suffering at work, a caring manner echoes the quality of life at work. The question, therefore, becomes that of the organizational configurations that allow this caring manner to be learned and expressed, prevent deviations, even perversions, and encourage cooperation. Such configurations exist. But one must be careful not to be naive; they do not arise spontaneously or through magical thinking. Similarly, we must beware of demagoguery; they do not thrive in a context where the promise of total autonomy left to the teams would take the place of a caring manner. A responsible organization does not rely on the natural goodness of some to make others happy. It is interested in the *work to be done* and in the best combination of resources of all kinds available to do it.

Let us move on to the object of care. To watch means to be vigilant, to be awake. To be caring is therefore to be attentive to well-being, in this case well-being at work. Why is this? Because understanding what is going on allows us to act on the sources of our *presence* at work. Being caring in management is the opposite of negligence or managerial incompetence, which we now know has a significant cost for employees, organizations and users, in this case patients. The quality of work is above all the concern for work well done, which satisfies both the recipient of this work (the customer, the user, the patient, etc.), its provider (the manager, the employer, the financier, the prescriber) and its producer (the staff, whether caregivers or not).

The caring manager certainly has values and beliefs but is not a Samaritan. They are aware of the causal link between the care given to the caregiver and the care given to the person being cared for. They are concerned about what builds the health of their employees at work. They know that the quality of the work done by the agents generates the joint recognition of the patient and their peers, and therefore self-esteem, one of the pillars of psychological balance. To this end, the manager *organizes the work,* that is, does their *organizational work*: they support the activity of their colleagues, seek to solve their problems, facilitate interactions with other services, allocate resources and regulate activity, in particular the workload; they are interested in the work activity itself, in the real work, not only in dictating it and in overviews. They reassure and relieve their team so that they can work in a framework that is conducive to the calmest possible deployment of an activity that is by nature trying; they listen and bring up for arbitration problems whose resolution goes beyond their sphere of decision, even if it means reporting on a postponement of the solution or even on a failure. Of course, they can bring croissants to the morning service meeting, but this care is anecdotal compared to the expectations of managerial care! This is a real professional skill, among and in the same way as the others. It is a skill in its own right, one of the essential conditions *of* work and one of the components of working *conditions*.

The French National Authority for Health (*La Haute Autorité de santé*) has recognized that there can be no quality and safety of care without quality of work and quality of life at work (QLW). It has made QLW one of the 15 criteria for the certification of health-care institutions for quality of care. Paragraph 3.5 of the certification standard states that, throughout the health-care organization:

> Professionals are involved in a quality of work life approach driven by governance with, on the one hand, a QLW policy, and on the other hand, measures to manage interpersonal difficulties and conflicts.

The implementation of such a policy goes far beyond a commitment to the principle, even if it is put on a charter. In addition to management's stated commitment, it must be dedicated in the *concrete*, *irreversible* and *constant* deployment of an approach that is appropriate for all. This policy, which has become binding and the filter by which actions taken will henceforth be judged, must be based on principles of action that dictate the conduct of everyone, at all levels of the institution. The result is never final and is constantly reexamined, and this is both the difficulty and the greatness of the work, which will be reflected in the environment. Although complex to describe, this climate is nevertheless perceptible, through the *experience* of employees, as well as *observable*, through absenteeism, turnover, commitment, etc. This climate will promote the performance of care and that of the establishment.

This attention, this care for the work, not only depends on the good will of the actors and does not fit well with the only incantation of care. It implies the respect of methodological requirements that give it substance on a daily basis. It is based on a work environment and organization that are conducive to it and therefore well thought out, because, in practice, the intention of caring quickly comes up against real life and the constraints of the *real activity*. The latter must find a space where they can be expressed and regulated. A caring manner must be deployed and constantly secured in dedicated places and times.

Among the methodological requirements known, there is that of an approach developed in consultation with professionals and their representatives, monitored and evaluated in a shared manner. Above all, this approach, even if it is driven and informed by their views, must not remain the business of specialists, or be reserved for the establishment's prevention or quality control officers. The worst pitfall of benevolence would be to be *separated* from the actual care activity and from everything that makes it possible in the field, at the patient level. Clearly, managerial benevolence is not the responsibility of a specialized department and cannot be guaranteed by a procedure. It is a working framework designed to ensure that each decision takes into account its impact on the work of the agents. For example, the purchasing department must bear in mind what the acquisition and generalization of a given piece of equipment will mean in concrete terms for the staff. This leads to a purchasing process that leaves room for consultation and experimentation, differentiation and collective validation rather than just price criteria, which can lead to unsuitable solutions that are a real source of irritation. Similarly, a department head will have to evaluate a priori what resources their clinical project will mobilize within their own department, but also in other departments, etc. In short, while benevolence cannot be prescribed, it cannot be improvised either.

On this point, Mathieu Detchessahar's work on the *deliberate enterprise* sheds light on the HAS reference framework when the latter invites the creation of a new system:

> within the work units of spaces – times for collective discussions that allow for a diagnosis and concrete proposals on the conditions and organization of work, as well as devices to support professionals in the search for solutions aimed at improving the organization of work as close to the field as possible.

It follows that management must be finalized. It is not good-natured, it does not shy away from controversy or confrontation and it is not naïve or manipulative. It is intended to solve problems, to improve situations, within a framework that is readable, intelligible and marked by organizational justice. When it fails, and it will fail in the future, the HAS says that prevention and regulation mechanisms must take over:

> The aim is to maintain the cohesion of the teams. Management, and especially local management, plays an essential role in this area and must be supported in this function.

In hospitals, Article L. 6143-2-1 of the Public Health Code also enshrines this managerial and collective dimension of QLW. It stipulates that public health establishments must adopt a *social project* dealing in particular with training, internal dialogue within the divisions, the right to within the divisions, the right of expression of staff, the improvement of working conditions, the forward-looking and prospective management of jobs and qualifications. A specific section must be devoted to the QLW of medical and non-medical staff. It is this whole that must be taken into account.

But, let us face it, benevolence is ultimately not a very normative concept and we should be careful not to want to qualify and circumscribe it legally in the hope of naming it, recognizing it and, if necessary, sanctioning its absence. Similarly, it is not encapsulated in a standardized process and cannot be reduced to compliance with a decisional logigram. On the other hand, as we have seen, it does not escape a methodological framework that includes rigorous managerial devices and equipment. Otherwise, the promise it holds will end up as wishful thinking and, worst of all, as a form of disenchantment. The difficulty lies in finding the right balance between a compassionate veil lance, which depends solely on the individual qualities of the manager, and a prescribed and *overdosed* institutional benevolence.

In the first case, it would be enough to recruit people with a natural gift for *care*, capable of getting out of any situation, whatever the organizational configuration in which they would be placed, like mercenaries of care in a hostile environment! Other professional sectors have tried this, deploying what has been called *dose-based management* of their personnel. This consists of selecting the most suitable for the job and then separating them when they are worn out... before noticing the catastrophic effects of such an approach on the skills and attractiveness of the said sector.

In the second case, it would be enough to enter into benevolence, as one enters into quality, by equipping oneself with a multitude of procedures, the success of which would be based on the respect of instructions and standards that would allow one to check the "caring" box in the checklist of the perfect manager.

The in-between is all the more difficult to find as reality constantly reminds caregivers. They see benevolence as a slogan that is contradicted daily by the facts, or even as an instrument designed to divert attention from the real difficulties: resources. It is true that the budgetary context seems to make the intention a paradoxical injunction. To advocate caring management would be like wanting to confirm, endorse or hide restrictive policies. Does this mean that well-manned organizations are by nature proximal and caring? That they always give due consideration to all staff? That they guarantee their development and thus the quality of care? Or should we admit that the means do not lead to well-being or at least do not suffice? The truth is that, locally, there are services that provide job satisfaction. They help each other; the target is not the happiness of the caregiver but the care of the patient. The quality of the latter produces a positive perception of the former, and it is the effectiveness of this coupling that we must be convinced of in order to hope to work on the irreducible tensions of the means/mission duality. The examples in this book provide an illustration of what such a framework looks like in practice.

To think otherwise would be to assume that there is no room for maneuver at the local level. The head of department would be deprived of any power to act on the organization of the work of their teams, a convenient solution for dispensing with the work of organizing their responsibility. To deny the existence of the constraint would be wrong, but to think only in terms of the constraint would be to deny the existence of the resources that can be mobilized through a cooperative, collegial and supportive approach. Yet, even at the height of the social crisis that shook a large telephone company in the early 2010s, there were pockets of resources where managers managed to build local compromises that made it possible to reorganize in a humane way, to the benefit of all. This observation is universal. It applies to all fields of activity. This is why this book is smart to have devoted its third part to the inspiring exploration of professional worlds "outside health".

In the end, benevolence is the expression of a non-gendered competence exercised in an organizational framework oriented toward the sustainability of the activity, which everyone – and this is the good news – can acquire through learning and collective experience, as well as to give an account in a logic of recognition of professionalism. This is what this book explains.

Hervé LANOUZIÈRE
Director of the Institut national du travail, de l'emploi et de la formation professionnelle
Inspecteur général des affaires sociales (IGAS)

Introduction

"Be kind" is the last instruction given to a manager.

Caring management, slow management, alternative management, etc. have gained ground in the last decade owing to the effects of multiple factors: the spread of new information and communication technologies, increased competition, intensification of work, aspiration to greater autonomy in the organization of work, evolution of markets toward an increasing personalization of needs and services, the development of independent work and so on.

These developments are encouraging traditional companies to adapt and to transform. We can see the development of liberated companies, telecommuting, autonomous teams, co-working spaces, etc. The objective is to find a certain compromise between performance and well-being at work. Compromise is understood here in the strong sense (Barel 1989) of a rewarding cohabitation between performance and well-being, generating value for the various stakeholders (beneficiary, employee, manager, suppliers, prescribers, etc.), and not a divisive fusion leading to a choice of sides (performance or well-being).

This search for compromise is not foreign to health organizations. Like other sectors of activity, the health and social sector is not exempt from the productivity contracts, which impose the search for efficiency, speed of execution or optimization of means, or from the constraints of quality, traceability or safety that create an intensification of work.

How then to reconcile performance and well-being at work? Is this possible? Are health-care organizations capable of transforming themselves and showing flexibility? Those working in the field seem to be limited in their actions by a work

---

Introduction written by Christelle BRUYÈRE.

organization that is restrictive in terms of workload, on the one hand, and reporting, on the other hand, which prevents the development of benevolence to this day. This lack of time, which has become even more of a problem today than it was 20 years ago, makes benevolence at work more essential but also more difficult to implement.

In some respects, talking about caring management in a context where changes in the world of work are resulting in an increase in employee health problems may seem provocative and illusory. Some 63% of caregivers suffer from one or more symptoms of professional burnout, according to the ONI survey (*Ordre national des infirmiers*, 2018). Just over 42% of respondents thus report feeling burned out very often at the end of the workday, and a nearly identical proportion report feeling tired in the morning before facing another workday. Is it then a malicious management that is the cause or a health-care system that is not itself caring? The weight of reforms and procedures, recruitment difficulties, the growing power of administration, the plethora of management tools, etc.

It is not so much the search for culprits that interests us, but rather the valorization of innovative managerial actions because, faced with these signs that we can no longer ignore, it seems necessary to project ourselves into the future. Indeed, despite all the professional difficulties inherent in health-care institutions, we simultaneously note testimonies from caregivers stating that work contributes to their happiness. There are no "ready-made recipes" or "models to follow", but rather contexts, people and teams that initiate and implement managerial innovations in their establishments.

It is with this in mind that a working group of researchers from different backgrounds (management sciences, medicine, sociology, psychology, education sciences, public health) and professionals in the field (health managers, nurses, health institution managers, project managers, health and social sector training center managers) decided to produce this book. This collective is not a passing phase. It is part of a history of nearly 20 years between three training institutes in the Loire working to develop managerial skills in health[1] and bringing together researchers, students and professionals in the health and social sectors.

In addition, a research team from Saint-Etienne in management sciences (COACTIS) is exploring the so-called "caring" managerial practices of local

1 Located in the southeast quarter of France, in the Auvergne-Rhônes-Alpes region, the three institutes are the IAE (*Institut des administrations et des entreprises*) Saint-Étienne (and, more particularly, the MOSS Master's degree in the management of health and social organizations), the IFCS (*Institut de formation des cadres de santé*) of the Saint-Etienne University Hospital Center and the ENSEIS (*École nationale des solidarités, de l'encadrement et de l'intervention sociale*) of Firminy.

organizations for better performance (economic, social and environmental performance). EHPAD[2] clinics and hospitals are all fields of study investigated by this team, and made part of in the managerial training of the IAE de Saint-Etienne in order to raise awareness among the managers of tomorrow.

The objective of the book is to defend the idea that sustainable performance is no longer an option in health-care organizations. It is necessary to capitalize on and disseminate "successful" caring management practices. The current context linked to the COVID-19 crisis only reinforces this position.

Management can certainly be harmful, but it can also be very caring, a vector of performance and recognition. It is not just a matter of happy washing and must be translated into concrete practices. This book takes an interdisciplinary look at the issue of caring management in health-care and is based on experiments carried out, for the most part, in the Rhône-Alpes region and on interviews with professionals and researchers involved in the subject.

The book is structured in three parts:

– Part 1 offers a political, historical and international look at "caring" management in health. It is composed of four chapters highlighting the committed visions of two medical managers, the founders of an association campaigning for the enhancement of the human relationship in health and researchers involved in the topic of performance in health-care. One of the chapters will focus on caring management in the context of a crisis, and in particular a health crisis during COVID-19, in order to identify how this managerial approach can be a lever for crisis management. Indeed, COVID-19 required radical reorganization, in a very short period of time. What remains of caring management in this context? Does it still have its place?

– Part 2 relates the successful experiences of health-care institutions that have opted for caring management with all its difficulties, pitfalls and riches. What could be better than management by evidence? Here, four chapters provide concrete experiences expressed, discussed and analyzed through the views of psychologists, sociologists, managers and researchers.

– Finally, Part 3 explores other sectors of activity beyond the health sector. Indeed, the subject of caring management not only in health-care institutions; issues of organization and sustainable performance are multisectoral and openness to other professional cultures fuels the debate. This is why three chapters are dedicated to

2 EHPAD: *Etablissement d'hébergement pour personnes âgées dépendantes* are the most widespread forms of residential care for seniors in France, what we would call nursing homes in English.

managerial issues in various national and international organizations, from sectors as varied as agri-food, industry and education.

Being kind is not a job! Neither is being caring! And managing with care: what is that exactly?

Enjoy your reading.

PART 1

A Committed Vision of Caring Management

Introduction to Part 1

The news of the last few years – social movements, conflicts, tensions and more – tends to show that the constrained context in which the staff of social and medico-social organizations develop is the cause of much dissatisfaction. Among them, we find, for example, feelings of lack of resources (human, material, financial, etc.), of a loss of meaning, or even of a deterioration in working conditions, a lack of time to provide quality care and a constant tug-of-war between economic objectives to be achieved and qualitative objectives to be satisfied. The COVID-19 crisis has only accentuated the debate around caring management. Is it a luxury that we can only afford when everything is going well? Or is it, on the contrary, what keeps our heads above water when everything seems to be falling apart? Is it a lever for achieving sustainable performance and well-being at work?

It is here in Part 1 that a political, historical and international look at the issue is proposed in order to define the stakes and limits and to see the favorable outcomes.

Chapter 1 takes a critical look at the very existence of caring management in the health sector based on interviews with two committed medical managers. The multiplication of reforms and procedures, recruitment difficulties, a hyper-competitive training system based on competitive examinations, strengthening of the powers of the administration and the massive deployment of management, control and surveillance tools are all among the factors that hinder the development of caring management of health-care institutions.

However, can we not project ourselves into a future where sustainable performance and well-being at work would be compatible? Under what conditions? With what means? Chapter 2 looks at the value of human relationships in health-care organizations, with a focus on Uruguay as an international exception with its care model centered on medical humanism.

Chapter 3 then provides a historical overview of the problem, reminding us that the question we are interested in is not a fad. It is rooted in our history and the current changes in work (intensification, productivity, traceability, etc.) make it all the more significant.

Finally, Chapter 4 raises the question of caring management as a lever for the anticipation, management and repair of crises in the health-care system, and the COVID-19 crisis in particular. We must learn from the current crisis and from past crises in order to be able to deal with them together in the future.

1

Caring Management and the Health-care System: The Vision of Two Committed Doctor-managers

At a time when the words "management" and "care" are increasingly used in everyday language, it seems interesting, to study the link between caring management and health, to interview operational managers at the heart of the French health system. These two practitioners, who have been and are still in management positions, define themselves above all as doctors and researchers and do not necessarily feel qualified to talk about management. On the contrary, their experience as field actors places them at the heart of considerations, especially since they belong to the hospital world, the hub of the French health system.

Michèle Cottier, university professor – hospital practitioner – has been head of the histology-embryology laboratory of the University Hospital of Saint-Étienne since 2003. Regarding her research activities, she directed the interdisciplinary laboratory for the study of aerosolized nanoparticles from 2011 to 2015. Franck Chauvin, university professor – hospital practitioner – has been head of the public health department of the *Institut de cancérologie Lucien Neuwirth* since 2004. In 2004, he contributed to the creation of the Hygée Center, whose mission is to develop cancer prevention in the Auvergne-Rhône-Alpes region. He has been its deputy director since its inception. The complementarity of their profiles is even stronger and more interesting in their recent appointments: Michèle Cottier has been dean of the Université Jean Monnet de Saint-Étienne since November 2015, and Franck Chauvin has been president of the *Haut-Conseil de la santé publique* (French High Council for Public Health) since April 2017.

Chapter written by Carole MURE and Cécile ROMEYER.

These two doctors, engaged in their different functions, have agreed to tell us, in the context of this book, about their view of caring management in the French health system, and more particularly in hospitals in individual semidirected interviews, conducted in parallel. The professional is at the heart of their reflections: whether it is through the quality of the care given to the people being treated or the well-being of the staff themselves. Both agree on the idea that it is difficult to talk about caring management without questioning the environment of people's work:

> What is our environment? Do we understand it? If we don't understand it, it doesn't seem to me to be a good basis for management. (Michèle Cottier)

In the hospital, it is therefore a question of questioning the health-care system.

Based on their reflections, we will explore how and why the health-care system is in crisis and what the possible ways forward are. We will then focus on the contributions of the health crisis linked to COVID-19. We will then conclude by highlighting their vision of caring management in health-care.

1.1. A health-care system that is insufficiently caring toward its staff and users

When asked about the notion of care and caring management, the responses of our two doctors were identical: it is difficult to talk about caring management in a system that is not caring itself. They both tried to explain to us how and why the health-care system is not caring enough in their eyes.

1.1.1. *From the training of hospital staff to compartmentalization between different professions*

One of the reasons for the lack of care in the health-care system is related to the way in which the training of health-care professionals is carried out. Let us consider that of physicians, which Michèle Cottier summarizes as follows:

> It's a hyper-competitive system where the principle of competition is permanent: you have to pass a competitive exam to get in, and pass a competitive exam to get out; whether you're a university hospital worker or a hospital worker, you have to be appointed to a hospital, etc. By definition, competition does not develop the collective spirit! It is difficult to manage in a caring manner without a collective spirit! Similarly, the fact that the different types of professionals never meet

> during their training does not facilitate communication between them afterwards and inevitably leads to difficulties in getting to know each other, understanding each other, understanding each other's issues and working together: in this context, how can we develop a team spirit?

This separation between the professions during their studies and professional training will contribute to the creation of compartmentalization in the hospital system: compartmentalization, for example, between the medical and nursing approaches, which "places the treatment and care of the patient before any economic consideration", and the economic logic promoted by the administrative staff, which "advocates the pooling of costs and the definition of activities according to revenues" (Vallette et al. 2015). Similarly, access to the functions of directors being reserved to the body of hospital directors may have contributed to reinforcing the gap between the two approaches.

To go further, we can highlight the compartmentalization of administration, paramedical staff and medical staff, which differ in particular by their organizational structure with their own operating rules, by their forms of recognition and ethics, by their place within the hospital community and by their feeling of belonging to a different entity (respectively, the hospital, the department and the medical profession) (Romeyer 2001). All this leads to a lack of dialog between doctors and administration or between doctors and carers, even though they are supposed to work together in a coordinated way to ensure good patient care. More particularly, the people in charge of these different professions do not develop any shared analysis of the activity, each remaining within its own logic and aiming at its own objectives:

> This whole system does not contribute to a dialogue between the people in charge and does not contribute to shared analyses. (Michèle Cottier)

Michèle Cottier also evokes the notion of trust: given the high level of responsibility a doctor has when faced with a decision (diagnosis, therapeutic decision), a responsibility that they bear alone and do not share, it is difficult to delegate under conditions that they do not control. Tensions and compartmentalization are thereby reinforced further. This issue of trust can also be found between management and physicians, as shown by Bérard (2013) and Gavault et al. (2014), with reluctance to consider that physicians can be managers responsible for their activity, which translates into difficulties in delegating this management to them at the level of the individual hubs, for example.

1.1.2. *The impact of the reforms on the governance and strategy of hospital establishments*

According to Valette et al. (2015), since 2005, reforms have aimed, on the one hand, to increase the involvement of physicians in the internal management of health-care institutions and, on the other hand, to strengthen the powers and responsibilities of directors of health-care institutions (see the Order of 2 May 2005 and the HPST Act of 21 July 2009). The objective is to encourage administrative and medical actors to take the economic impact into account more in their decisions and in their medical and health-care practices (Domy et al. 2014).

The words of our two doctors reveal the consequences of the implementation of these reforms on their activity and practice. Several ideas put forward in the interviews show a certain loss of points of reference on the part of nursing and medical staff.

A loss of points of reference linked primarily to the impression of a lack of a clear vision of the rules within the hospital, particularly due to the contradiction between the two logics (medical and economic) with which doctors are confronted. This is referred to as "role tension", which has significant negative effects:

> Decreased job satisfaction, organizational involvement and engagement at work can also manifest when the employee perceives their role as ambiguous or conflicting. (Loubet 2011)

The two physicians interviewed reveal throughout the interviews these tensions of role and this lack of understanding of the system, going thus far as to speak of a "nebula where nothing is understood" (Michèle Cottier), specifying that "the system does everything to hide the keys; physicians lost the keys a long time ago" (Franck Chauvin). In their roles as managers, they highlight the paradoxical injunctions resulting from the system, which is a "jungle in which there are no rules" (Franck Chauvin) and where "procedures have been piled up" (Michèle Cottier). Since the system is incomprehensible, health-care professionals have difficulty understanding the decisions made because they seem to be out of step "with the reality of the field and the reality of needs" (Michèle Cottier). This can generate behavior that can be perceived as violent, adding to the system's lack of care: "people therefore force their arguments" (Franck Chauvin).

The loss of points of reference can also be linked to a loss of meaning. For doctors, it corresponds to the absence of a clear medical vision on the part of those in charge of the hospital:

> There is already this question at the foundation of the hospital: the capacity of the person in charge to really manage and give direction to an activity that is the care of patients, because we must not forget that everything must be done from there. (...) Management is not necessarily imbued with what caring for a patient entails. (Michèle Cottier)

This lack of medical vision seems all the more regrettable in the eyes of the practitioner as he/she compares this situation to that of the university, where the definition of the institution's strategy is in the hands of a teacher-researcher. This person is thus able to give direction and define a project that will make sense to the community of teacher-researchers (in terms of training and research) and students.

This loss of points of reference generates a certain uneasiness among health professionals, particularly among those in management positions. "I find the system aggressive (...) it is no more caring towards managers than towards agents" (Franck Chauvin). This malaise is explained by De Pouvourville (2010) as the injunction to be made of management, which would cause a weakening of identity among doctors. The malaise is also acute among university hospital doctors, who depend on both the hospital and the university institution and find themselves lost between the two, whereas until now they felt more involved in the hospital, making the project very meaningful to them.

In addition to a loss of points of reference, the reforms have resulted in a strengthening of the powers of the administration. Indeed, the HPST law of 2009 gave hospitals a supervisory board and an executive board, strengthening the powers of the director at the same time. The representation of the medical profession on the supervisory board is relatively weak, although its role is strategic (it decides on the strategic positions of the establishment and exercises permanent control over the management and financial health of the establishment). Within the board of directors, medical power is balanced by the fact that, on the one hand, the doctors – although they are in the majority – are appointed by the director and, on the other hand, by the fact that they have fewer duties compared to the executive council, which they replace. The director also appoints the doctors who head the divisions. The hospital administration is therefore seen by medical and nursing staff as a body "which controls, which supervises in the repressive sense of the term; it receives orders from above and is itself supervised" (Michèle Cottier). Hospital professionals have the impression that the objective of profitability of the activity (by contributing, for example, to the removal of beds) takes precedence over the main vocation of the hospital: to take care of the patients. Michèle Cottier notes that patients find themselves "in hellish conditions of care". A documentary made by a teacher-researcher based on interviews with doctors from various public hospitals illustrates very well the impact of the implementation of activity-based pricing on the daily lives of caregivers (Marie-Astrid Le Teule 2020, "Le prix de la vie"). Moatti noted in 2018 these same impressions:

> Caregivers are unwillingly thrown into a race to the bottom that rations time for patients, undermines the quality of care, and alters the meaning of their mission. (Moatti 2018)

This strengthening of the administration's power is also reflected in the implementation of management tools that reinforce the impression, mentioned by Michèle Cottier, of having tools for control and monitoring in the hospital. She deplores the management charts implemented by the administration, which health-care professionals do not understand and which they find very difficult to analyze (or even have no time to analyze). These tools are not seen as helping to manage the activity or a service. Here, we find the vision of Moisdon (2012), according to which the tools are conceived with an evaluation and incentive purpose to prevent the regulator from meddling in the organization. They do not help internal actors guide themselves in a real reconfiguration of their organization; the purpose is not adapted to the actors in the field and, in particular, to doctors in positions of responsibility. The latter thus have "often limited confidence in the data often limited in the data produced by management, which makes a common diagnosis difficult" (Aubert 2014).

1.1.3. *A saturated and weakened health-care system*

In addition, both practitioners speak of a health-care system that is saturated. On the one hand, they note an increase in chronic diseases in connection with an increase in life expectancy and a stability of life expectancy in good health, that is, an increase in chronic pathologies linked to the aging of the population. They also point out the difficulty in recruiting care providers in hospitals, whether they are doctors or paramedics. Finally, they underline the paradox of the health system, from a financial point of view, by referring to the activity-based pricing of health establishments: "the worse a patient is, the happier the system is because he is working" (Franck Chauvin). As a result, "we will no longer be able to take care of everyone if there are so many patients" (Franck Chauvin). This observation has a direct impact on doctors, who feel that they are losing their professional ethics. The idea of not being able to care for everyone clashes with their commitments stemming from the Hippocratic Oath: "I will give my care to the indigent and to anyone who asks me for it", and from the Declaration of Geneva:

> I will not permit considerations of age, disease or disability, creed, ethnic origin, gender, nationality, political affiliation, race, sexual

> orientation, social standing or any other factor to intervene between my duty and my patient.

As a result, their medical values are affected, making their professional practice conditions more complex. This observation does not stop with physicians but extends to all caregivers, as indicated by the President of the French Republic, Emmanuel Macron, in his speech on the transformation of the health-care system "Taking care of everyone," (*Prendre soin de chacun*) delivered at the Élysée Palace on September 18, 2018: "malaise has now taken hold deeply".

The French health-care system, built after the Second World War, was inspired by the Beveridgian (welfare) and Bismarckian (insurance) models. It is based on three axes: social insurance, assistance and universal public services. Franck Chauvin speaks of "three prongs of social insurance". Its foundations are today undermined by the emergence of risks such as unemployment and dependence, the increase in inequalities such as salaries and career paths and by the difficulty of financing social protection. For Michèle Cottier, "the roots of the problem are deep and pervasive". She also points out the importance of the social mission of the hospital forgotten by the budgetary system.

Finally, the French health-care system is recognized as performing well from the point of view of the health-care system, but it is weakened and under pressure. Indeed, it was designed for the needs of a society that are no longer those of today. This observation was also mentioned by Emmanuel Macron in 2018. Moreover, Franck Chauvin specifies that doctors themselves have played a role in bringing about this situation, particularly by refusing to "transfer part of their activity to non-physicians, to caregivers" for fear of competition and therefore for fear of a decrease in their income.

1.2. Some ways to make the health system more caring

Following this assessment, it seems necessary to project ourselves into the future. Franck Chauvin specifies this idea: We always say to ourselves that it will be for later, but there is a moment when we are faced with it. This urgency to work on the system is also put forward by Michèle Cottier: "it is now that we must invest for the future". Above all, the two doctors talk about the importance of sharing this assessment to give meaning to the strategy to adopt. It is a matter of agreeing on the starting point to "agree on where we want to go" (Franck Chauvin). It is therefore a matter of conducting "an informed, broad and open debate, involving all stakeholders, first and foremost caregivers and patients" (Moatti 2018) with the aim of finding ways to reform the health-care system. A desire for sharing between the different actors is thus put forward to "recreate trust to create a link" (Michèle Cottier). This projection requires the involvement of all to define objectives for the benefit of all and to redefine the reasons for being and the roles of each of the actors in the health system.

From there, the two testimonies put forward and question different axes of reflection.

1.2.1. *Establishing medical or shared governance between physicians and administrators*

Michèle Cottier would like to see a system of governance for the hospital that is closer to the university model in which the president (teacher-researcher) assumes responsibility for the whole and then delegates to the director general of services (administrative). Delegation favors the maintenance of a link and a certain degree of accountability that allows the president to have the legitimacy to intervene when necessary. She emphasizes the importance of delegating to a person with complementary competitive skills, as well as the importance of trust between the president and the director general of services, between whom dialog must be of high quality and allow for shared analyses. Michèle Cottier mentions the example of cancer centers in France, in which the physician has regained a more central position in the governance system through a repositioning of the health-care offering (similar to the central role of the teacher-researcher with respect to the training offering in universities). These private, not-for-profit, monothematic hospitals are in fact run by a pair of doctors and a deputy director general with a managerial background, often a hospital director. As a result, "cancer centers constitute a model of private non-profit hospital that seems to be performing well" (Aubert 2014). However, it should be remembered that this type of establishment is special in that practitioners treat a single pathology, unlike public hospitals:

> The authority of the chief medical officer is then close to that of a department head in a hospital; a chief medical officer is legitimate insofar as the establishment they direct carries out one or more activities with which they are familiar at the clinical level. This refers more to the role of a head of a division who would be a decision-maker than the head of a multidisciplinary establishment. (Aubert 2014)

The practitioner also mentions the case of establishments in English-speaking countries, some of which are still run by doctors. Indeed:

> In the past, hospitals were routinely run by doctors. That has changed. In the United Kingdom (UK) and the United States (US), most

> hospital chief executive officers (CEOs) are non-physician managers. Of the 6,500 hospitals in the US, only 235 are led by physicians. (Goodall 2011)

However, the results of a study in the *US News and World Report on best hospitals*, reported by Amanda Goodall (2011), show that physician-led facilities are not more efficient.

Another solution could therefore be to promote a balance of power within the hospital. This is the view of François-Jérôme Aubert in his thesis entitled "*La décision à l'hôpital public: quelles relations entre directeur et médecin?*" "The creation of a situation of trust between directors and physicians is essential to increase the quality of decision-making within the hospital" (Aubert 2014).

The next step, as Michèle Cottier and Franck Chauvin recommend, would be for directors and physicians to jointly and clearly define the institution's strategy to enable each to work for the benefit of the whole, according to their skills. The establishment of such a dialog could facilitate the construction of management tools adapted to the needs of health professionals and the institution's strategy.

1.2.2. *Developing prevention*

"Improving the health of the population while ensuring fair financing and meeting the expectations of the population" is the primary goal of a health system (Chevreul 2015). However, as previously mentioned, given the increase in the number of chronic diseases and the rise in life expectancy, the current system is reaching its limits. It is therefore necessary to consider it differently, that is to say, to solve the problem of the number of patients to receive care. Consequently, the idea is to develop prevention to reduce the number of chronic diseases to increase life expectancy in good health and to diminish the number of patients to be treated.

Public health therefore concerns all individuals without exception. As early as 1920, in the journal *Science*, C. E. Winslow, an American bacteriologist and public health expert, defined it as

> The science and art of preventing disease, prolonging life, and promoting physical health and efficiency through the community's ordered co efforts for environmental sanitation, control of infections in the population, education of the individual in the principles of personal hygiene, organization of medical and nursing services for the early diagnosis and preventive treatment of pathologies, development of

social arrangements that will assure each person an adequate standard of living for the maintenance of health.

Then, in 1986, the Ottawa Charter, adopted at the first international conference for health promotion, clarified this notion: "health promotion is the process of enabling people to increase control over, and to improve, their own health". The implementation of a health promotion policy, including prevention in all settings, is a key focus of the 2018–2022 national health strategy. To date, "the system is unequal on prevention, on risk factors and egalitarian on health expenditures" (Franck Chauvin). It is therefore necessary to increase the psychosocial skills of individuals to enable them to influence the determinants of their health. "If people feel that we are concerned about their health, they feel that they are in a caring environment. They feel valued, considered" (Franck Chauvin). It is then possible to modify the factors that impact health to change the health behaviors of individuals. Health education appears to be a key to implementing prevention actions adapted to the needs of individuals. For Franck Chauvin, "the health system must be given a population-based responsibility. We must say [to health professionals]: you are no longer responsible simply for the fact that the sick are well, you must be responsible for the fact that the population is well". This shows that prevention must become part of the core business of health-care providers, as an activity in its own right. This is a new mission for some professions and a skill to be reaffirmed for others. Caregivers are also concerned, as individuals, by health promotion. A European movement, for example, talks about health-promoting hospitals. In France, this trend – which began in 1997 but is still in its infancy today – has taken on the name "health-promoting place of health" since 2019. It aims to show the interest of implementing a real health promotion policy in establishments, involving all actors and resulting in multiple concrete actions at different levels (and in particular on prevention and the well-being of users and staff). Franck Chauvin explains the findings of this experience: "Hospitals that implement health promotion policies for professionals are hospitals that are themselves becoming much more concerned about the health of their patients and where the climate inside the hospital is improving".

In France, "we treat very well but we are not healthier than our neighbors because we prevent resolutely less well" (Emmanuel Macron, speech of September 18, 2018). In Chapter 2, Julia Gudefin and André Simonnet of the association DanaeCare will provide an international perspective on this issue by drawing on international work or experiences.

1.2.3. *Acquiring new skills*

During the two testimonies, the physicians expressed ideas for change and specified that these should be made with the support of professionals because "being trained is different from having learned by feeling" (Michèle Cottier).

On the one hand, the dual function of doctor and manager requires skills in medicine and management. Michèle Cottier explains that "we really need to be able to put students who are destined for the health sector into double degrees in management, economics, law or sociology. I am a great believer in the strength of the double degree, which allows you to go further than just a veneer that comes as an accessory to your studies". To occupy positions of responsibility, it is therefore necessary to have skills that are in line with the functions occupied. This vision also echoes the complexity of these dual professions, which are nonetheless inseparable for the proper functioning of health-care institutions.

On the other hand, before developing prevention, it seems essential to give meaning to this new role for health students who are the professionals of tomorrow. Franck Chauvin emphasizes that we must share this observation: "In France, life expectancy is increasing and life expectancy in good health has not changed, so there are more and more chronic diseases. We need to educate and explain that caring for patients is good, but it is not the only thing. We must re-focus on primary care because France is doped up on hospitals". A change took shape with the June 12, 2018 order on health service for health students, which includes prevention in the initial training of health students. It specifies that "the training objectives of the health service are to introduce students to the challenges of primary prevention, defined by the World Health Organization as all the actions implemented with the aim of reducing the incidence of a disease or health problem by reducing the causes and risk factors; to enable the implementation of concrete primary prevention actions that participate in the policy of prevention and the fight against social and territorial inequalities in access to health set up to integrate prevention into the practices of health professionals". Furthermore, the training of physicians could have as its objective to take care of people's health, including curative and preventive care, in their daily practice. This training in preventive clinical practices already exists in Quebec, for example.

Finally, it is also important to learn to work together. Until now, health students studied in a compartmentalized way during their theoretical training and, during their internships, they worked together without any identified objective. One of the training objectives of the health service is to "promote interprofessionality and interdisciplinarity during the training courses followed" (Order of June 12, 2018, Article 1). Beyond asking students to train in preventive care by building and conducting a preventive action together, it is a question of enabling them to know and recognize the skills of other professionals and to develop team spirit between the various training courses. The 2019 reform of health studies aims to "decompartmentalize the health-care fields and allow for training time in common". This first step in bringing together training courses and professions should be followed by the opening up of training courses between managers and doctors. Training would provide keys to understanding the system and therefore give meaning to practices that would be part of a caring training system that would encourage the implementation of a caring manner and caring management in the practices of tomorrow's professionals.

1.2.4. *Intermediate conclusion: a vision of caring management in the health system*

The prospect of profoundly changing this care system toward a health system is the essential prerequisite, according to Michèle Cottier and Franck Chauvin, for implementing caring management.

The preceding remarks allow us to better understand the vision that the two doctors have of caring management. According to them, it is first of all giving meaning, for the managers themselves as well as for their team, by allowing a better understanding of the work environment; "it is giving the keys to understand" (Franck Chauvin). It then means respecting individuals, recognizing their skills and giving them the means to carry out their activity to promote their well-being. It means putting the professional back at the heart of management and stopping "extremely mathematical management with indicators" (Franck Chauvin). In addition, the caring manager facilitates the collaborative work and coordination that are essential to the care of all patients in their singularity. He creates the conditions for a caring environment where the establishment of a relationship of trust becomes possible. Frédéric Pellegrin will return to the notion of caring management in Chapter 3, based on a semantic analysis.

1.3. The impacts of the health crisis on a caring manner in the health-care system and potential lessons learned

The interviews with Michèle Cottier and Franck Chauvin were conducted in December 2019, and the chapter was written between December and February 2020, that is, before the pandemic. While at the time of adding this third section we are in the middle of the COVID-19 epidemic, it seems interesting to consider the question of the link between crisis management and the caring, or not, character of the French health system, as questioned by our two doctors. Indeed, health, in terms of the need for care, took a central place in the daily life of everyone during the health crisis, disrupting the health system.

Faced with the appearance of a new pathology and the scale of the epidemic, hospitals had to react on all fronts: patient reception, logistics, communication, human resources, etc. All areas were affected, involving all hospital professionals. During the first wave of the crisis, several researchers wanted to understand how the crisis had been managed in health-care institutions. We will thus draw on the recent writings of Brunet (2020), Dumez and Minvielle (2020), Le Boterf (2020) and Nobre (2020a) to draw lessons from the way in which establishments have organized themselves to deal with the crisis and to study the impacts on the benevolence of the health system.

Hervé Dumez and Etienne Minvielle (2020) conducted a field survey by meeting with professionals – actors in the management of the crisis – to gather their testimonies. Their report on the French hospital system in the COVID-19 crisis highlights "the commitment of all categories of health personnel" to enable patient care in this unique context. "It also demonstrates the importance of putting operational responsibilities as close to the field as possible, in order to gain agility, a critical value in times of crisis, in order to meet, often urgently, the many challenges of daily life, whether it be to anticipate, to develop the necessary support management, to adapt collectively to a changing environment, to encourage creativity or to establish cooperation with other players in the healthcare ecosystem". The way the hospital operates is adapting to the crisis it is facing, reinventing itself by reorienting the special of its services, setting up specific missions such as managing stocks of sensitive or even very sensitive products, reassigning staff to new positions and so on. The roles and missions of the actors are thereby modified. A crisis cell is systematically set up in health-care establishments; it brings together professionals with complementary medical and managerial skills, before being hierarchical: it thus constitutes a multidisciplinary, or even omni-disciplinary, decision-making body in health-care establishments (Brunet 2020; Nobre 2020b). It is a privileged place for exchanges and reflections leading to decision-making and promoting internal communication. The real interdisciplinarity observed in the field is a strength, and the collaboration between the players makes it possible to achieve the objective of caring for all patients.

At the University Hospital of Strasbourg, for example (Clavert and Saint Hilary 2020), the steering of this crisis unit, at the institutional level, is shared by the general manager of the institution and the president of the institutional medical committee in close coordination with the operational level, which is characterized by a decompartmentalization of the various professions, where each one has its place. Greater trust between management and doctors, on the one hand, and between doctors and paramedics, on the other hand, is taking hold in this period of crisis.

Another striking observation of this period is the sharing of a common objective by all professionals in the health sector and centered on the patient: saving lives

(Le Boterf 2020). This shared objective gives the actors the meaning that they had sometimes lost in their daily work and that Michèle Cottier and Franck Chauvin denounced.

It should be noted that the management of this crisis did not remain compartmentalized in hospitals, and there was real cooperation between establishments and non-hospital health professionals. To deal with the situation, health-care staff demonstrated creativity and adaptability, overcoming the barriers between inpatient and outpatient settings: teams in homes for the dependent elderly were reinforced by school and private nurses, screening centers were created, and teams calling on professionals from different sectors were set up. Their professional awareness and their individual and collective skills are major assets for maintaining the continuity and quality of care.

In Alsace, the cessation of outpatient activity as of March 16, 2020 made it possible to make health professionals available for other sectors and thus to cope with the significant absenteeism during the period (Rossini et al. 2020). In addition, a mobile medical team, composed of four doctors specialized in physical medicine and rehabilitation, was created during the first wave of the pandemic. This team traveled to the Strasbourg University Hospital sites "to help assess patients and their potential for referral to the locomotor, neurology and respiratory follow-up care and rehabilitation streams". In addition, a regional admissions unit was set up to optimize downstream care thanks to a call center with a single number.

While this city-hospital linkage has improved during the various waves of the pandemic, it still shows that there are many points to be developed and that there is still a need to think about how to avoid placing the hospital at the center of the health system, as recommended by Franck Chauvin.

At the same time, public health messages have multiplied around barrier gestures. These have sometimes been presented more as a means of helping the hospital and, more particularly, the caregivers, than as a health education action specifically. The importance of the second wave questions the understanding of these messages in relation to individual behaviors. Do people have the keys to understand what is being asked of them in order to choose whether or not to adopt certain recommendations? The application of barrier actions is based on the notion of obligation "to have the right to... be obliged to...". The need to develop prevention to encourage the adaptation of individual behaviors is thus highlighted and remains a focus for future work.

While the health crisis is a very trying time for health system actors, it does create some conditions to address many of the health system issues that Michèle Cottier and Franck Chauvin raised in December 2019, as shown in Table 1.1.

System problems raised by M. Cottier and F. Chauvin	Organizations set up in establishments during the crisis
Compartmentalization between administrative and medical spheres; between professional bodies	Decompartmentalizing the different worlds involved in the hospital
Lack of trust between management and physicians	Operational responsibilities, decentralization
Lack of trust between physicians and paramedics	Commitment of all toward the patient
Loss of points of reference and meaning	Common goal, focused on the patient and their recovery
Strengthening the powers of the administration	Setting up of multidisciplinary crisis cells multidisciplinary crisis cells, shared decisions
Saturation of the health-care system	Prevention system deployed on the national territory

Table 1.1. *Organization during the health crisis, mirroring the health system problems*

In this context, the avenues for making the health-care system more caring in section 1.2 make sense. Their relevance is even enhanced by the fact that several of the authors who have analyzed the health crisis have reached the same conclusions (see Table 1.2).

Health system problems	Possible solutions
Partitioning	Reconciliation of training (Nobre 2020b)
Lack of trust between physicians and paramedics	Development of collective competence (Le Boterf 2020)
Lack of trust between management and physicians	Management training for physicians + effective managerial delegation to physicians (Nobre 2020b)
Loss of points of reference and meaning	Shared governance → care and management are at the heart of decisions, with a desire to optimize resources and to coordinate (Brunet 2020; Nobre 2020b)
Strengthening of administration powers	Setting up of multidisciplinary crisis cells multidisciplinary crisis cells, decisions shared
Saturation of the health-care system	Development of prevention

Table 1.2. *Permanent solutions to dysfunctions in the health-care system to make it more caring*

Nobre (2020b) raises the question of the transposability to the post-COVID era of the crisis cell, which favors shared decision-making between the administrative and medical management of the establishments. Brunet (2020) goes further and proposes the introduction of a new form of governance in hospitals with the creation of a strategic council distributing power among all the strategic players in the hospital. These people would be grouped into colleges with decision-making powers and not simply consultative bodies. This council, chaired by the hospital director assisted by the president of the CME, "would take over the missions of the board of directors and the supervisory board, which would disappear, since the strategic council has countervailing powers within it, and therefore validation but also control and monitoring bodies". In this way, "the sharing of skills, intelligence, methods, opinions, experiences and divergent opinions makes it possible to take the best final decision within a given timeframe".

For Thierry Nobre, the delegation of part of the management to the medical profession ("medicalization of management") implies the implementation of a "managerialization of the medical profession", which involves reinforcing the management training of doctors and bringing them closer to the training of health-care decision-makers (interns and student directors), thus contributing to a cultural rapprochement between the two professions.

Le Boterf (2020) highlights the fact that the organization has been transformed on the basis of a logic of cooperation not only between doctors-nurses-nursing assistants but also between all the personnel of the establishments:

> The ethical decisions on prioritization were made collegially. (...) The confrontation of the different points of view allowed a more informed ethical judgment to be made on a case-by-case basis. The actors succeeded in finding and deciding together on solutions to reorganize the hospital, adjusting or creating care protocols, sharing relevant professional practices, inventing new modes of communication with patients and their families, and setting up training courses for new learning. They were able to develop a collective capacity to study problems, to search for and sort medical information together, to take stock of the lessons of experience together and to carry out therapeutic assessments as a team. All these shared cognitive operations were essential in the cooperation processes that were set up. (Le Boterf 2020)

We would add the last avenue mentioned in section 1.2, which proved to be effective during this crisis, as mentioned above, even if it still needs to be reinforced: the development of prevention to promote the adaptation of behaviors and avoid upstream contamination within the population.

1.4. Conclusion

While the two physicians we interviewed to write this chapter thought at the end of 2019 that the system needed to be changed to be able to create the conditions for caring management, the health crisis provides an opportunity to experiment on a large scale with some of the proposals for changes in health organizations made in section 1.2. Similarly, the intermediate conclusions that we drew from the interviews with a view to a more caring system appear, in light of this crisis, to be valid and relevant: respecting individuals, putting health professionals back at the heart of management, facilitating collaborative work, etc. It is to be hoped that some of the practices implemented during this crisis and moving toward a more caring health system and management system and a more caring management style will be able to continue and that room for maneuver will remain possible for middle managers in their daily activity. This book contains a number of experiences of good management in different sectors (health, education or mass distribution), which can also be used as inspiration by health-care institutions.

1.5. References

Aubert, F.J. (2014). La décision à l'hôpital public : quelles relations entre directeur et médecin ? PhD Thesis, Université Bordeaux-IV, Centre Émile Durkheim, Bordeaux.

Barel, Y. (1989). *Le paradoxe et le système*. Presses Universitaires de Grenoble, Grenoble.

Bérard, E. (2013). Les pôles d'activité à l'hôpital vus comme un système cybernétique : une analyse en termes de contrôle de gestion. *Journal de gestion et d'économie médicales*, 3(4), 187–205.

Brunet, J. (2020). Pour la création d'un conseil stratégique hospitalier. *Gestions hospitalières*, 597.

Chevreul, K. (2015). Système de santé. In *ABCDaire de santé publique*, Brault, N. (ed.). Ellipses, Paris.

Clavert, P. and Saint Hilary, N. (2020). Quelles leçons organisationnelles et managériales de la Covid pour les blocs opératoires ? In *L'hôpital pendant la Covid-19 : innovations, transformations et résilience*, Nobre, T. (ed.). Éditions EMS, Caen.

De Pouvourville, G. (2010). La crise d'identité des médecins face au nouveau management de l'hôpital. *Le journal de l'école de Paris du management*, 86(6), 22–29.

Domy, P., Moulin, G., Frechou, D., Matrineau, F., Müller, C. (2014). Bilan et évaluation du fonctionnement des pôles dans les établissements de santé. Rapport des Conférences hospitalière, Ministère des Affaires Sociales et de la Santé, Paris.

Dumez, H. and Minvielle, E. (2020). Comment le système hospitalier français a-t-il géré la crise Covid 19 ? Une contribution des sciences de gestion. PhD Thesis, École polytechnique, Palaiseau.

Gavault, S., Laude, L., Baret, C. (2014). L'institutionnalisation des pôles d'activité médicale entre agir stratégique et agir projectif. *II*[e] *Congrès ARAMOS*, Marseille.

Goodall, A.H. (2011). Physician-leaders and hospital performance. Is there an association? *Social Science and Medicine*, 73(4), 535–539.

Grenier, C. and Bernardini, J. (2016). Strategic and enforced logics hybridization: An agency view within French hospitals and universities. In *Towards a Comparative Institutionalism? Forms, Dynamics, and Logics across the Organizational Fields of Health and Higher Education*, Pinheiro, R., Ramirez, F., Vrangbæk, K., Byrkjeflot, H. (eds). Emerald Group Publishing, Bingley.

Le Boterf, G. (2020). La prise en charge des Covid-19 : quelle situation professionnelle, quelle réponse en termes de professionnalisme ? *Gestions hospitalières*, 597.

Loubet, G. (2011). D'Hippocrate à Mercure : praticiens hospitaliers ou médecins gestionnaires ? Évolution du métier et tensions de rôles ? *Communication au 32*[e] *séminaire de l'Association Française de Comptabilité*, Montpellier.

Moatti, S. (2018). Un système en souffrance. *L'économie politique*, 80, 5–7.

Moisdon, J.-C. (2012). Le paradoxe de la boîte noire : réformes hospitalières et organisation. *Droit et Société*, 80, 91–115.

Nobre, T. (2020a). *L'hôpital pendant la Covid-19 : innovations, transformations et résilience.* Éditions EMS, Caen.

Nobre, T. (ed.) (2020b). Vers un management partagé, une organisation responsabilisante et une structure agile ? In *L'hôpital pendant la Covid-19 : innovations, transformations et résilience*. Éditions EMS, Caen.

Romeyer, C. (2001). Système d'information fondé sur une traçabilité des activités : intérêts et difficultés de mise en œuvre dans les hôpitaux. PhD Thesis, Université de la Méditerranée, Marseille.

Rossini, E., Vivet, L., Genatio, D. (2020). Quelles leçons organisationnelles et managériales de l'offre de soins en SSR ? Le cas de l'Ugecam Alsace. In *L'hôpital pendant la Covid-19 : innovations, transformations et résilience*, Nobre, T. (ed.). Éditions EMS, Caen.

Valette, A., Grenier, C., Saulpic, O., Zarlowski, P. (2015). La fabrication du "médico-économique" à l'hôpital français : une analyse de la littérature. *Politiques et management public*, 32(3), 241–264.

2

Valuing Human Relationships in the Organization of Care: An International Approach

In a variety of countries, numerous reports reveal a growing malaise among caregivers in their profession, both students and working professionals. For example, they report an alarming number of strikes and hunger strikes, burnout and suicide (Thomas et al. 2018). The causes identified by researchers and reporters focus on difficult working conditions, the stress involved and the pressure generated. However, what is most revealing is the caregiver's internal contradiction or the "value conflict" between the desire to "do one's job well" and the impossibility of doing it because of working conditions that do not allow it (Girard 2009).

From this perspective, how can we bring together a desire for innovation in the medical sector and transformations in the role and posture of health-care personnel while guaranteeing working conditions that do not undermine the well-being of caregivers, students and patients? At first glance, this issue might only concern the restrictive framework of medical consultation and practice. In reality, it has a much more global impact on the organization of care in that it defines the relationships between managers and management, caregivers and patients, and the way in which care is integrated into these work organizations.

In this context, would not one of the solutions be to enhance the value of the caregiver–patient relationship? From the point of view of caregivers, this would certainly have the advantage of reducing sick leave for caregivers and thus limiting the costs of replacement and turnover, reducing professional reorientations and suicides to prolong careers and invest in long-term training, and, ultimately, giving

---

Chapter written by Julia GUDEFIN and André SIMONNET.

back the taste and the sense of the profession to students who discover a medical sector in distress. From the patient's point of view, enhancing the value of the caregiver–patient relationship would certainly have the advantage of reducing the consumption of medication (especially in light of antibiotic resistance), reducing the number of consultations and, ultimately, regaining confidence in the caregiver.

At a time when the health-care system is being rethought, should not the caregiver–patient relationship in particular, and the human relationship in health-care in general, be seen as key indicators for responding to the economic, societal, health and philosophical issues that are shaping the future of our health-care system?

To outline the contours of this reflection, several elements will be addressed. First, the problems related to the humanization or dehumanization of health-care systems are not limited to France and are not specific to its health-care system. On the contrary, they concern a large number of countries and are part of a societal context marked by a tendency to devalue the human relationship in health-care organizations, the most important of which is the caregiver–patient relationship (section 2.1).

However, the generalization of the devaluation of the human relationship in health-care organizations is marked by some exceptions. Indeed, pioneering practices have emerged elsewhere in the world, and in particular in Uruguay in response to this observation, and have progressively drawn up a model for organizing care that favors humanism at all levels of the care system: between the caregiver and the patient, between the caregivers themselves, between the caregivers and the managers, and between the care staff and the administrative staff of health-care institutions. Thus, in Uruguay, medical humanism has become a real practice to generate quality care and a caring organization of care (section 2.2).

From this perspective, the humanization of the health-care system in response to a devaluation of the human relationship in health-care is an issue within our reach. It represents a missing indicator in the chain of care, from the stage of medical training to the organization of care, and includes medical practice. Giving a prominent place to the human relationship in health-care would have positive effects on health economics, public health and the organization of care. It would therefore be a criterion for determining the health status of a health-care system and a strategy for organizing care. In this context, the human relationship in health would embody a new performance indicator for benevolence (section 2.3).

2.1. The devaluation of the caregiver–patient relationship at the level of the health-care organization: a worldwide observation

Whether in Europe, America or the Asia-Middle East, caregivers and health-care professionals are increasingly subject to burnout, with increasing rates of depression and suicide. In the different parts of the world where we have conducted our investigations[1], the observation is the same: there is a correlation between the devaluation of the caregiver–patient relationship at the systemic level and the lack of a sense of belonging. Without protection, the relationship has been relegated to the background, leaving a dominant place to other elements: the hypertechnification of medical practices, the ever increasing number of administrative procedures, a mountain of overtime and an ever-increasing pressure on practitioners justified by a short-term vision of the health economy. With so much pressure, how can one remain a positive actor in a relationship?

In general, the diversity of the caregivers we met in some 15 countries shows the difficulties that this situation causes both for the caregiver and for the patient: a clear regression of trust between the caregiver and the patient, and an increasing decrease in the time per patient, which does not allow for the creation of a relationship. For example, there is a close relationship between, on the one hand, the increased – and in some cases unnecessary – use of drugs and medical imaging and, on the other hand, the devaluation of the caregiver–patient relationship. Indeed, in many testimonials, the point was raised that, when the relationship is under pressure, the means of the caregiver and the patient's expectation are oriented more toward the prescription of medication, even though the consultation did not allow for the pathological problem(s) to be expressed conveniently and in complete confidence.

All of these difficulties often lead to conflicts that arise, in most cases, following a medical error, which leads to a judicialization of the provider–patient relationship, especially in countries with procedural laws such as the United States or, more recently, Lebanon or Brazil.

In this generalized context, the caregiver–patient relationship is dominated by a mutual mistrust whose consequences are harmful both for the caregiver, who loses the meaning of their work, and for the patient, who loses confidence in their doctor. Now, in a medical environment pressurized by economic questions and, in particular, those of the profitability of care, how can we not wonder about the multitude of the direct and indirect costs generated by an organizational strategy that results in the devaluation of the caregiver – patient relationship?

1 For a map of the shoot and video clips, see: danaecare.com.

However, it is important to remember the reality of each of the two protagonists who suffer from this "lack of relationship", which raises questions about what is expected of a care organization that would welcome a quality relationship between the caregiver and the patient. We still need to agree on what these terms mean.

Out of more than 100 hours of interviews with actors in health training, practice and organization conducted between 2012 and 2018 in three continents (Europe, America, Asia-Middle East)[2], the elements that emerged with the most prevalence on the question of what characterizes a quality relationship between a caregiver and a patient were: first, trust, then active listening and third, sufficient time for the relationship. These three elements are shared by caregivers (all specialties and professions) and patients (all pathologies). This observation provokes two reactions: on the one hand, the three elements identified are interdependent. Trust develops with active listening made possible by sufficient time given to the relationship. On the other hand, they are not valued at all in the care system. When questioned, hospital and clinic managers tell us that the technology made available to caregivers compensates for the lack of time in the relationship and provides the confidence necessary for the care given by the carer. In other words, a technical response is provided to a human need.

However, can we imagine today that the lack of a human relationship in the caregiver–patient relationship and the lack of appreciation of the human relationship in the organization of care are two of the elements that constitute the distress felt by both caregivers and patients? Certainly, questions of profitability guide the technical responses of managers who see human relationships as a non-monetizable and therefore non-profitable time. However, this vision of care is detrimental to both the medical staff and the health-care system and its economy, in which the patient is the final link. Indeed, placing caregivers in timed working conditions, particularly through timed care, is the best way to cause them to lose the meaning of their profession and to dehumanize the organization of health care in which the patient no longer feels considered as such, even though many measures have been put in place to improve their care and safety. In this sense, the French National Authority for Health (HAS) issues good practice guides to develop quality in the health, social and medico-social field, and in particular, quality and safety indicators for care.

For the health-care workers, managers and trainers we interviewed, this situation gives rise to organizational problems, the most important of which are work stoppages and staff turnover, which raise the question for managers of how to retain health-care staff in their health-care organization and therefore the very functioning of their health-care institution. This situation also generates public health problems, particularly with regard to the physical and mental health of health-care workers, given

2 For a list of stakeholders by country, see: danaecare.com.

the prevalence of burnout and, in the most serious cases, suicides among caregivers. This is all the more alarming because this malaise is occurring at an increasingly early age and concerns students who, having idealized their future profession, are subjected to a real trauma when they discover the daily reality of their work.

In this context, is it possible to imagine a humanistic organization of care in which the human relationship is no longer perceived as a factor that can be cut back but as a necessary indicator for generating an efficient and effective care system? While this may seem utopian to some, integrating humanism into the organization of care has become a real practice elsewhere in the world and precisely in Uruguay. Let us, therefore, examine Uruguayan pragmatism and its practice of medical humanism.

2.2. An example of a caring organization: medical humanism in Uruguay

Inspired by his own experience and the work of some of his colleagues, Professor Humberto Correa has been developing a medical curriculum focused on medical humanism since 2006 in the Faculty of Medicine at the University of Latin America Center for Human Economics (UCLAEH). Initially, it was aimed at medical students. However, since 2018, it has been extended to health professionals and administrative staff of Uruguayan health institutions in view of the positive impact of medical humanism on the health ecosystem for the past 14 years. This approach is unprecedented in Uruguay. The goal is to increase empathy and generate more humane physicians, care and health-care organizations, thus limiting the negative impacts of their dehumanization on patients, caregivers, the health economy and public health policy.

The inspiration for this project came from Professor Humberto Correa's own experience as an intensive care physician and from the work in medicine on the suffering of the physician working in the intensive care unit (ICU). Among the results of this work, a number of potential types of damage caused to caregivers by ICU work are mentioned: emotional distortion, physical disorders (sometimes very serious), loss of vitality and cancellation of development. Professor Humberto Correa emphasizes that all these potential negative consequences diminish the caregiver as an integral, empathetic and growing human being and, as a result, dehumanize them. For this reason, he believes that the active practice of medical humanism in the ICU should not only be aimed at the patients but also at all the people who make up the ICU care team, which should lead to the search for remedies to all the harmful situations and to the creation of new conditions that limit them and tend to the healthy development of the physicians, nurses and teams that make up the health-care institutions.

Other works in medicine that he mentions in his book show that doctors, even if they do not wish it, are affected by the suffering of others and by death. There is an empathic identification with pain and loss, which is exacerbated in predisposed physicians and can lead them – if not encouraged by the organization of care – to "emotional abstinence" or "compassion fatigue". As a result, it will lead them to practice care that is not compassionate, distant and not interested in patients, especially in regard to the dying and their family members. It is the loss of empathy and its transformation into coldness and cynicism.

He also notes that the empathy of physicians – natural and common at the beginning of medical school – can be greatly diminished by the educational model received during undergraduate and residency training (e.g. internship in France). Then, in the ICU, it can be further eroded due to several factors: contact with serious situations, pain and death, increasing dependence on technology, economic limitations, limited care resources, intragroup dysfunction and time pressures.

Some of the authors quoted in his book point out that doctors are vulnerable beings like all human beings and that they can become non-empathetic, cold and alexithymic without realizing it, due to certain individual blindnesses favored by the organization of care and one's own culture. Professor Humberto Correa therefore highlights that if the organization of care includes special attention to the human relationship, it is possible to recognize in time the effect that the many factors of damage have on those who are exposed to them.

For these authors, the main causes that generate vulnerability and admission of caregivers to the ICU are fear of death, aspects of their religious convictions or atheism, previous traumatic experience, solitude in making critical decisions, fear of error, guilt, chronic stress from working too much under pressure, working with inadequate resources, team conflict, rigid hierarchies and stress in their personal lives.

To complement this work, a Uruguayan study was conducted in 2014 to investigate the prevalence of burnout among Uruguayan critical care physicians. The research was conducted in 12 units involving 82 physicians working in intensive care and the use of the Maslach Inventory, whose main markers are maintained fatigue, depersonalization and lack of achievement. The Maslow Burnout Inventory (MBI) is one of the descriptive models of burnout that assesses psychological impairment at work by studying the consequences of chronic stress. The original version of the MBI asks 22 questions that explore three dimensions: emotional exhaustion (how the person feels about their work), dehumanization (their ability to manage relationships with others, depersonalization, loss of empathy) and the degree of personal accomplishment at work (loss of meaning at work).

Their results indicate that 51% of the physicians surveyed had elements of burnout or were completely burned out. The common symptoms encountered among the ICU physicians surveyed that present burnout were sleep disturbances, eating problems, lack of memory, mood disturbances and a desire to leave their place of work. As a comparative, in France, 46.5% of the same physicians have elements of burnout, and in the UK, 29% suffer from stress, 12% suffer from depression, 3% suffer from suicidal ideation, and almost all are dissatisfied with their careers.

In summary, sustained stress, that is, leading to burnout produces psycho-physical damage, identity disorders, underestimation of one's own worth, loss of security and ability to control, and the disruption of family, professional and social life. As a result, poor defense mechanisms (denial, dissociation) are also established. They erode sensitivity and empathy and lead to alexithymia.

This is why Prof. Humberto Correa felt it was urgent to act at the institutional level to stop the erosion of empathy and generate a more humane medicine, not only in the organization of care but also upstream, in medical training. This approach was welcomed and approved by the Uruguayan Ministry of Education and Culture in 2006.

Medical humanism, as it is conceived in Uruguay, centers on the concept of empathy. The objective is to value and explain it, not only through theoretical courses but also and above all through practice via modules that put into real application the behaviors and attitudes that question empathy. It is a real cooperative, introspective and multidisciplinary work that medical students, as well as health professionals and the administrative staff of health institutions, carry out. Through this work, they question their own feelings and emotions faced with the feelings and emotions of the patient. The aim is to describe, accept and analyze them during group work supported by a tutor. This is to demonstrate the value of empathy in the caregiver–patient relationship and within the teams of health-care institutions, not only for the patient but also for the caregivers themselves, to create quality care in a caring and efficient organizational system.

As Prof. Humberto Correa explains:

> The educational project in humanized medicine emerges as a response to a socio-cultural and historical context that has profound implications for the practice and teaching of medicine. It is useful to recall that medicine is the daughter of the culture in which it develops, of the socioeconomic conditions that shape it and of the social imagination that results from it. From them, it obtains its characteristics and orientations. During the last fifty years, the dominant tendencies of our western society have privileged the consumption, the realization of the

> economic success, the obtaining of the power and the satisfaction of personal-individual goals. Young people entering medicine participate to varying degrees in this imaginary decline. But these young people will be on a journey of change in search of a new identity: that of a physician. They will be in a process of transformation and thus they will be very subject to the influence of their teachers, curricula and teaching and the care environment on them. Their future medical personality will depend on the character of these influences. That character will be absorbed and incorporated into him. (Correa 2016)

After 14 years of operation with medical students, feedback studies have shown that students who have graduated from are more empathetic with their patients, less emotionally vulnerable and have a stronger sense of meaning in their work, without their scientific and technical knowledge being diminished compared to students who have graduated from other health training institutions. The experience is therefore largely positive for the caregiver, for the patient and, more globally, for the health ecosystem in which they evolve.

This feedback is consistent with the results of a 2014 study (Chou et al. 2014) in which the characteristics of physicians whom residents (e.g. interns in France) consider to be humanists were determined through surveys and interviews. The attributes manifested by these physicians are as follows:

– thanking their patients for their trust;

– taking a keen interest in the patient's history;

– the satisfaction of doing quality work;

– considering that being a physician goes beyond just treating illness and dispensing medication.

In the interviews, physicians considered to be humanistic explained the factors they think help them to maintain their humanistic posture and behavior:

– practicing self-reflection;

– trying to be role models for their students;

– seeking their own life balance (professional and private life).

All of these characteristics and factors are reflected in the "Charter on Physician Well-Being" published in 2018 in JAMA (Thomas et al. 2018), which notes that the cost of turnover related to the burnout of physicians represents one-third of the cost of the health-care system. Beyond the individual character that the humanist physician may represent, it is therefore undeniable that the well-being of the caregiver – understood as their mental health – is closely interconnected with a more humane and caring organization of care. In this context, medical humanism, or at least the humanization of care, should be one of the organizational objectives for improving care from both a health and economic point of view. From this perspective, the humanization of care, which is conveyed by the human relationship in health-care, could become a new performance indicator of care organizations.

2.3. The human relationship in health: toward a new indicator of performance of a caring manner in organizations

At a time of innovation in health-care and the evolution of the patient's place in the care process, at a time of profound changes in the medical profession, it is important to question the place of the human relationship in health-care, the consequences and the stakes involved.

The preceding discussion highlighted the essential nature of the value of the human relationship in the health ecosystem, both at the level of medical consultation and practice and at the more global level of the organization of care. While the human relationship has been relegated to the background in the vast majority of the countries studied, we can now see the importance of putting it at the forefront of the different strata of the healthcare system.

From then on, the objective is to generate an efficient and effective care system that cannot be developed without including the human relationship at all levels of care: between caregiver and patient, between caregivers, and between caregivers and management. As we have seen, enhancing the human relationship in health-care is a lever on which to rely to structure an organization of care – at the level of a country or a department – that generates the economic viability of the care system and efficiency of care. In this way, a multitude of hidden costs, direct or indirect, are taken into account and integrated for a more efficient care system.

Consequently, the humanization of care is a challenge within our reach. To meet this major societal challenge, it is necessary to enhance the human relationship in health-care on three levels.

2.3.1. *At the level of medical training*

As mentioned in section 2.2, whether students or health professionals or even the administrative staff of health institutions, it is essential to offer time for reflection or a time to reconnect with the very heart of the nursing profession: care understood not only in its scientific and technical aspects but also in its human and relational aspects. Uruguay is a typical example. It is the first necessary step, upstream of medical practice and the organization of care, to give meaning back to one's work and to limit conflicts of value among caregivers and medical teams.

The duplication of medical humanism in France would not be an irresistible obstacle insofar as the health system and health training system in Uruguay is largely modeled on the one in France. With regard to training for health professionals and the administrative staff of health institutions, the question is even simpler insofar as modules for the promotion of human relations in health could be included in the obligatory continuing vocational training.

2.3.2. *At the level of medical practice*

At the level of medical practice, the feeling of dehumanization is all the stronger because it is part of an increasingly technical context. A predominantly technical response to a profoundly human need is not desired since it is the human support that will allow a better appropriation and acceptance of the technical nature of care. This is a major issue in today's society, where artificial intelligence tools predominate among health innovations and are intended to replace caregivers in their medical acts.

2.3.3. *At the level of the organization of care*

At this more global level, care, caregivers, patients and their mutual relationships are organized. This pyramidal organization, which is steered by managers and which is deployed over all health-care actors, acts with the aim of producing efficient and effective care, that is, with the aim of treating, curing and supporting. However, as we have mentioned, organizational dysfunctions linked to the dehumanization of care cause negative effects that impact caregivers, patients, the health economy and public health. These organizational dysfunctions are mainly based on contradictory injunctions based on two aspects:

– the lack of appreciation for "caring" – in a place that is nevertheless precisely intended to do so;

– the conflict of values among caregivers who oscillate between a desire to do their work well and the impossibility of doing so due to a lack of resources or, broadly, due to working conditions or a work organization that does not allow for the realization and generation of quality care and therefore effective care.

In this context, an alignment between, on the one hand, the meaning of work, that is, the desire to "do well" or the desire for efficiency and quality in care, and, on the other hand, the quality of life at work, that is, a care organization that takes care of health professionals in all the components of their work, and in particular the relational components (horizontal and vertical), will inevitably have positive effects on the quality of care provided to patients and on the loyalty of caregivers to their health-care institution. This organizational strategy applied at the level of a health-care institution will contribute to the overall health of a country's health-care system.

When we talk about quality of life at work, it is therefore essential to make the link between the meaning of the work of health professionals and the human relationship in health.

Consequently, the human relationship in which not only the caregiver–patient relationship, but also the relationship between health professionals and management, is valued is a key indicator of the health of a health-care system. From this perspective, it is necessary that each health-care actor, at the forefront of which are those responsible for the planning and organization of the health-care system, seize this formidable lever to design the health-care system of the future: a caring health-care system putting people back at the heart of care.

However, in times of crisis, what place is left for "taking care"? Can the value of human relations and benevolence in intragroup and interprofessional relations endure when the health, economic, social or political crisis disrupts the organization of care? Are they swept away by a profound rupture in the organization of care? Or are they the foundation on which crisis management is based?

In France, long before the COVID-19 health crisis, the culture of prevention and crisis management was introduced in all public and private health establishments to prevent and manage serious health threats and emergency situations. Indeed, since 2004, health-care institutions have been obliged to have white plans drawn up in the form of guides (law No. 2004-806 of August 9, 2004 on public health policy, Official Journal of August 11, 2004). This requirement is based on "the context of increasing health threats, linked to epidemics, technological or climatic accidents or malicious acts"[3]. The context in is clearly described by the white paper and crisis management guide:

> The normal functioning [of health-care institutions] is compromised, if not inoperative. The head of the institution finds themselves isolated in

3 Ministry of Solidarity and Health, white paper and crisis management, 2006, p. 7. Statement initially made in report No. 1092 on behalf of the Commission for Cultural, Family and Social Affairs on the bill No. 877 on public health policy, by Mr. Jean-Michel Dubernard, M.P., registered at the Presidency of the National Assembly on September 25, 2003 (Marra 2018).

> an environment that generates great tension, and the basic balances on which the organization is usually based are missing. This type of management hardly supports improvisation, hesitation or doubt. (Marra 2018)

To integrate these realities into the managerial culture and beyond the operational measures they describe, the crisis management guides of health-care institutions draw the attention and vigilance of managers and directors to the relational concerns and loss of trust that crisis situations induce crisis situations:

> Crisis management of crisis is the result of a culture to be acquired, a state of mind to be reinforced and a serene vigilance that is permanent, documented and operational. The form and nature of human relations, the complexity of problems and the media coverage, among other factors, induce uncertainty that we must learn to manage collectively. To deny these phenomena would lead to crises that would increasingly destroy the trust which is essential to any social and professional structure. (Marra 2018)

To deal with these situations, the guide for health-care institutions under stress recognizes that crisis management must be based, first and foremost, on "a good knowledge of the people with whom we work, the workplaces, the technical networks and the human, professional and institutional environment", as well as on the skills and daily availability of managers to detect emerging crises or potentially dangerous situations. Consequently, the human dimension is the foundation on which crisis management is based and organized. Since a crisis is by definition unpredictable, it is essential that the human, relational and caring dimensions be developed and valued beforehand in health-care institutions to deal with emergency situations and the tension generated by crises. Thought out and planned in this way, crisis management relies on a resilient care system supported by human relationships.

However, in a health-care system where human relations are not or hardly valued, crisis management risks being based on an unstable foundation that amplifies the phenomenon of organizational destabilization and disruption generated by the crisis. The deployment of operational crisis management systems is therefore limited in its application, reactivity, relevance and, ultimately, acceptance.

Take the example of Lebanon, which has experienced repeated major political, social, economic and health crises, from the civil war between 1975 and 1990 to the double explosion of ammonium nitrate storage in the port of Beirut in August 2020, resulting in thousands of victims, and the health crisis linked to COVID-19, to name but a few examples. The vast majority of caregivers interviewed in Lebanon between 2017 and 2018[4] were medical interns during the civil war and are still practicing today. They have experienced these multiple crises from the inside, being tossed between tension, exhaustion and improvisation in the face of destruction and a lack of human and material resources. According to their testimonials, great solidarity between caregivers emerged during the civil war, strengthening mutual aid and ties in the face of upheaval. However, as the crises and political choices impacted the socioeconomic models, the health sector evolved toward greater competition between structures and between health actors based on a model of economic profitability, even the commodification of care. The solidarity that emerged during the civil war has thus been eroded by a model of competition between caregivers and a race for profit for the structures. It is therefore with nostalgia that some people remember this solidarity; although it was born out of a time of major crisis, it was meaningful in their profession in contrast to the current competition that generates interprofessional, intergenerational and patient conflicts.

Human relationships, care and benevolence are therefore not a luxury that only a normal functioning health-care system could covet. It would even be imprudent to do without them. What we learn from times of crisis is that human relationships, care and benevolence must be integrated into all levels of care to generate a high-performance care system in normal times and a resilient care system in times of crisis.

2.4. Conclusion

Finally, valuing the human aspect of care, which is notably conveyed by empathy in the caregiver–patient relationship--patient relationship, is not impossible. Whether in Uruguay, or in the Netherlands[5] or France[6], where similar initiatives have emerged, experience shows that valuing human relationships generates quality care in a caring health ecosystem for both the caregiver and the patient, beyond the cultural and historical differences that cross each country and each locality. The human

4 For a list of stakeholders by country, see: danaecare.com.

5 In the Netherlands, the Buurtzorg association has developed a revolutionary model for home nursing based mainly on the human relationship between caregiver and patient. It was founded in 2007 by Jos de Blok, with a team of four nurses and a computer scientist friend. The project is now being implemented in other European countries, notably in France with the association "Soignons humains". See: www.soignonshumain.com/buurtzorg/.

6 Dominique Pon, director of the Pasteur clinic in Toulouse, advocates the human side of the hospital sector through a cooperative group called "SantéCité", which brings together independent private clinics with no capital ties, with the aim of putting people back at the heart of care. See: santecite.fr.

aspect of care is therefore a universal value that must be protected to preserve a quality care system and organization.

In conclusion, from the point of view of both caregivers and patients, human relationships are at the heart of care at all levels of the health-care organization. It begins at the individual level, when the caregiver meets the patient. This approach is so often relegated to the background in the organization of health-care that it deserves to be recalled. However, our research has shown that if the relationship is created on the small scale of a meeting between two individuals, the issues involved cannot be confined to the consulting room. In contrast, they emerge from there to become essential issues on a systemic scale, that of the health system and its organization at the economic, social and cultural levels. From this perspective, the human relationship in health could become an innovative and effective indicator of tomorrow's care organizations.

2.5. References

Assunção, A.A., Machado, C.J., Cano Prais, H.A., de Araújo, T.-M. (2014). Depression among physicians working in public healthcare. Belo Horizonte. *Social Psychiatry and Psychiatric Epidemiology*, 49, 1219–1229.

Casagrande Riganti, C.V. (2016). Estrés laboral en médicos que trabajan en Centros de Tratamiento intensivo, Pre-proyecto de investigación. PhD Thesis, Université de la République orientale de l'Uruguay [Online]. Available at: https://www.colibri.udelar.edu.uy/jspui/handle/20.500.12008/8581.

Chou, C.M., Kellom, K., Shea, J.A. (2014). Attitudes and habits of highly humanistic physicians. *Acad Med.*, 89(9), 1252–1258.

Coomber, S., Todd, C., Park, G., Baxter, P., Firth-Cozens, J., Shore, S. (2002). Stress in UK intensive care unit doctors. *Br. J. Anaesth*, 89(6), 873–878.

Correa, H. (2016). *Humanismo médico.* Fin de siglo, Montevideo.

Fleury, C. (2019). *Le soin est un humanisme.* Gallimard, Paris.

Girard, D. (2009). Conflits de valeurs et souffrance au travail. *Éthique publique*, 11(2), 129–138 [Online]. Available at: https://www.colibri.udelar.edu.uy/jspui/handle/20.500.12008/8581.

Kornig, C., Levet, P., Ghadi, V. (2016). Revue de littérature : qualité de vie au travail et qualité des soins. Report, Haute Autorité de santé, Saint-Denis-La Plaine [Online]. Available at: https://www.has-sante.fr/jcms/c_2610262/fr/revue-de-litterature-sur-qualite-de-vie-au-travail-et-qualite-des-soins.

Legault, G.-A. (2009). Dialoguer sur la souffrance des soignants : pourquoi est-ce si difficile ? *La souffrance des soignants*, Béland, J.-P. (ed.). Presses de l'université Laval, Quebec.

Marra, D. (2018). Rapport sur la qualité de vie des étudiants en santé. Rapport, Ministère des Solidarités et de la Santé, Paris [Online]. Available at: https://solidarites-sante.gouv.fr/ministere/documentation-et-publications-officielles/rapports/sante/article/rapport-du-dr-donata-marra-sur-la-qualite-de-vie-des-etudiants-en-sante.

Mehanna, Z. and Richa, S. (2006). Prévalence des troubles anxio-dépressifs chez les étudiants en médecine : étude transversale chez les étudiants en médecine de l'Université Saint-Joseph de Beyrouth. *L'encéphale*, 32, 976–982.

Pierron, J.-P., Vinot, D., Chelle, E. (2008). *Les valeurs du soin*. Seli Arslan, Paris.

Serres, M. (2006). L'éducation médicale vue par un philosophe. *Revue internationale francophone d'éducation médicale*, 7, 135–141.

Thomas, L.R., Ripp, A.J., West, C.P. (2018). Charter on physician well-being. *JAMA*, 319(15), 1541–1542.

3

The Search for a Caring Nature at Work throughout History

In this book dedicated to caring management, why devote a chapter to the search for a caring nature at work throughout history? Beyond the health and social sectors, the organization of work and, in particular, management, through the search for a certain compromise between the performance and well-being of workers, is far from being a new phenomenon limited to a single sector.

With regard to this observation, which we will develop more widely in the following parts, it seems to us opportune to turn to history because the memory can sometimes fail us, and the lights of the mass media blind us by the illusion of the false novelty.

This chapter will first give some definitions of the concepts of management, benevolence, work and their corollary: caring management.

In the second part, followed by a discussion, we will invite you on a journey through time to analyze how different organizations and companies have mobilized around this search for benevolence at work. We will move from a traditional and historical approach to other horizons qualified as more modern toward “alternative management“.

Chapter written by Frédéric PELLEGRIN ROMEGGIO.

3.1. Management, a recent discipline and function

3.1.1. *Management*

> Sharing the same Latin root as *ménagement*, a 17th century French word derived from *ménager*, or to arrange and regulate with care and skill, management can be defined as the way to lead, direct, structure and develop an organization (...). Management concerns the organization of groups of men and women who must work together with the aim of a finalized collective action (...). The main problem of management is knowing how to allow social groups to live so that they can produce a collective beyond the simple addition of individual expertise. (Thietart 2003)

> Management is not simply a function, but a position. Each manager would adopt, in a more or less stable way, one of them according to the situations with which he would be confronted and the organizations in which he would exercise his function (...). We can then consider position from the point of view of "role". (Barabel et al. 2008)

Henri Fayol, considered one of the founding theorists of modern management, does not use the term "management" directly but rather "industrial and general administration" (1916) in terms of five major functions: the technical function (to produce, transform, manufacture), the commercial function (to buy, sell, exchange), the financial function (to seek and use capital), the security function (to protect goods and people) and the accounting function (to plan, organize, order, coordinate, control). In other words, Fayol's "general administration" or "management" is truly a matter of strategic choices and not just a simple problem of "human resources management" and involves all the disciplines traditionally associated with management or "management sciences".

3.1.2. *Benevolence and other terms often associated*

Many terms are often associated or confused with the word "benevolence". To better enlighten us, below we share the contribution of Matthieu Ricard, who has dedicated a large part of his life to it. Matthieu Ricard studied cellular genetics before turning to Buddhism. Ordained a monk in 1978, he is one of the world's leading specialists in Tibetan Buddhism and the French interpreter of the Dalai Lama.

Benevolence, from the Latin *benevole*, "wanting the good of the other" is a favorable position toward others, accompanied by a willingness to act (...).

Positive emotions such as joy, contentment, gratitude, wonder, enthusiasm, inspiration and love are more than just the absence of negative emotions. Joy is not the simple absence of sadness, and benevolence is not the simple absence of unkindness. Positive emotions have a supplementary dimension that cannot be reduced to neutrality of mind: they are sources of deep satisfaction. This means that, in order to flourish in life, it is not enough to neutralize negative and disruptive emotions, one must encourage the blossoming of positive emotions (...).

Altruism, derived from the Latin *alter* "other", was used for the first time by Auguste Comte; it supposes "the elimination of egoistic desires and egocentrism, as well as the fulfillment of a life devoted to the good of others". Among the other modalities of altruism, benevolence corresponds to a way of being that is spontaneously translated into acts as soon as circumstances allow (...). Solicitude consists of being permanently and watchfully concerned about the fate of others: concerned about their situation, we take care to provide for their needs, to promote their well-being and to remedy their suffering. Devotion consists of putting oneself selflessly at the service of people or of a cause beneficial to society. Benevolence is a form of gentle thoughtfulness that manifests itself in the way we relate to others. Fraternity (...) comes from the feeling of belonging to the great human family of which every representative is perceived as a brother or sister whose fate is important to us; fraternity also evokes notions of good understanding, cohesion and union (...). The feeling of solidarity with a more or less extended group of people is born when we have to face common challenges and obstacles together (...). Love is the supreme emotion (...), love allows us to see the other with concern, benevolence and compassion. It is thus related to altruism insofar as one becomes sincerely concerned by the fate of others and by one's own good (pp. 87–88) (...). Empathy refers to the ability to "feel the other from within" (...), empathy can be triggered by an affective perception of the other's feelings or by the cognitive imagination of his or her experience.

Box 3.1. *The importance of words and their meanings (Ricard 2013)*

3.1.3. *Work: suffering or a means of personal fulfillment?*

From an etymological point of view, the origin of the word "work" still arouses many controversies among linguists, synonymous with suffering or even enslavement for some, or conversely achievement and pride for others. For example, in French, the word "*travail*" means torment, pain, fatigue and evokes the pains of childbirth, the "work" of the woman who gives birth. The verb "*travailler*" comes from the popular Latin *tripaliare*, action to torture by means of *trepalium*, a sinister instrument of torture with three legs and three stakes (Paquot 2007). Work is also sometimes associated with the divine curse: "By the sweat of your brow you will eat your food" (Genesis, Chapter 3, verse 9). Since antiquity, powerful people have refused to work and made others (slaves or serfs) work. Work is generally perceived as a tedious, enslaving, degrading activity and is not at all seen as a means of self-realization, except for certain master craftsmen or artisans (stonecutters, luthiers, instrument makers, printers, etc., as well as trades relating to architecture in particular).

Generally, and from an etymological point of view, the terms *"travail"* or even "management" (which share the same Latin root *manus*, hand, also found in the terms "manipulate" or "maneuver") can have, depending on their meaning, a very negative connotation, far from benevolence. Also, would the expression "caring management" (to which we will return later) not simply be antinomic and meaningless?

3.1.4. *The "scam" of the etymology of the word "work"?*

> Just as serious is the principle of constructing, within the framework of these purely ideological steps, false etymological paths. This is most probably what happened to the word "travail". Indeed, the passage from Latin "*tripalium*" to Old French "*travaillier*", close ancestor of the modern verb "travailler", via a hypothetical verb "*tripaliare*", is highly improbable. Everything suggests that this story is an ideological scam, fraudulently using linguistics (...). The verb "*travailler*", from which the noun "*travail*" derives, is said to come from the medieval Hispanic words "*trabajo*" (= to work) and "*trabajar*" (= to work), which express a "tension that is directed towards a goal and that meets resistance". This semantic description could be related to the Latin prefix trans-, which is often reduced to "*tra-*" ("tramontane", to cross, traboule, etc.), which expresses a principle of passage from one state to another, not suffering.[1]

Beyond the semantic and etymological explanation of the word "work", some authors praise or criticize the supposed virtues of work. For example, the philosopher of work Simone Weil (1909–1943) advocated the realization of man through work; it is necessary to liberate work and not to be liberated from work, contrary to Hannah Arendt (1906–1975), for whom it was necessary to liberate men from work by separating the work realized from the work needed for its realization.

1 Available at: https://blogs.mediapart.fr/flebas/blog/240316/l-arnaque-de-l-etymologie-du-mot-travail.

Work would thus present a double face with both negative and positive realities through a dolorous and constructive vision.

3.1.5. *Benevolence at work? From "classic" management to "caring" management*

Recently, the concept of "caring management" has been defined as follows:

> Transposed to the corporate world, benevolent behaviors allow the development of a "caring management" that is, active benevolence oriented towards action and performance" (Rodet and Desjaques 2019)

However, is this apparent and ubiquitous quest for benevolence at work just a new development, a fad?

3.2. The search for benevolence at work throughout history: representations that evolve over time

3.2.1. *The historical approach to benevolence*

Contrary to what one might think, the search for benevolence at work is not a contemporary phenomenon. Although despised for centuries, because it was considered as an enslaving and degrading activity, work was finally considered by the Enlightenment in Europe in the 18th century. For example, Diderot's Encyclopedia rehabilitates work by praising the quality of "useful men" (editor's note: craftsmen and other manual workers). For the Enlightenment, work was no longer seen as a divine punishment but as an essential factor of civilization. Already in the 17th century, the Protestant Reformation led by Martin Luther and John Calvin was in complete contrast to Catholicism, claiming that work is by no means an expiatory punishment for original sin but a privileged means of drawing closer to God (in the Protestantism of that time, work was also associated with economic success, thus postulating that the rich entrepreneur is blessed by God) (Weber 1964).

At the beginning of the 19th century, work even became a symbol of liberation for the people. For example, for Henri de Saint-Simon (1760–1825) and for his disciples, the "industrialists" (e.g. Auguste Comte), who fight for the abolition of privileges and against the phenomenon of rent, it is necessary to give "to each according to his capacity and to each capacity according to his works". Work thus becomes the pivot of human activities. However, this somewhat idealistic vision is very quickly overtaken by reality and the appalling living conditions of the workers.

With the industrial revolution in Europe, the feudal, agrarian and artisanal society evolved into a commercial and industrial society. Work became the main engine of economic growth under the "invisible" (and benevolent?) hand of nascent capitalism (Adam Smith, 1723–1790). However, it is clear that the worker is once again at the service of a new "lord", the capitalist entrepreneur, holder of the capital and organizer of the production of manufactured goods. Thus, far from being liberated by work, the worker is more than ever chained to his/her precarious and miserable condition. Moreover, Karl Marx and Friedrich Engels strongly denounced this state of affairs, advocating a pragmatic "scientific socialism" (also called "communism" or "historical materialism" in opposition to "utopian socialism" and its idyllic vision). Despite everything, they dreamed of "a society without compulsory work, where each person goes about their business according to their mood and inclinations". Marx fights against wage-earning and alienation, which imprisons the wage earner and forces him to sell his labor power instead of realizing himself by carrying out "the activities that reveal his personality". For Marx and Engels, it is necessary to reconcile the individual with himself, whereas the social and technical division of labor aims "to divide him and to make him alien to his own expectations and desires" (Engels 1973). This thought totally contradicts the idea of Stakhanovism that will appear later under Lenin and Stalin, with which productivism transcends the individual. The disastrous and pitiful situation of the wage earners of this period will lead, in particular, to calls to the "proletarian revolution" (Karl Marx) or to anarchy (Pierre-Joseph Proudhon) from many intellectuals or political personalities of the time. Therefore, in this chaotic period of the 19th century, in a context where work is experienced mainly as enslavement and alienation, is it still possible to imagine a more just and humane society with its employees, and what about benevolence at work?

Like some utopians of this period, such as Saint-Simon or the first French "socialists" (a neologism coined by Pierre Leroux in 1831), Charles Fourier (1772–1836) also proclaimed that work is not degrading; in contrast, "it belongs to human nature, it mobilizes energies, nourishes passions, provides satisfaction, in short, it contributes to self-fulfillment" (Paquot 2007). Through his theory of "passionate attractiveness" in which pleasure and work form a whole, Fourier proposes organizing work, as well as society, within "phalansteries" (the phalanx is a community of 1,620 people, 810 men and 810 women living in harmony in the same place of habitation and work, the phalanstery) with "phalansterians" who choose their work according to its attractiveness. However, what is this utopian socialism worth in the face of the miserable condition of the workers of the 19th century?

Jean-Baptiste André Godin (1817–1888), the famous French stove maker, put most of Fourier's principles into practice in his "*Familistère*" (the operational version of the phalanstery) in Guise, Aisne, France, from 1859 until 1968. Godin devoted his entire fortune to the realization of an "original social system", valuing the employees of his firm through profit sharing (1877), before bequeathing all his capital to them (a system of "*sociétaires*" and "*auxiliaires*"). Godin innovated socially by allowing mothers to breastfeed during working hours by creating a pension fund and a mutual insurance company that functioned in cases of illness. His "*Familistère*" or "social palace" was entirely dedicated to the work and well-being of all (sanitary facilities on all floors, comfortable living spaces, warmth, light). A theater opera was built (access to culture), gardens and spaces for animals were created, and a heated swimming pool was built on the site with swimming lessons to avoid drowning nearby (in the Aisne river, which passes through the site), as well as a school and more. The organizational principles of the *Familistère* are cooperation, association, the cult of work, a certain level of initiative left to the workers, access to culture and the permanent search for the well-being of the individual, wherever they may be and at any moment of their life (Lallement 2009). For Godin, taking into account all the needs of his employees went beyond simple paternalism, insofar as his personal motivations went far beyond the sole objectives of productivity and profitability of the company. Its commitment is more of a deeply humanistic dimension and even a "Christian" mission.

A few years earlier, in England at first, Robert Owen (1816), an English industrialist, decided to drastically reduce working hours in his factories and greatly improve working conditions. Like the philosopher Fourier or the industrialist Godin later on, Owen was convinced that the happiness of people depends on the perfect integration of harmonious and motivating work in a suitable environment and living environment. To put his convictions into practice, and driven by a humanist ideal in January 1826, he founded the New Harmony community in Indiana, USA (10,000 hectares, 1,000 sympathizers, 3 h of work per day, for example, which was ultimately a failure, mainly because of the permanent disputes between the leaders of the community village and the very low productivity, which led to the collapse of economic activities). Here, again, the motivation of this idealistic business leader went far beyond the sole concern of profitability to the permanent search for the general well-being of the people. Numerous examples of "Owenian" community villages followed throughout the world (Paquot 2007).

All these experiences of community villages mixing work and pleasure to be the concretization of an ideal, "a realized utopia", eventually failed after a few years of existence due to deplorable management, a form of deplorable management, a form of administrative negligence, incompetence, lack of cohesion, shared vision, cooperation or simply and paradoxically a lack of goodwill toward each other. The only real case that has successfully endured over time (almost 110 years) is undoubtedly that of Godin's *Familistère*. Such longevity could be explained, on the one hand, by two important economic characteristics: permanent technological innovation and leadership in its sector of activity, or at least the holding of a significant market share, and, on the other hand, by the presence of a charismatic leader who allows a certain degree of autonomy and a capacity for initiative to the workers. It is important to emphasize that we find these characteristics today in certain leading innovative companies, such as W.L. Gore & Associates (inventor of Goretex, among other things), Harley Davidson, 3M, FAVI (a French company, European leader in gearbox forks), Sun Hydraulics, etc., which are often presented as "liberated enterprises" and atypical social models that reconcile economic performance and job satisfaction (Getz' economic performance and job satisfaction (Getz and Carney 2013; Laloux 2015)). However, apart from these few examples, it was not until the end of the 19th century, with the Third Republic and the government of Félix Faure, that the state began to care about its workers (e.g. a law guaranteeing workers against the risks of industrial accidents in 1898).

Following these major political changes in our history, it was not until the beginning, or even the middle of the 20th century, that scientific research proposed various models of organizational or management theories. After a first attempt at managerial organization with the classical school (the scientific organization of work proposed by Taylor (1911)) and Fordism, the principles of sound administration by Fayol (1916), or Weber's bureaucratic administration (1904), it was initially the school of human relations that theorized the first modern reflections on a certain benevolence at work. The theory of human relations is, in a way, a response to the unbridled search for productivity of the classical school and its social and human consequences (absenteeism, general demotivation, high staff turnover, etc.). Elton Mayo's experiments at Western Electric in Hawthorne (1924–1932) demonstrate the importance of social relations in a group, the social climate, the quality of interpersonal relations and the consideration of others for their work. Abraham Maslow (1908–1970) establishes a hierarchy of human needs in organizations to better understand the motivation of man at work. He proposes a hierarchy of needs around five elements (physiological needs, security, belonging, esteem recognition and fulfillment) and underlines the difficulty of satisfying higher needs. Like Mayo, Maslow shows the limits of financial motivation alone and emphasizes the intrinsic interest in the content of work. Frederick Herzberg (1923–2000) distinguishes between factors of satisfaction and dissatisfaction in work (bifactorial theory). The factors of satisfaction are assimilated to motivational elements (interest in the work, self-fulfillment, responsibilities, etc.), while the factors of dissatisfaction are qualified as hygiene or atmosphere factors (company policy, remuneration, control, etc.). For Herzberg, the factors of dissatisfaction can be easily eliminated, notably through demands, unlike the factors of satisfaction, which involve more the content of the work and its interest for the worker. Douglas Mac Gregor (1906–1964) has shown that there are various forms of corporate governance linked to the manager's attitude and perception of management. Mac Gregor contrasts two implicit attitudes that he formulates in two theories, theory X versus theory Y. Theory X is similar to the management advocated by the classical school, in which the work is tedious by nature and not very motivating for the workers and therefore requires permanent monitoring by the management. The attitude required in this case is a system based exclusively on sanction-reward (financial). In contrast, theory Y postulates that people can be involved in their work in the long-term, provided that they find a genuine interest in it (and not just a financial one) and a means of personal fulfillment. In theory Y, people can find satisfaction in their work, self-direction, creativity and increased responsibility. Mac Gregor advocates a Y-type management rather than an X-type management from the perspective of sustainable efficiency.

In the tradition of Mac Gregor, Ouchi (1981) identifies three types of organizations. Ouchi describes firm A (Anglo-Saxon model), characterized by individual decision-making without any real consultation with employees, which he contrasts with firm J (Japanese model), which favors group work and decisions, and then proposes firm Z, which would be a combination of the other two models, associating individual responsibilities and collective decisions. In the school of human relations, we can also cite authors such as Lewin (1890–1947), on group dynamics and the different styles of leadership (authoritarian, permissive, democratic), and Likert (1903–1981), on management styles (authoritarian exploitative, authoritarian paternalistic, consultative, participative), the participative style being the most effective because it releases the potential of individuals. Mary Parker Follet (1868–1933) also worked a lot on the empowerment and participation of workers, the question of authority and power, notably through leadership, the "win–win" relationship in professional relations, advocating "power-with" versus "power-against. We can also cite authors such as Blake and Mouton (1970), who, by crossing two dimensions, interest in people and interest in tasks, identify five management styles (controlling, laissez-faire, compromise, social and integrating). Tannenbaum and Schmidt (1958) present a continuum in decision-making, ranging from authoritarian decisions made without any consultation to decisions made in consultation with the employees.

3.2.2. *The new management theories: "classical management versus alternative management"*

Talking about alternatives implies a choice. This choice would a priori oppose two options: either to apply a "classic", traditional, historical management or to choose another, more "modern", form of management.

When we speak about alternatives, we often make parallels with the "alternative economy" (supposedly more just, more equitable, more united, the SSE [social and solidarity economy]). We can also refer to the economy in general and look for an alternative to the classical economy (liberal, capitalist). Similarly, we could also evoke the choice of alternatives in sectors totally outside the field of management sciences, such as energy with alternative solutions (cleaner, preserving the environment, renewable, alternative to fossil fuels condemned). But what about management? What alternative could be proposed?

Recently, some authors have proposed the concept of "slow management" (Honoré 2004; Bruch and Ghoshal 2005) as a set of managerial practices aimed at creating cooperative, stable and sustainable work environments that promote human flourishing. Slow management is opposed to the classical theories described by these authors as "fast management", which favors individualism, short-term strategic vision, extreme financialization, urgency and immediacy of results. On the other hand, slow management is part of a sustainable development approach, the societal and social responsibility of organizations, alternative movements such as collaborative production and consumption, fair trade, and even the economic theory of degrowth. It is interesting to note that this area of thought adopts a very relative position with respect to time. The passing of time should no longer be a constraint that is suffered and oppressive because it is up to each person to reappropriate time to become the master of their own time. This is the opposite of certain managerial practices that some would describe as "time-stealing", such as consulting and writing e-mails and "infobesity" (Sauvajol-Rialland 2013). Detchessahar and Grevin (2009) even speak of "*gestionnite*", or *management-it is*", when they denounce the time spent in organizations feeding "management machines" instead of devoting themselves to more value-creating activities. Indeed, we can legitimately question the totality of the time spent in most organizations filling in tables, writing memos, preparing and organizing reports under the commonly accepted pretext of contributing to the steering of organizations. Is this particular and enslaving relationship to time a characteristic of Western countries, linked to a certain Anglo-Saxon culture of work and human activities, as opposed to other cultures (e.g. African culture, which gives more importance to the passing of time and human relationships, or even, in some respects, the Scandinavian model) (Hofstede 1994)?

3.2.3. *Alternative management: various experiences*

Since the 1970s, new management theories have been developed, such as lean management, autonomous teams, sociocracy (origin of Auguste Comte, 1798–1857), sociodynamics (Jean-Christian Fauvet, the inspiration for Favi, a "holomorphic" company), servant leadership (which consists of putting the manager at the service of the employees and not the other way around, Robert K. Greenleaf, 1970), socioeconomic management (Henri Savall 1976), CSR participative governance (e.g. Steria), deep democracy (e.g. in postapartheid South Africa), the Go Rowe method (result only work environment), Theory U (Otto Scharmer, 2012), appreciative inquiry (an approach centered on solutions to achieve a state of success rather than solutions to eliminate a problem), holacracy (Brian Robertson: placing the organization, its needs and purpose, as the center of gravity, viewing the company as a whole entity that exists for itself, managing all tensions and differentiating people from their roles) and so on.

Some companies or organizations have also proposed "alternative" visions of management (principle of Grounded Theory or theory "anchored" in practice, "lay" theory), such as Google, which redefined the role of leader through the "oxygen" program by identifying the skills required to be a good manager (being an excellent educator (coach), delegating decision-making power to the team and avoiding "micromanagement").

Some companies go much further in implementing "alternative" management, as the following examples show.

Favi is a French company (400 people) that has been particularly profitable, especially for the past 30 years, in the highly competitive car market. There is very little hierarchy and control; the staff is autonomous and organizes itself to meet the needs of its customers. The company is divided into mini-factories with an experienced leader at the head, who is co-opted and does not impose decisions. The leaders explain the "what to do". For the "how to do", they trust their teams.

We cite many other examples of "alternative" companies or organizations, such as Chronoflex (France, hydraulic hoses, 270 people), Hervé Thermique (France, 1,450 people), Gore (USA, textiles, 10,000 employees), Harley-Davidson, Poult (French cookie factory, 1,600 people), SOL (industrial cleaning, Finland, 11,500 employees), Sun Hydraulics (USA, 900 employees), AES (worldwide, energy, 40,000 employees), BSO/origin (worldwide, IT consulting, 10,000 employees), Buurtzorg (health-care, Netherlands, 7,000 employees), Morning Star (USA, food processing, leader in tomato processing, 2,400 people), Patagonia (textile, USA, 1,350 people), SEMCO (Brazil, 3,000 people) and HCLT (India, IT services, 55,000 people, slogan: "employees first, customers next"), as well as administrations, schools, hospitals (Laloux 2015) and so on.

Some general principles emerge from these "alternative enterprises":

– the principle of subsidiarity (the responsibility for an action decision lies with the competent person closest to those who are directly concerned by that action);

– the elimination of subordination and power hierarchies by other forms of "talent" hierarchies;

– autonomy, trust, the right to make mistakes, the reduced size of the teams, a certain way of thinking "backwards" with, for example, "reverse delegation (sociodynamics)", "backwards Taylorism", "the pyramid backwards", etc.

3.2.4. *A quick look at the "liberated enterprise" concept*

These numerous examples testify to the interest and success of an increasing number of people around the world in implementing new ways of managing organizations and breaking free from certain dogmas and the dominant managerial doctrine on power sharing and work distribution.

In recent years, the concept of the "liberated company" has been highlighted in the professional and scientific press as a new way of bringing greater well-being or benevolence to the workplace. It seems appropriate to us to address this concept briefly in this chapter, highlighting its main characteristics and limitations:

> Corporate liberation consists of promoting employee responsibility by freeing them from what may impede their margins of decision and action. (Verrier and Bourgeois 2016)

The concept of the liberated enterprise was mainly theorized by Tom Peters (1993) and was put back in the spotlight recently by Isaac Getz and Brian M. Carney (2012).

3.2.4.1. *Why liberate the company?*

The theorists of liberated companies emphasize the need to adapt to the ever-changing socioeconomic environment through greater freedom of action. "The species that survive are not the strongest or the most intelligent, but those that adapt best to change" (Charles Darwin). By invoking Darwin, these authors use the theory of Contingency (Woodward, Perrow, Buns, Stalker, Lawrence, Lorsch, Chandler, Mintzberg), which legitimizes constant adaptation to one's environment and to one's era within the framework of management sciences.

They also highlight the current desire to go beyond the classic hierarchical and bureaucratic systems of organization. According to these authors, the Taylorian model was not bad in itself and rather corresponded to the context and the needs of its time: mass industrialization.

3.2.4.2. *Liberate it from what, and for what?*

It is about freeing ourselves from the hierarchy of power to move toward other forms of hierarchy (talent, knowledge, etc.) (Getz and Carney 2015). It is also about freeing ourselves from time and space (Lean spirit), freeing employees and managers from "time thieves" (reporting, control, command, risk management (illusion of being able to master uncertainty, etc.). Freeing oneself from space and time constraints by a new organization of work (e.g. telecommuting, collaborative spaces, etc.). Beyond the physical, it is also about freeing the mind, unleashing initiatives, freeing creativity and innovation of everyone (and not only of those who are paid for it (R&D)). It is also the need or the opportunity to capture (and then disseminate) innovation wherever it is found (e.g. SNCF, which has created a global mechanism aimed at identifying innovation among suppliers and internal employees). It is no longer necessary to distinguish between those who innovate and those who do not (= Taylorian approach). Moreover, it means accepting the right to make mistakes and capitalize on the feedback from managerial mistakes (e.g. mismanagement of idea boxes). It also means identifying the qualities, skills, new behaviors and roles of each person, the levers necessary to unleash creativity (autonomy, trust, etc.) and the obstacles and "irritants".

Before, work was mostly "prescribed" and "standardized" due to the predominance of industry. Today, work is increasingly dominated by "knowledge workers", with a strong capacity for initiative, creativity and so on. As a result, new aspirations are emerging for employees (meaning, fulfillment, respect, commitment) with a digital revolution (telecommuting, virtualization, workspaces, etc.), logic of networks and communities of practice (horizontal exchanges).

Moreover, to use the words of Matthieu Detchessahar (2009), many companies are "sick", suffering from "*gestionnitis*" ("management-it is") by constantly feeding the management machines. Most managers are too busy with a very time-consuming form of management under the pretext of controlling risk and uncertainty to devote themselves to the real work, that of the "managed" which has now become the "invisible work" (Gomez 2015).

And the managers? "Managers should not disappear, they are essential to organizing "empowerment" and leading the transformation project" (Verrier and Bourgeois 2016). According to Verrier and Bourgeois (2016), the legitimacy of managers is based on five key notions:

– Freedom and responsibility (e.g. management by trust).

– Elements of culture and meaning (e.g. principle of subsidiarity, values).

– The valorization of skills ("it is the one who does who knows, but it is also the one who knows who does").

– Organizational choices (Michel Crozier: freedom is more organization rather than less).

– The ethical framework (respect for private life). It is a matter of dealing with three issues: the overall structure (the work units), the interactions between people and entities and the ethical framework (building a strong corporate culture while respecting the freedom and privacy of each individual).

Theorists and practitioners of the liberated enterprise propose a few principles of action to liberate the company: make pragmatism central (trial and error). There is no such thing as a ready-made solution, but rather a tailor-made one; rather than liberating, we need to adopt an approach to human and organizational transformation; we need to make an effective analysis of power issues, power relationships and conflicting interests, not denying them; starting with people, not proposing something ready-made from above (freeing oneself from the Taylorian culture, from the "push" logic), knowing how to listen to and understand what employees are saying.

What levers should be used for implementation? Define and organize elements of meaning (compass and source of commitment, management by values); formalize a strategy built and carried by all; ensure the rise in responsibility and competence (replace the "job description" logic with a "path to competence" logic); set up facilitating structures (e.g. develop "intrapreneurship"); regulate interactions (relationships, decision-making processes, example of management book, red lines, etc.); building shared HR policies (creating employee value propositions consistent with customer value propositions); repositioning managers (replacing the command-and-control model with a manager model), becoming a resource for teams, a facilitator, a leader (pedagogue), inspiring, etc., repositioning managers (replace the command-and-control model with a manager model), becoming a resource for teams, a facilitator, a leader (pedagogue), giving desire, etc.; centering support functions on value creation (stop controls, gendarmerie, etc.); reminding people who the functionary is not at the service of the operational staff (the opposite of the current relation) but at the service of the customer; rethinking the role and posture of the leader (the man of strategy, organization, culture, transformation, he is no longer a "hierarchical superior") (Verrier and Bourgeois 2016).

It is therefore by no means a question of eliminating managers but of redefining their roles (facilitator, helping people to "do their job well"; Clot 2015, 2021).

3.2.4.3. *What are the limits and perspectives of the liberated enterprise?*

One of the main criticisms of the liberated enterprise is that it focuses on individual determinants (a psychological approach to the issues), with man being considered good by nature (Mac Gregor, Rousseau, etc.) or, conversely, bad (Hobbes). However, this is a very deterministic approach, and the debate is not there; the company often makes workers what they are. Moreover, the company does not have to make its employees happy; the purpose of the company ("liberated" or not) is not this. More broadly, we can also criticize the liberated company for the place of the "liberating leader", the responsibility (counterpart of freedom) decreed, the criticism (or even the disappearance?) of managers, the criticism (or even the elimination?) of support functions, the all-or-nothing logic (the company is either free or not), the absence of regulation of interactions (how to coordinate actions, how to make decisions) (Verrier and Bourgois 2016). In addition, several authors and organizations propose some very specific forms of liberated enterprise, such as the "opal enterprise" (Laloux 2015), which would be part of a long historical process of evolution-transformation of companies toward a kind of ideal symbiosis between their different stakeholders.

3.3. Is history a perpetual restart?

For some, "history is a perpetual restart" (Thucydides, 460 BC). In terms of human organization, this aphorism could seem totally true and, in a certain sense, very pessimistic. However, the history of management, which can be defined as the organization of a work group, is in fact relatively recent. In addition, notwithstanding the fact that we have known the same classical practices for slightly more than a century and, despite a more humanistic approach the 1930s, this could only be a "historical parenthesis". It is quite legitimate to wonder about the fact that, despite our longstanding knowledge of certain levers of benevolence at work (e.g. meaning, achievable objectives, freedom of action, autonomy, gratitude, encouragement, forgiveness, the right to make mistakes and so on), a managerial model has not clearly emerged and become widespread.

However, we can no longer remain deaf to the positive signals sent throughout the world by these so-called "alternative" organizations, which are successful at all levels and naturally invite us not to remain prisoners of the same "managerial recipes" *ad vitam æternam*. Another choice is possible. This apparent "resistance" or persistence of the classic management model can be explained by different reasons. It can be a cultural reason due to the prevalence of the Taylorian model, the common representation of the leader and their authority, their protection (parent–child, teacher–student, leader–subordinate relationship) and respect for the hierarchy. However, this can also be explained by the financialization of the economy: the manager, the leader must respond to short-term objectives (immediate profitability, intermediation of financial markets).

In fact, managers have very little room for maneuver; they are merely executors in charge of controlling performance and are themselves controlled in an environment where the real decisions are made elsewhere, beyond the sphere of "real" work. Here again, management sciences explain this very well through the "agency theory" (Jensen and Meckling 1976) in which an "agent" (the manager) carries out what the "principal" (the owner of the capital) asks of them. In short, it is not a question of questioning the concept of authority but simply of substituting the notion of subordination and therefore of hierarchical authority for other forms of authority (talents, skills, expertise, relational intelligence, the ability to bring together, to encourage, to coordinate-organize, etc.).

Indeed, the classical representation of authority generally takes the form of highly normative hierarchical structures that have been part of history since time immemorial (feudal, Roman, Greek, Egyptian systems, etc.) with "leaders" and subordinates ("masters and slaves"?) We thus speak of N+1, N+2, and so on, and a contrario of N-1, N-2, etc., a system in which authority is legitimized mainly by a privileged position in an organizational chart. If we take it literally, this type of very fixed organization can sometimes be the ground for a lot of "N" (hate). Therefore, at the end of this historical journey, let us dare to imagine a next step toward a more peaceful working world, in which the number of "N" (hate) would be reduced in favor of more "P" (peace) in interpersonal and interorganizational relationships.

3.4. Conclusion

The search for benevolence in the workplace is certainly a historic quest that, admittedly, has not yet been able to offer us a unique or normative managerial model. However, is it truly desirable? History teaches us that there are certain levers likely to develop benevolence at work, but this is by no means an ultimate *vade mecum*. It is undoubtedly up to each of us to reinvent our own roles in this new theater of the *commedia del lavoro* (the comedy of work).

3.5. References

Barabel, M., Meier, O., Teboul, T. (2008). *Les fondamentaux du management.* Dunod, Malakoff.

Bruch, H. and Ghoshal, S. (2005). *A Bias for Action*. Penguin Books, London.

Clot, Y. (2015). *Le travail à cœur : pour en finir avec les risques psychosociaux*. La Découverte, Paris.

Clot, Y., Bonnefond, J.Y., Bonnemain, A., Zittoun, M. (2021). *Le prix du travail bien fait. La coopération conflictuelle dans les organisations*. La Découverte, Paris.

Detchessahar, M. and Grevin, A. (2009). Un organisme de santé malade de "gestionnite". *Annales des Mines – Gérer et comprendre*, 4(98), 27–37.

Engels, F. (1973). *Socialisme utopique et socialisme scientifique*. Éditions sociales, Paris.

Getz, I. and Carney, B.M. (2013). *Liberté & Cie – Quand la liberté des salariés fait le succès des entreprises*. Flammarion, Paris.

Gomez, P.Y. (2015). *Le travail invisible. Enquête sur une disparition.* Éditions François Bourin, Paris.

Hofstede, G. (1994). *Vivre dans un monde multiculturel*. Les Éditions d'Organisation, Paris.

Honoré, C. (2004). *Éloge de la Lenteur*. Marabout, Nanterre.

Jensen, M. (1976). Can the corporation survive? Center for Research in Government Policy and Business, University of Rochester, Rochester.

Lallement, M. (2009). *Le travail de l'utopie. Godin et le familistère de Guise. Biographie*. Les Belles Lettres, Paris.

Laloux, F. (2015). *Reinventing Organizations*. Diateino, Paris.

Paquot, T. (2007). *Utopies et utopistes*. La Découverte, Paris.

Ricard, M. (2013). *Plaidoyer pour l'altruisme. La force de la bienveillance*. Nil Éditions, Paris.

Rodet, P. and Desjaques, Y. (2019). *Le management bienveillant. La bienveillance est l'indicateur d'un monde encore humain*. Eyrolles, Paris.

Sauvajol-Rialland, C. (2013). "Infobésité", le mal du siècle. *France TV Info* [Online]. Available at: https://www.francetvinfo.fr/economie/entreprises/video-infobesite-le-mal-du-siecle_348052.html.

Thietart, R.A. (2003). *Méthodes de recherche en management*. Dunod, Malakoff.

Verrier, G. and Bourgeois, N. (2016). *Faut-il libérer l'entreprise ? Confiance, responsabilité et autonomie au travail*. Dunod, Malakoff.

Weber, M. (1964). *L'éthique protestante et l'esprit du capitalisme, 1904–1905*. Plon, Paris.

4

Caring Management: A Lever to Anticipate, Manage and Repair Crises in the Health-Care System? Lessons Learned from the COVID-19 Health Crisis

Bayntun et al. asked, as early as 2012, whether the health-care system was well prepared for health disasters. Were our companies, our public services and our public authorities more generally prepared to manage the COVID-19 crisis as well as possible? The answer, no, leads us to wonder how all these systems can prepare themselves to face new crises or new disasters, especially those predicted due to global warming. We must learn from the current crisis and from past crises to be able, from now on, to "take care of thousands of people suddenly in mortal danger, as humanely as possible" (Fessler 2020). Health crises (avian flu, H1N1, SARS 2003, COVID-19, etc.) are becoming more frequent, larger in scale and, in some cases, rapidly transforming into real health, economic and social disasters.

For a long time (Lagadec 1991), it has been recognized that crisis management relies to a large extent on the trust of the parties involved, including victims, stakeholders, experts and public authorities. It seems, however, that relying on the existence of such a climate of trust, which would be established tacitly and spontaneously during a crisis, is no longer sufficient. Our health systems, our organizational systems and our state systems need a genuine proactive policy of crisis preparation, crisis management and postcrisis restoration. This policy must be focused on protecting everyone from the risks and stresses caused by the many

---

Chapter written by Manel ABDELJALIL-DINÉ, Christelle BRUYÈRE, Nelly MASSARD and Martine SÉVILLE.

hazards with increasingly serious consequences. Could caring management be the basis of such a proactive policy, allowing us to strengthen our systems and their capacity for resilience in the face of hazards?

Management is now at a crossroads. Faced with the COVID-19 crisis, it must now show that it is ready to fully assume, even in times of crisis such as COVID-19, and a fortiori in this period, its primary function of being a form of alternative management to ensure the protection and "care" of stakeholders.

In the first section, this chapter aims to show how a caring management style, centered on the recognition of each of each person in their work, caring for others and sharing a common view of activities, as well as identification and reduction of vulnerabilities and the search for a peaceful social climate, could and should be a lever for anticipating, managing and repairing crises. Based on data collected on a panel of health-care institutions in the Auvergne-Rhône-Alpes (AURA) region, we provide, in the second section, examples of this proposal from the health-care system.

4.1. Caring management can be a lever for anticipating, managing and repairing crises, but it must assert itself as such

Crisis, catastrophe or disaster occurs when hazards or shocks affect vulnerable systems or people. Consequently, a crisis management policy consists of working both on the occurrence of hazards, which must be anticipated and reduced, and on the vulnerability of systems or people who could be affected by these hazards. Once the risk of a crisis has been identified, it is also necessary to find solutions to the crisis in a context of urgency and great uncertainty as to the short-term and long-term effectiveness of these solutions. Finally, once the crisis is over, one must know how to rebuild the people – the "survivors" as they are called in the literature on crisis management – and the damaged systems and give them back the capacity to rebuild what was affected by the crisis. To what extent can caring management intervene at these three levels of prevention: preparation, management and repair of crises?

It seems that it should be more strategic, extended to other stakeholders rather than just employees and focus more on the survivors of the crisis and on the reassessment of professions that are ignored (the "heroes in the shadows") but very important in the restoration of the postcrisis social link.

4.1.1. *Caring management to better anticipate and prevent crises: toward a more strategic caring management?*

Many of the hazards that cause crises today are exogenous shocks (health, economic) that affect our companies and our health systems and on which they have little influence. They must therefore prepare themselves by being less vulnerable to avoid these hazards turning into disasters through cascading effects. On the other hand, it is increasingly clear that, as the work on the Anthropocene[1] indicates, humans themselves can be the source of crises in an endogenous way. Caring management will not be able to completely eliminate these hazards; it must, however, be able to act as a lever for the care and protection of stakeholders (Rodet and Desjacques 2019), including in these periods "outside the normal functioning of organizations", and thus contribute to strengthening the resilience of each individual in the face of them. Caring management could thus help to identify and reduce the vulnerabilities of people and systems exposed to crisis risks. It can also help to reduce the risk of malicious acts or eliminate endogenous sources of disaster. It must therefore become strategic.

Many crises originate in shocks that are exogenous to organizations. It is therefore difficult, as Rodet (2019) points out, to eliminate the stress inherent to these hazards or, more generally, to the growing uncertainty associated with not knowing where and when the crisis will come from. It is no longer possible to think that "humans could have absolute control over these hazards" (Akanni 2020); however, it is no longer possible to consider crises such as the COVID-19 crisis as an epiphenomenon (Akanni 2020). On the contrary, the more vulnerable people and systems are, the greater they will be affected by these hazards. To prevent or anticipate crises and increase their resilience, it is necessary to identify the vulnerabilities of people and systems.

However, while disasters and their contexts are different, many of them evoke similar system vulnerabilities, particularly in the health sector (Bayntun et al. 2012). Common practices and policies must therefore be put in place to learn how to identify and address these vulnerabilities through genuine individual, collective, organizational and interorganizational learning. It is also important to integrate multidisciplinary perspectives (medical, health, economic, political, etc.) in this learning process and in a global risk-based approach to avoid cascading crises. Each component of the health system must have the freedom not only to identify, recognize and prevent its sources of vulnerability (Lagadec 1991) but also to address

1 The Anthropocene is a term relating to a new geological era in which man has acquired such an influence on the biosphere that he has become its central actor (source: https://www.geo.fr/environnement/geologie-quest-ce-que-lanthropocene-193622).

vulnerabilities linked to problems of coordination or connections between the components or the actors.

Bayntun et al. (2012) refer to this as the need for "multidisciplinary health systems" in disaster management. It is therefore important to develop true collective intelligence and trust and mutual trust to learn about past crises together and better prepare for future crises by considering possible scenarios. Even if these scenarios will not necessarily be those used during the crisis because of the high level of uncertainty and because nothing that was planned will work (Lagadec 1991), establishing these scenarios can make it possible to test a vast range of solutions together by imagining their potential consequences and to detect previously hidden vulnerabilities of the systems facing them, such as the difficulties in mobilizing certain resources in the event of a crisis (i.e. masks or gowns in the case of a health crisis). This collective intelligence is thus part of a true strategic perspective of crisis preparation. However, as Lagadec (1991) points out, it is very difficult for the various actors to recognize their vulnerabilities or the failures encountered during previous crisis episodes. In fact, there is a need for an environment that encourages them to take a step back and consider their weaknesses. Caring management by recognizing the right to fail, to trial and error, must be able to encourage the expression and management of these different levels of vulnerability in a strategic perspective of developing collective awareness of extreme situations that the health system may encounter in the future due to exogenous shocks.

Some crises can also arise from malicious acts, from dissident behavior within organizations or from people in a situation of failure. Caring management should reduce the likelihood of this happening or of these acts multiplying. In addition, and in a more tacit way, it also seems that, by their very activity and in an involuntary way this time, systems or people are endogenous sources of crisis. As Ferar indicates in 2020 (p. 191), "management, though reputedly strategic (Beaumont 1993), of knowledge (Cook and Brown 1999), was unable to recognize and prevent this health crisis and, like the previous financial crisis, it is a management that produces crisis cells, which has become 'sick at heart', out of the race, out of the game".

It is therefore essential that caring management, by posing as an alternative source to traditional management, can consider the human, social and environmental consequences of the activities of the organizations it leads. Focusing on a sustainable performance and the creation of value through partnership can help to reduce these endogenous sources of crisis. More specifically, crises within the health system may have arisen from several paradoxical tensions:

> There are tensions between budgetary imperatives and public health objectives, tensions between the centralization of public health

policies and the need for local adaptation, and tensions between a "republican" vision of the hospital and a more managerial vision based on the development of budgetary management tools. (Bréchat et al. 2010)

A proactive policy aimed at reducing these endogenous sources of crisis must seek to find a strategic balance between these different paradoxical forces, which must be possible for a caring management style in search of a calm environment through a convergence of interests, visions or interpretations of situations that are sometimes divergent but must be taken into account. Faced with the rise of strategic uncertainties, it must also put in place a more interactive management system (Simons 1995), more focused on the task to be accomplished than on efficiency (Naro and Travaillé 2020), than what has been developed until now to stimulate organizational learning and the suggestion of new ideas. Promoting collective intelligence to increase the resilience of our systems in the face of disasters is now a concern for many researchers, and a number of avenues are being considered: technical, notably through digitization or the role of social networks (Chamberlain et al. 2020) or crowdsourcing (Song et al. 2020) but also linked to the development of social capital (Koh et al. 2008) based on the construction of communities (Agani et al. 2010) of supportive groups in the face of difficulties to which caring management should be able to contribute.

Collective learning about past crises, transparency as to the main sources of vulnerability and the development of a calm social climate by finding a balance between paradoxical tensions must be articulated with the definition of common action logics. The existence of a common sense of purpose for each person's activity, a mission that generates support and transcends the obstacles of the moment, can help to transcend the difficulties and vulnerabilities of each person when a crisis occurs and facilitate the choice of solutions to manage it. Trust that each person can, at their own level, grasp the issues and the solutions to be implemented to accomplish their task, whatever happens, in the face of the crisis, according to a principle of subsidiarity is part of this. Benevolence must therefore be able to play a strategic role in defining these courses of action.

Finally, it is essential that, in the face of crisis or disaster threats, leadership within the health system – or, more precisely, within health-care institutions or facilities – be involved in building the resilience capacity of their organization, bearing in mind, at their level, all the potential sources of strong vulnerability if the crisis or disaster occurs; the leader must play a pivotal role in learning from past crises and in defining or redefining the common logic of action (the mission) within the organization. Some authors speak of transformational leadership (Bass 1999), "magnanimous" leadership (Patapan 2016), or even shock management (Shufutinsky et al. 2020).

Being a leader committed to caring management by fostering an environment that motivates employees to stay and contribute to the resolution of crises certainly presupposes, as for any employee retention, "a systematic effort" (Mandhanya and Agrawal 2017), a real voluntarist policy, but it must allow for achieving these objectives. The leader or the management team must therefore be able to maintain the following:

> Interpersonal relationships, mediate apologies and provide encouragement, provide opportunities to divert attention, encourage self-determination, and increase interdependence among organizational members. (Mandaya and Agrawal 2017)

This seems to fall, at least in part, under the characteristics advocated in the framework of a caring management.

4.1.2. *Caring management to manage crises: the need for caring management to be extended to more stakeholders than just employees*

It seems that now the current crises pose real pernicious problems (McMillan and Overall 2016), that is, ones that are difficult to understand truly and impossible to solve completely. The COVID-19 crisis has demonstrated the difficulty of articulating solutions that are agreeable to all stakeholders (business leaders, physicians, government, etc.). It is therefore no longer a question of trying to resolve these crises but rather of limiting their destructive effects by finding solutions that are acceptable to a group of actors with different points of view and interests.

To the extent that the crisis implies the impossibility of relying on what was planned (Lagadec 1991) because decisions have to be made in a hurry and because a certain number of actors reveal during the crisis the vulnerabilities that they had hidden until then, it is mutual trust in the teams and with the partners that will count; trust in the way they will proceed, if not to find solutions, at least in the way they will approach the crisis. The notions of shared trust of the legitimacy of decisions made by some will all be greater if caring management within the system has been put in place.

However, crisis management also requires trust in external partners (experts, neighboring governments, etc.) who will help to resolve the crisis. For example, the care of COVID-19 patients in other regions that provide intensive care beds, or the provision of masks and gowns to health personnel by certain companies, all of which may have appeared to be "do-it-yourself" solutions, but which helped to save lives. However, caring management seems to have dealt less with the issue of management of external parties than with team management. It would therefore be interesting to analyze whether an organization's internal policy of caring management can be extended to its external partners (customers, suppliers, partners), especially since this is part of the search for sustainable performance claimed by caring management.

Finally, Lagadec (1991, p. 200) warns of the need to remember, in cases of crisis management, the need to "sort" both the solutions to the crisis and the beneficiaries of those solutions. As demonstrated by the COVID-19 health crisis but also by other health crises or migratory crises, the question of who to accept as sick, who to treat, who not to treat and what treatment to give to which patient (like the questions asked, for example, by the UN agencies in charge of migrants, as to which migrant can be housed and which must be deported because the camps are unable to accept them all; Lecadet 2020) pose major problems in large-scale health crises. For example, it was decided to reserve beds for COVID-19 patients by postponing certain surgical interventions scheduled for other patients. However, as Lagadec (1991) points out, "sorting must be done delicately so as not to generate unnecessary resentment".

Crisis management therefore requires creating a dynamic of adherence to the choices and decisions made (Lagadec 1991) and building a system of cooperation on the basis of a mutual adjustment that can be done in an emergency. This must be based on a real collective strength or capacity that can contribute to the development of caring management.

More generally, caring management must be attentive to the cascading consequences of crisis management: the psychological distress of health-care workers who must continue to work while the pandemic explodes and they themselves are subject to the risks of contagion, the need to isolate themselves so as not to contaminate their families, and the feeling of guilt at not being able to treat everyone (Walton et al. 2020). This situation has already been encountered during other pandemics, such as the Severe Acute Respiratory Syndrome (SARS) in 2003, after which many health-care workers experienced psychological distress (Tam et al. 2004; Lee et al. 2007).

Overall, crisis management assumes that both internal and external stakeholders are managed, that they adhere to the chosen solutions and that they are open to solutions that may be "cobbled together" depending on the situation and the means available but that are accepted by all. Management must therefore be caring in nature toward both internal employees and other, more external stakeholders.

4.1.3. *Caring management in the face of the challenges of crisis recovery*

The COVID-19 crisis has shown the importance of "forgotten" or "invisible" jobs, the role of certain actors (e.g. garbage collectors) who have contributed a great deal to maintaining social links or creating connections in a crisis marked by ruptures. Some authors (Chanlat 2020, p. 120) call for the following:

> The "anthropological turnaround" at the end of COVID-19 to put forward the virtues of proximity, social ties, speech, the return of long time and long-term thinking, the preservation of resources, prudence, culture and a wisdom based on an ethics of finitude.

It is also a question of rethinking the organization of work for more autonomy because, as Bachelard (2020) points out:

> Decision-makers will have seen the value of unleashing the imagination, commitment and autonomy of employees through flexible, agile organizations, freed from bureaucratic constraints, adapted to the 21st century and its uncertainties, in the service of global performance and the fulfillment and well-being of employees.

Resilience is unlikely to be sufficient in the post-COVID-19 world. The crisis will lead organizations to rethink their management methods in depth to create more humanistic management (Alemanno 2020), an alternative management more focused on the fragility of people at work but also on their potential for creativity, their key role in the achievement of the overall task even when they seem a priori in a less visible position, which can be caring management.

However, caring management will have to provide concrete answers to various problems inherent to the postcrisis period. It must, first of all, address the issue of revaluing forgotten or invisible jobs (Fessler 2020) in the health sector, not only there (garbage collectors, for example) but also those of the "heroes of the shadows" according to the expression of Besseyre des Horts (2020). This requires a rethinking of the relative value of jobs in relation to each other, because according to him (2020):

> It is undoubtedly in the area of jobs that a real challenge should be made to the certainties that have been based for decades on the relative value of jobs in relation to each other: jobs in the social sphere have the greatest precariousness and the lowest salaries, and jobs in the economic sphere have the greatest stability and the highest salaries. (Besseyre des Horts 2020)

It will also be necessary to look at the "survivors", those who have escaped the health or social consequences of the crisis and who will feel guilty for having escaped or for not having done enough for others. We must give meaning to their work by including them in the achievement of a collectively rethought mission of the system.

Finally, caring management, while focusing on the issue of people within work groups, will have to address the issue of financing the consequences of the crisis in the health-care system and, once again, on the question of the balance between human and economic concerns. There will therefore be a need for renewed management at the end of the large-scale COVID-19 crisis; will caring management be able to meet these challenges?

4.2. Caring management in the face of the COVID-19 crisis: case studies of health-care institutions in the AURA region (Auvergne-Rhône-Alpes)

Caring management must be able to meet the challenge of being strategic to develop collective intelligence to prepare for the crisis, extended to stakeholders other than the employees seen in a homogeneous way (victims, survivors, solution-creators, heroes in the shadows, unexpected or expected partners, experts from different backgrounds), during and after the crisis and taking up the challenge of valuing professions that are overlooked but that contribute to achieving the aims of the health system.

Are there any indications of the role of caring management as a lever for anticipating, managing and recovering from the COVID-19 crisis experienced by health-care institutions? This is what we will try to determine in this second study through a panel of health-care institutions in the Auvergne-Rhône-Alpes region (AURA). Table 4.1 provides a summary of the main theoretical elements set out in section 4.1, which characterize the ideal case of a health-care organization that includes caring management in its overall strategy (management internal to the system, not just linked to individuals). This grid was used to read the data collected from the experience of 12 managers (health-care executives, institutional management) in a health crisis management situation in 2020 in various structures from the public or associative sector: seven hospital centers, one university hospital center, one residential establishment for dependent elderly people and one medical-educational institute. Their feedback on their experience was transcribed in their master's dissertation (Master in Management of Health Organizations at the Saint-Étienne Business Administration Institute). In addition, three individual interviews lasting a total of 4 h were conducted with two nursing home directors and a senior health executive in charge of a bed management unit of a university hospital.

	Before the crisis	During the crisis	After the crisis
Use of caring management	Develop collective intelligence (ability to work together)	Strengthen the climate of trust to legitimize decisions	Comfort the "survivors" and giving meaning to work
	Have an active partnership approach, particularly in the area of intervention	Build solutions with internal and external multidisciplinary stakeholders (HR, health-care professionals, managers, supervisors, etc.)	Develop organizational agility (toward less bureaucracy and more autonomy and more autonomy, proximity)
	Stimulate creativity of employees, encourage initiatives		Promote professions with a poor image or invisible, and yet indispensable
	Develop organizational learning (learn from past crises, produce scenarios)		Steer the strategy of the establishment by reconciling economic and human logic for a sustainable performance

Table 4.1. *Potential roles of caring management in crisis anticipation, management and recovery*

Among the cases studied, one health-care facility approaches the theoretical ideal (we will call it PYA). We will begin by analyzing PYA and then the other facilities to test the theoretical elements previously identified in the field.

Several questions will be addressed: can caring management truly be a lever for anticipating, managing and recovering from the COVID-19 crisis? Is it limited to an attractive discourse with no proven effect? Is it finally a luxury that can be afforded only when everything is going well, and which shatters with the tumult of the crisis?

4.2.1. *When caring management deployed in the organization before the crisis promotes resilience and organizational learning to cope: the case of PYA*

Among the cases studied, we identify an institution that has implemented caring management within the system. This is the PYA nursing home (Chapter 6). Its director, whom we could describe as a "liberating leader" (Getz and Carney 2016) or a "committed leader" (Mandhanya and Agrawal 2017), has had, since the creation of the establishment, the will to exercise, with the management team, caring management. With regularity and conviction, she has put in place mutual trust, collaborative work, transparency, the right to make mistakes and the principle of subsidiarity as key elements of the institution's management style. At times, she was bullied by internal and external actors who were used to the authoritarian role of the leader in the organization, but she always stood her ground.

The COVID-19 crisis was, for this nursing home director, a piece of evidence that caring management works: "I have the proof, it backs up my way of managing: this mode of management works". She also confides that managing the establishment during the crisis "has given even more meaning to her job". We propose making PYA a case study. Well-monitored management is at the heart of the governance of the establishment, whereas the other cases studied propose a rather classic mode of management. Through this PYA case, we show how caring management can be a lever for anticipating, managing and recovering from the crisis.

Before the crisis, the nursing and care teams worked together and were used to taking initiatives and making decisions because "decisions are made by the people who are competent to make them and the management is not in the institution 7 days a week, unlike the nurses". Organizational learning is developed and can be illustrated, for example, by the pairs formed by an orderly and a nurse, who are specialists in a given field, with the task of disseminating good practices to their colleagues (e.g. oral hygiene specialist). Collaborative work is also expressed through the projects carried out in the establishment. Several projects are carried out by multidisciplinary teams (e.g. the 4M project, section 6.3).

The collaborative mode of operation and the experience acquired during the projects were levers for managing the crisis:

> We used what we learned during the 4M project during the crisis. The crisis brought the employees and the management into the same situation as at the beginning of the project: when the crisis arrives, we all had the same level of knowledge, the same level of feelings. We were all faced with the same difficulty, whether it was a nurse, a nurse's aide, or management. We need support and find solutions on an ad hoc basis (...). The teams, in complete autonomy have thought about the organizations. It is a shared management. It's shared management.

The 4M project, with its horizontal management, taught them that, to move forward, it was necessary to rely on the expertise of each person and to develop a true collective intelligence:

> We all learned things during the project we did together, we were all on the same level, we needed each other's expertise to cope, we sort of

> used our collective intelligence during the crisis like we did during the 4M project.

Management also played a role in facilitating the choice of solutions to manage the crisis when ethical issues arose. Solutions were chosen as a team, re-evaluated if they did not work, creating buy-in to the choice finally made: "The decision is a compromise and we support the team's solution". For example, the team was faced with the deaths of residents. In the absence of funeral companies (overwhelmed) to take care of the deceased, it was up to the establishment to take care of putting the body of the deceased in a body bag while respecting the relevant hygiene rules. Caring management made it possible to overcome the vulnerabilities of each person and the difficulties faced in these dramatic situations. As a team and with the support of the management, the caregivers were all able to share their fears or their (in)ability to do this "unexpected" work in their profession as caregivers.

Before the crisis, kindness, respect for one another and mutual aid were already very present in the establishment and were part of its DNA. The right to make mistakes is one of the principles of the management style, and mistakes are accepted and perceived as a form of learning for the employee: "We learn from our mistakes". We can qualify them as crisis management levers:

> The solidarity effect seen during the crisis is a defense mechanism. This mechanism was put in place very quickly in the institution, but it was all the stronger because it was already very present. This solidarity has been maintained over time. But it is part of our positioning, so the mutual aid, the work climate, and the collaboration are already there. These are activities that we know how to do, so their effects were accentuated during a crisis.

In addition, these same levers have, during the crisis, allowed the team to take a step back from the vulnerabilities of each individual. The virus brought fears and anxiety to the caregivers, exacerbated by family pressure (families fear the virus entering their homes). The objective of the caregivers was to not get sick and some of them refused to work in fear. Caring management made it possible to collectively accept these numerous stoppages and to welcome and train newcomers very quickly: "The management in place allows the teams to become resilient. For example, we might be three people short of the workforce for tomorrow, but the team was able to adapt (...). We also recruited students who quickly integrated (...). But we also had to make sure that the teams rested: the director must be vigilant about stress and fatigue". Caring management also leads the manager to be optimistic, to encourage: "Fear is transmitted, so we had to be optimistic to rebalance the climate against the pessimists".

The proximity of management with its teams has also been a lever for managing the crisis because it allows the teams to be reactive when it is necessary to adapt the organization to deal with absences:

> Management communicates through proximity. I, and the health executive, are very close to the teams, so decision-making is faster. We were more reactive (...). We find the solution together; it is shared and it is an area of satisfaction for all members.

This transparent communication goes beyond the walls of the nursing home by continuously informing external stakeholders (e.g. families, administrators, etc.), thus generating empathy and mutual support.

The COVID-19 crisis showed the importance of "forgotten" or "invisible" jobs. Some jobs within the nursing home were valued after the crisis. This is the case of the linen department, whose work has never been so important:

> During COVID, there was a focus on the caregivers with the clapping ritual, but for example, within the institution, we highlighted the work of the laundry: their work was needed. This crisis showed that we needed each other.

Caring management led the team to evaluate its practices after the crisis and to capitalize on its experiences as after a project. The team has experienced a different way of relating to the resident and is currently thinking about putting more personalization into future care. The establishment, like many, had to isolate the residents. It was therefore necessary to adapt the activities, the animations and to make them in smaller groups.

Members of the institution were stretched thin during the crisis. Caring management promoted the resilience of the actors and the organization. It allowed them to "hold out over time (...), it allows the team to resist (...), it lives and overcomes things. They recover afterwards and are satisfied to have succeeded in doing difficult things". Care management seems to be a lever for crisis recovery since it strengthens the team and gives them a sense of satisfaction.

The PYA case illustrates the role that caring management within the system can play in crisis management and recovery. It does not yet make it possible to anticipate crises, as PYA is not in the process of building scenarios to guard against future crises. However, we note that well-monitored management facilitates organizational learning and resilience to prepare for future crises.

4.2.2. *When caring management based on the goodwill of work groups in normal times is imposed on everyone in times of crisis*

Among the cases studied, management practices remain mostly focused on team management, with the exception of the PYA case. In other words, it is not a question of a global strategy of an institution in search of sustainable performance but of individual strategies that vary from one care service to another, depending on personal preferences and work groups.

As a result, before the COVID-19 crisis, the "traces" of caring management identified in the feedback from managers were more a matter of individual choices made by some health managers. The latter feel "responsible" for their teams and implement projects on their own initiative to improve the well-being of the team and their daily professional practices. For example, in one of the memoirs analyzed, a health executive observed, when she took up her post, that her team of carers was very concerned about the quality of care and was constantly questioning the therapies offered to patients. However, nothing in the department is formalized or charted. To respond to these concerns, this manager, in collaboration with her hospital's quality department, set up a project to evaluate care practices and their traceability to get her team to formalize and trace all practices in the patient's journey from entry to exit. The objective of this project was to encourage learning organizational learning within the unit, to establish cooperation and collaboration between the different professionals and to promote the care of the patient as a whole. According to this framework:

> This work of formalizing the roles and missions of each person was necessary (...), the professionals also had to learn to work in cooperation toward a common goal: quality of care. (...), this project has also helped to promote and develop the dynamics and cohesion of the team.

Benevolence then appears to be an individual and "spontaneous" strategy linked to the sensitivity of the health executive and their ability to take the initiative but also to the team of professionals in the field and their willingness to follow the executive and to become involved in the executive's projects, which, as seen previously in the literature, makes it possible to redefine the logic of common actions and reduce the possible risks of malice. These individual choices for caring management constitute favorable predispositions to manage the crisis. However, they are "restrained" by the system within the framework of its normal functioning, which does not encourage the dissemination and sustainability of these managerial practices.

However, if before the COVID-19 crisis, the place of caring management seemed to depend on the goodwill of the managers, in times of crisis, it seems to have imposed itself as a necessity for all. "It's what keeps our heads above water" (nursing home director). Caring management is understood here in terms of "taking care" of patients, professionals, oneself, relatives, etc. Listening, collaboration, pedagogy (explaining the decisions made), and mutual aid have become essential levers for managing the COVID-19 crisis, as if taking care of others and oneself had become indispensable in an environment that puts people at risk. Because the professionals felt in danger in front of this new virus:

> We had to constantly reassure them, some nurses refused to work in the COVID unit, new information came in every day and we had to deal with it. (Health executive)

Crisis cells were set up to "take stock of the morale of the troops, provide information and take decisions together" (health executive). Internal and interfacility collaboration was facilitated during the COVID-19 crisis. Two health-care managers in charge of setting up a bed management cell (with associated software), before the crisis, testify to the ease with which they were able to obtain the information necessary for its proper functioning during the crisis (which was not the case in normal times). Indeed, the bed management units and the Bed Manager functioned perfectly during the crisis. To take care of the COVID-19 patients within territories, there was collaboration between different hospitals, as well as between internal services. The reliability of the feedback from the services to these units enabled the patients to be put "in the right place, at the right time":

> In this crisis, the bed management unit made it possible to create and strengthen the link between our institution and the other institutions in the GHT, as well as between the emergency department and the hospitalization services. (Senior manager, bed manager unit leader)

Services and hospitals coordinate and share information because, as the literature points out, the crisis gives a common meaning to everyone's activity, a mission that generates support and makes it possible to transcend the difficulties. The crisis pushed the actors to operate in a collaborative mode.

In addition, faced with this anxiety-provoking context, some health managers have had to adopt a directive management style, unusual in their practices, to reassure their teams, as the following testimony from a manager indicates:

> At the time of the health crisis, the national injunctions, which had to be implemented quickly, the fatigue, the uncertainties of the caregivers, the anxieties of the patients pushed me to adopt a more

> directive management. This allowed me to guide the teams through the vagaries of regularly modified management notes, to organize changes in operations and to control the proper application of directives.

While this directive management style may be perceived in an ordinary context as authoritarian, it was nevertheless very much appreciated by the caregivers in this context and allowed them to have a precise and reassuring framework in managing this crisis.

Similarly, the health crisis has the financial, organizational, and strategic constraints that weigh on health managers on a daily basis. They have witnessed an administrative simplification of all the processes that are usually time consuming in their missions (recruitment, training, financing, etc.). The following testimony illustrates this unprecedented situation where the structure in general and the management more specifically gave them all the means to face this crisis. The result of this "freedom to act" in this context of crisis has led to a real awareness on the part of the health executive of his or her role as manager:

> The disappearance of budgetary restrictions, combined with a simplification of administration, has greatly facilitated the management of human resources. We have been able to recruit according to needs without the usual procedures of discussions and waiting for approval (...). The results were convincing and quick. On the other hand, it is important to note that this lack of financial restraint was not synonymous with useless thinking. Rigor was the order of the day. Financial management is the responsibility of each manager, especially since public money is involved. This flexibility and the rapid arrival of reinforcements after the activation of the white paper had an immediate effect on the staff: they felt supported and not left to their own devices.

During this crisis, the managerial logic of the framework has taken all its meaning:

> From stock management, to recruitment, to the realization of new schedules, new work organization, the implementation of training, project management: creation and opening of a COVID service with a dedicated team and all this in record time. (Department manager)

After the crisis, the question arises as to what will remain of all this experience. To what extent will the caring managerial practices identified during the crisis persist? Will the organization learn from this crisis? And at what level? A director of a nursing home confided to us her isolation during the crisis management: "I never want to go through this again". This independent community nursing home notes the necessity and urgency of joining forces to cope. The request has been expressly made to the board of directors and contacts are underway. From the same perspective, all the feedback from experiences highlights the importance of strengthening collaboration with internal and external stakeholders, thus inviting professionals to invent new modalities of coordination. The crisis has highlighted the added value of the network and the need to maintain social links over time (links with families, volunteers, guardians, local partners, etc.). "Establishments with ties to their local area and with real and active partners have generally fared better than the others" (nursing home director). Introducing digital tools to enable families to keep in touch with residents, conducting the social life council by video, strengthening the rest time for caregivers, establishing a permanent link with guardianship authorities and sharing good practices between establishments are all illustrations of new collaborative practices that create real social capital born of caring management practices. Nevertheless, the question of the sustainability of these practices remains.

If the postcrisis period is full of hope for some, it is, in fact, no less painful for most of them, who leave exhausted, even discouraged, at all levels of the hierarchy (management and team). Aware of this reality, the management of one institution has decided to increase the working time of the psychologist to provide support during the postcrisis period: exhaustion, return to normal ("we are once again prevented from carrying out our tasks") or even professional retraining. The internal system takes over again, and the reappearing institutional frameworks prevent the formalization of feedback from this crisis and the institutionalization of caring management practices.

The question of valuing health professionals and the meaning of their work is also at the heart of the discussions because, beyond the applause at 8 p.m., what institutional and political recognition is given?

> After the lockdown, I wrote a thank you letter to the staff thanking them for their presence, availability and investment. It was important to me that their work was recognized. It was my one and only lever. (Health executive)

4.3. Conclusion

To the question "is caring management only a luxury that can be afforded when everything is going well", the answer is finally no. We have seen that the opposite is true, that during crises, caring management practices became a necessity when things were going badly and were not seen in calm periods. The crisis changes the rules of the game and the context of action: it shakes up practices, reinforces care, removes institutional locks and highlights the power of collaboration.

We also found that while all the facilities studied experienced the same pandemic, not all professionals came out of it with the same mindset. At PYA, "there were no fewer deaths; caring management does not remove the problems of recruitment or absenteeism during the crisis. But we manage them differently; it protects the team, the managers, the management, the users, etc., and we come out of it better". In the other establishments, the feedback from managers shows a general exhaustion.

Caring management therefore seems to be able to mitigate the effects of the COVID-19 crisis. However, the institutionalization of caring management practices within the health system seems more difficult. It will undoubtedly be useful, after the COVID-19 crisis, to share feedback from each component of this system on the benefits and risks associated with these caring management practices, both in normal and crisis contexts.

4.4. References

Agani, F., Landau, J., Agani, N. (2010). Community-building before, during, and after times of trauma: The application of the LINC model of community resilience in Kosovo. *American Journal of Orthopsychiatry*, 80(1), 143.

Akanni, A. (2020). Il faudra être vertueux. In *Les répercussions durables de la crise sur le management*, Frimousse, S., Peretti, J.M. (eds). *Question(s) de management*, 28, 159–243.

Alemanno, S. (2020). Vers un management humaniste : une issue de la crise sanitaire mondiale de 2020. In *Les répercussions durables de la crise sur le management*, Frimousse, S., Peretti, J.M. (eds). *Question(s) de management*, 28, 159–243.

Bachelard, O. (2020). Le coronavirus réussira-t-il à affaiblir la bureaucratie organisationnelle ? In *Les répercussions durables de la crise sur le management*, Frimousse, S., Peretti, J.M. (eds). *Question(s) de management*, 28, 159–243.

Bass, B.M. (1999). Two decades of research and development in transformational leadership. *European Journal of Work and Organizational Psychology*, 8(1), 9–32.

Bayntun, C., Rockenschaub, G., Murray, V. (2012). Developing a health system approach to disaster management: A qualitative analysis of the core literature to complement the WHO Toolkit for assessing health-system capacity for crisis management. *PLoS Currents*, 4.

Beaumont, P.B. (1993). *Human Resource Management: Key Concepts and Skills*. Sage Publications Ltd, London.

Besseyre des Horts, C.H. (2020). Les héros de l'ombre : vers une nouvelle hiérarchie des emplois ? In *Les répercussions durables de la crise sur le management*, Frimousse, S., Peretti, J.M. (eds). *Question(s) de management*, 28, 159–243.

Bréchat, P.H., Leenhardt, A., Mathieu-Grenouilleau, M.C., Rymer, R., Matisse, F., Baraille, D., Beaufils, P. (2010). Des pôles d'activités hospitaliers entre gestion de la crise et mise en œuvre d'une politique de santé publique. *Santé publique*, 22(5), 571–580.

Chamberlain, J., Turpin, B., Maged, A., Chatsiou, A., O'Callaghan, K. (2020). Designing for collective intelligence and community resilience on social networks. *Human Computation*, May 13.

Chanlat, J.F. (2020). La nécessité d'un retournement anthropologique. In *Les répercussions durables de la crise sur le management*, Frimousse, S., Peretti, J.M. (eds.). *Question(s) de management*, 28, 159–243.

Cook, S.D.N. and Brown, J.S. (1999). Bridging epistemologies: The generative dance between organizational knowledge and organizational knowing. *Organization Science*, 10, 381–400. [Online]. Available at: http://dx.doi.org/10.1287/orsc.10.4.381.

Ferar, D. (2020). Le management responsable de la crise sanitaire. In *Les répercussions durables de la crise sur le management*, Frimousse, S., Peretti, J.M. (eds). *Question(s) de management*, 28, 159–243.

Fessler, J.M. (2020). Le respect mutuel. In *Les répercussions durables de la crise sur le management*, Frimousse, S., Peretti, J.M. (eds). *Question(s) de management*, 2, 159–243.

Getz, I. and Carney, B. (2016). *Liberté & Compagnie, quand la liberté des salariés fait le succès des entreprises*. Flammarion, Paris.

Koh, H.K. and Cadigan, R.O. (2008). Disaster preparedness and social capital. In *Social Capital and Health*, Kawachi, I., Subramanian, S.V., Kim, D. (eds). Springer, New York.

Lagadec, P. (1991). *La gestion des crises. Outils de réflexion à l'usage des décideurs*. Édiscience International, Paris.

Lecadet, C. (2020). The IOM's crisis management and the expulsion of Ethiopians from Saudi Arabia. In *The International Organization for Migration*, Geiger, M., Pécoud, A. (eds). Palgrave Macmillan, London.

Lee, A.M., Wong, J.G., McAlonan, G.M., Cheung, V., Cheung, C., Sham, P.C., Chua, S.E. (2007). Stress and psychological distress among SARS survivors 1 year after the outbreak. *The Canadian Journal of Psychiatry*, 52(4), 233–240.

Mandhanya, Y. and Agrawal, B. (2017). A study of impact of leadership practices in retaining talent with special reference to automobile sector. PhD Thesis, University of Applied Sciences, Indore.

McMillan, C. and Overall, J. (2016). Wicked problems: turning strategic management upside down. *Journal of Business Strategy*, 37(1), 34–43.

Naro, G. and Travaille, D. (2020). Les leçons de la crise sanitaire du Covid-19 pour le contrôle de gestion des hôpitaux publics : d'une logique de l'efficience à une logique de l'efficacité. *XX USP International Conference in Accounting, Accounting as a Governance Mechanism*, São Paulo.

Patapan, H. (2016). Magnanimous leadership: Edmund Barton and the Australian founding. *Leadership and the Humanities*, 4(1), 1–20.

Rodet, P. (2017). Le management bienveillant n'est pas une utopie [Online]. Available at: https://www.francetvinfo.fr/economie/emploi/carriere/vie-professionnelle/management/le-management-bienveillant-n-est-pas-une-utopie_2340553.html.

Rodet, P. and Desjacques, Y. (2017). *Le management bienveillant*. Eyrolles, Paris.

Simons, R. (1995). *Levers of Control: How Managers Use Innovative Control Systems to Drive Strategic Renewal*. Harvard Business School Press, Boston.

Shufutinsky, A., De Porres, D., Long, B., Sibel, J.R. (2020). Shock leadership development for the modern era of pandemic management and preparedness. *International Journal of Organizational Innovation*, 13(1), 20–42.

Song, Z., Zhang, H., Dolan, C. (2020). Promoting disaster resilience: Operation mechanisms and self-organizing processes of crowdsourcing. *Sustainability*, 12(5), 1862.

Tam, C.W., Pang, E.P., Lam, L.C., Chiu, H.F. (2004). Severe acute respiratory syndrome (SARS) in Hong Kong in 2003: Stress and psychological impact among frontline healthcare workers. *Psychological Medicine*, 34(7), 1197–1204.

Walton, M., Murray, E., Christian, M.D. (2020). Mental health care for medical staff and affiliated healthcare workers during the Covid-19 pandemic. European Heart. *Journal: Acute Cardiovascular Care*, 9(3), 241–247.

PART 2

Management in the Health Sector: What Feedback Do We Get?

Introduction to Part 2

The objective of this Part 2 is to anchor caring management in reality by investigating concrete experiences of caring managerial practices.

Chapter 5 takes a critical sociological look at the hypocrisy of "marketed" approaches, based on a conference by Danièle Linhart, invited to the fourth annual study day on the caring management of local managers[1]. Altruistic and virtuous approaches are thus questioned and their paradoxes highlighted.

Based on this critical analysis, the following management practices are presented: benevolence in health-care institutions, with a recognized impact on both the economic and social performance. A first case (Chapter 6) shows that the implementation of an innovative project based on collaborative and co-constructed work, confidence and the principle of subsidiarity can bring convincing results for all the stakeholders in a nursing home.

Next, Chapter 7 presents a study conducted on the determinants of happiness at work at work with a population of 145 paramedics. The aim is to analyze the capacity of managers to act on the determinants of happiness at work in order to define the keys that can enable them to act in a constrained environment in both an individual and a collective dimension. This study shows that the levers of autonomy, recognition, professional relations and the feeling of a job well done can, under certain conditions, allow managers to influence perceived happiness.

Finally, Chapter 8 highlights the determining role of health-care managers in the development of the quality of work life of their staff. In particular, it explains how,

---

1 Fourth annual study day on the management of local managers, February 8, 2019, jointly organized by the IFCS de Saint-Étienne, the ENSEIS de Firminy and the Université Jean Monnet.

and in what conditions, discussion and decision-making spaces can support managerial action in the service of team health, based on an experiment in a nursing home.

Beyond the disappointments, palpable and measurable in a certain number of medical, medico-social or para-medical organizations, this part thus lays the groundwork for a renewed management and the conditions for a close supervision that can bring shared values and lead structuring projects in service of the satisfaction of patients and caregivers.

5

Between Illusion and Disillusionment: A Critical View by a Work Sociologist

This chapter is based on a conference given by Danièle Linhart, a sociologist of work, director of research at the CNRS and member of the "Gender, Work and Mobility" team of the CRESPPA laboratory (*Centre de recherche en sociologie et politique de Paris*), who was invited to talk about caring management during an annual study day on the management of local executives in health-care institutions[1]. She works on transformations in the organization of work and management, focusing on their effects on employees in the private and public sectors.

She immediately expressed her distrust of this notion, which, according to her, finds its source in the very principles and foundations of contemporary management. Sifting through the characteristics of the latter, she denounces the illusion of a break with Taylorism and analyzes the consequences of a managerial ideology centered on individual performance, injunctions to autonomy, creativity and personal development.

While company management, she tells us, is taking less and less account of the professionalism of employees, they no longer hesitate, to use her terms, to "coddle" the workers. In return, they expect the latter to adhere completely to the corporate values of the company blended with unlimited involvement in their work. She thus denounces the paradox of a management who would like to "take care" of employees while denying their professionalism, and takes the expression "caring management" in the opposite direction by investigating the origins of suffering and malaise in the workplace, and the nature and causes of burnout.

Chapter written by Marc BERNAUD and Marie-Cécile LEGAY.

1 Fourth annual study day on caring management of proximity managers. February 8, 2019, co-organized by the IFCS de Saint-Étienne, the IREIS de Firminy and université Jean Monnet.

We propose here to compare her reflections with our experiences in the hospital world.

5.1. The contradictions of modern management

5.1.1. *A desire to break with Taylorism*

Conducting a reflection on caring management, Danièle Linhart situates it at the turn of the 1980s, in the wake of the exhaustion of the Taylor model and the questioning of it following the strikes of May 1968. It is indeed during this period that this system, "based on a dehumanizing aim of putting workers to work", showed all its limits, both at the economic and ideological levels. At the economic level, it was weakened by a succession of strikes, practices of "casting off the chains", massive turnover and absenteeism, all of which indicate a model that is less and less effective (Dejours 1998). At the ideological level, Taylorism is prey to a sharp criticism of its foundations and is radically out of step with the new aspirations of society. It was then accused of all sorts of vices, in particular that of "denying the moods and states of mind of workers". According to Taylor, the scientific organization of work (SOW)[2] should not take into account the subjective dimension of individuals. It must work regardless of the employees and their state of mind. Faced with a system at the end of its tether, a new management mode, more human but also more competitive, will impose itself.

The first characteristic of this management transformation according to Linhart, "is precisely a focus on the human dimension". It is true that working conditions are also being discussed, particularly in the demands of trade unions, but the key words of managers were quickly oriented toward the development of creativity, the involvement of individuals in the work, their reactivity, their unreserved commitment and so on. This was followed by the appearance of methods and systems that promoted an individualization of the relationship between each person and their work and even a "psychologization of relationships" in which employees were solicited on a personal and intimate level. Gradually, it is no longer enough for employees to perform their jobs with professional awareness and professionalism; they must also "respond to new demands, centered on their behavior and state of mind".

From then on, they are expected to "get out of their comfort zone", to take up the challenges of the modern world, to taste for adventure and to show a passion for the challenges. According to the sociologist, we are witnessing an overhumanization of work based on the idea that "everyone should be able to improve themselves, to

2 SOW: read everywhere as scientific organization of work.

discover potential that they did not even imagine and to approach an ideal version of the self". In fact, management no longer conceives of companies only as places of production but also as places of personal development and fulfillment. The idea that "work is a matter for men and women and that we must take charge of their fantasies, their impulses, their desires, and that we must also manage their fears and weaknesses" quickly emerges.

This evolution is illustrated by the words of an admiral during a conference for the DeciDRH association. To the question from the floor:

> How to ensure the unwavering and unconditional support of the soldiers, the latter replies: [...] I'll tell you how I do it, I take care of everything! I take care of all the problems of these little guys [...]. He then gives the example of the submariners who go on a campaign lasting several months on board submarines. He describes the confined life and the lack of privacy to which the sailors manage to adapt. However, he says: there remains a fundamental source of anxiety and uneasiness [...]. Well, what works on my guys when they are in the field, it is the problem of the fidelity of their wife! Yes, it sounds trivial, but it can poison the mind, and the guy can't do his job anymore. So what to do? [...]. What is the most perilous moment for a wife's fidelity? Well, when a household appliance breaks down, that's the dangerous moment, because an electrician, a repairman or a plumber comes into the home and who knows what can happen? [...]. So I went looking for mechanics, plumbers, etc., to make a partnership with the Navy. You call a number and you get home help for work. That's the "Wellness *à la Carte*" program. And so that relaxed my guys, and there you go, so you see you have to take care of everything. (Linhart 2019)

This managerial solicitude, described by Danièle Linhart as the "overhumanization" of the company, can also be found in the health and social sector, where under the guise of the development of quality of life at work, the boundaries between "work time" and "non-work time" are sometimes blurred, and there is confusion between what is part of the organization of work within an institution and what belongs to the domain of the private life of the employees. It was in this vein that, wanting to "take care of her employees"[3], the director of a nursing home in the Saint-Etienne region has developed various services for her employees. She has renovated a break room equipped with a television and armchairs. In addition, she offers a relaxation area with rooms and beds for caregivers whose schedule includes

3 To use the expression used by the director of this establishment.

a break at lunchtime that requires them to stay on site. The latter can also benefit from a visit from a hairdresser or a beautician at their own expense. Finally, as part of a "quality of life and comfort" approach (to use her words), she has set up a partnership with an association managing a short food circuit (bringing together local farmers and consumers) to offer fruit and vegetable delivery once a week. All of these measures were designed, she says, to indirectly bring "comfort" to the private lives of employees, "improving their quality of life", and, in her view, compensate for the existence of unattractive working hours in her institution.

This is a strange reasoning given the hardship that can be caused by the type of schedule and rotation proposed in this establishment. In fact, traditionally, in health-care organizations, daytime caregivers are offered a continuous schedule: a "morning" shift that runs from approximately 7:00 a.m. to 2:00 p.m., and an "evening" shift that covers the 1:30–8:30 p.m. period. In this nursing home, the care assistants have special schedules that require a 2 h break in the middle of their working day. This system allows the institution to make substantial savings: where there should be, for example, two people in the morning and two in the evening, one person in the morning, one person in the evening and one person as back-up are used, while maintaining a sufficient number of staff at the peak times of activity, that is, at the beginning and end of the day.

For obvious reasons, this type of "split" schedule is not very popular with caregivers. They complain of having a "double day" because they provide heavy morning care (getting up, toilets, meals) and evening care (getting up from naptime, changing pads, snacks, then meals, bedtime and final nighttime changes). This organization also questions the quality of the care of the residents by the caregivers. One can easily imagine the state of mind and the degree of patience of these caregivers at the end of the day when they have just spent more than 10 h working without leaving the nursing home and they have to deal with the refusal of care, the slowness or the night-time anguish of the residents. From this reality, it is perplexing to imagine that all of this physical hardship and mental burden can be compensated for by providing a comfortable room so that workers can remain in the workplace during their lunch break.

However, the quality of life at work for these caregivers is not the only thing their director is concerned about. Concerned about "good understanding" among the staff, the latter has also decided to set up "team-building" events. In this way, she joins the ranks of companies that, as Danièle Linhart points out, strive to "transform the workplace into a second home, a second family", and to this end she organizes escape games for the members of her management team and dance parties for the rest of the team. Finally, she would like to point out that she regularly offers personalized gifts to the members of the management team "according to the character and uniqueness of each person".

Overall, in this example, we are not thus far from Google, which, in its Zurich facility, has provided its young engineers with slides to move from one floor to another and rest areas in the shape of flying saucers in which they can listen to music and enjoy chocolate bars (Linhart 2015).

Ultimately, in the three cases mentioned above, "everything is done to make life around work pleasant and to take care of it in such a way as to try to convince us that whatever the contradictions [in the organization of work], there are still [within the institutions] zones of happiness and benevolence" (Linhart 2019). This overinvestment in the human, this attention to the happiness and quality of life of employees, would easily lead us to believe in a radical break with Taylorism and its dehumanizing vision of the organization. However, as we shall see, it would be a delusion to believe that our institutions have totally emancipated themselves from the spirit of the scientific organization of work. "The idea of a change and a break with the Taylorian philosophy is not correct; it is even totally false", explains Danièle Linhart.

5.1.2. *The illusion of a break with Taylorism*

In the constant search for profitability and cost reduction, Taylor tracked down the autonomy, the room for maneuvering and the "loitering" of employees. In his SOW, he set out to analyze the different operating modes of workers and to select the most efficient processes to eradicate idle time and gain in productivity. At the same time, SOW has contributed to standardizing all work methods, leaving less room for the variety of practices, know-how and individual expertise of employees. Everything is calculated and meticulous. Modern management, on the other hand, emphasizes the autonomy and responsibility of all. In this respect, it responds to a desire expressed since the 1968 movement through what Boltanski and Chiapello have identified as an "artistic critique of work" (Boltanski and Chiapello 1999). However, this leads to individualization and competition, with a considerable cost in terms of burnout, says Danièle Linhart:

> Everyone must become an office of time and methods in order to apply the philosophy of time and cost-saving to themselves at all times. Everyone must ensure that they make the most effective use of themselves from the point of view of the efficiency and quality criteria decided by their management. (Linhart 2019)

Above all, it would be illusory to think that this is incentive to autonomy. The sociologist Marie-Anne Dujarier has shown that, since the 1980s, quality measures have been developed and imposed in the various spheres of work, both public and private, with perverse effects on employees. These quality approaches, she points out, "combine mechanisms of purpose, process and enrolment; they require the achievement of quality scores on precise criteria, scrupulously following procedures, standards, approaches and rules of certification in the name of the moral and economic imperative of satisfying the consumer" and, one might add, the user or patient (Dujarier 2006).

This corpus of rules, injunctions and formalization of work constitutes what ergonomics, then sociology or even psychodynamics of work, globally call "prescribed work". Its main characteristic is that it is developed outside the places where the work is produced by methods offices, quality engineers or accreditation agencies far from the reality of the field. Above all, as a result of an accumulation of prescriptions from various sources (laws, regulations, the Public Health Code, charters, accreditation manuals, good practice guides, etc.), prescribed work produces numerous paradoxical injunctions that "the front lines" must resolve in real time. A striking example is given by the researcher, who shows to what extent the feeding of elderly people in a nursing home can present a large number of contradictions. On the one hand, it is necessary to respect the taste and eating habits of residents while taking into account their needs and medical instructions. On the other hand, it is necessary to have the approval of the nurse (who is often not on the same floor) to change the contents of a meal while serving the trays as quickly as possible. Finally, it is necessary to respect the rhythm and autonomy of the elderly while limiting the time it takes to eat. "All of these prescriptions are formulated for caregivers who work in hospitals where catering is centralized and menus are largely imposed" (Dujarier 2006).

Faced with these paradoxical instructions, one may wonder how caregivers deal with them on a daily basis. When asked about this during a training session in January 2020, nurses working in nursing homes confessed their powerlessness to resolve the contradictions surrounding the residents' supper. In their institution, the most tired elderly are "exempt" from going to the common dining room in the evening to have their meal. Instead, they are served in their rooms by the nursing assistants, who also help them with their food intake. There are approximately 15 of these residents, and the care team in charge of them is, at best, composed of three people. The general organization of the structure foresees a meal time of about half an hour, we deduce that each elderly person benefits from 6 min, watch in hand, to be able to ingest the total contents of their tray. In this case, it is difficult to respect their rhythm and habits.

To meet the demands of a time-constrained organization, there is only one solution left for caregivers: spend as little time as possible with residents who report having no appetite so that they can spend slightly more time with those who seem more inclined to eat. In doing so, caregivers develop a sense of "not doing their job well". This feeling of not being up to par, of not being the "good professional" they would like to be, is a source of ethical suffering (Dejours 2015) and can lead them to burnout (Linhart 2019). Thus, by advocating autonomy, responsibility and the maximum involvement of employees while leaving them to fend for themselves in the face of contradictory work organization demands, modern management is faced with its own paradox: introducing a certain form of dehumanization where it knows how to make work more human.

5.2. Consultants to the "rescue" of management

5.2.1. *Consultants at the service of sponsors*

Beyond this false break with Taylorism, and a certain perversion of autonomy in the workplace, the context of globalization and exacerbated competition has imposed the supremacy of economic logics to the detriment of the logics of production of goods or services. Public sector establishments have not escaped these developments, and hospitals, like all health establishments, have had to face a succession of reforms designed to restore balance to public accounts. In the wake of the general review of public policies (2007), the so-called HPST law (*hôpital, patients, santé et territoires*: hospital, patients, health and territories) of 2009 marked a turning point in hospital management, placing increasing emphasis on the accounting side of patient care (see section 5.1).

At the same time, modes of governance from the private sector are taking hold in hospitals and open the door to consultants who happily transfer their know-how to the public arena (Belorgey 2014; Juven et al. 2019). As a result, manuals of good managerial practices "benchmarked" by consultants from large national or even international consulting firms start to appear in hospitals, transferring a "turnkey" way of thinking, at a distance from the reality of the field to which it applies (Linhart 2019). These international consulting firms, such as McKinsey, Capgemini or the Boston Consulting Group, remain little-known players in the implementation of HPST law, even though, as Frédéric Pierru demonstrates, they played a major role in the birth and implementation of regional health agencies (Pierru 2012).

According to a leader of the ARS project group at the time, their request was dictated "by the fact that we had to move quickly, with only a dozen people available to work on this project. It was therefore a lack of resources that forced the State to outsource part of the work to consulting firms. Although the latter were heavily involved in the restructuring of hospitals, their missions nevertheless gave rise to numerous disputes within the ARS group itself, some members of which are now denouncing their lack of knowledge of the health sector and the massive use of consultants when internal resources were available.

According to the Court of Accounts report of April 28, 2018, the use of these expert firms and services is now widespread in all public health establishments. However, "the consultants' productions rarely provide results that match the expected services", and the analyses carried out by the regional audit chambers show that "many reports of missions essentially use internal data and simply copy known information, repeating existing notes or conclusions". The daily newspaper *Le Monde*, on June 6, 2020, reported the experience of a university hospital director: "They [the consultants] arrive everywhere with the same Excel tables, the same slide shows, but they know little about the reality on the ground". In reality, the data produced and invoiced are rarely questioned, rarely contextualized and sometimes even erroneous. Nevertheless, the data are passed on to the supervisory authorities and used as a reference to propose new organizations.

Our experience corroborates these observations. This was the case for a consultancy firm hired to verify the number of hours of vacation time allocated to the practitioners in an operating room and whose presentation and results merely repeated the work and conclusions of a project written upstream by the senior management. Indeed, during a change of general management, the new management showed mistrust toward the project to reorganize the operating rooms, as carried out up to that time, and suspected a volume of shift hours too advantageous for the surgeons. It therefore requested the intervention of a consultancy firm for an audit. The team of consultants took up the project developed by the management under the responsibility of the previous management by increasing the volume of hours by 4% to the benefit of the surgeons. These conclusions will not be retained.

In another case, a firm of external auditors submitted to the Ministry of Health occupancy rates for an operating room that were so aberrant that a simple consistency check could have invalidated them; this rate, which usually fluctuated between 75% and 82%, was calculated by the consultants at less than 20%! Surprised by these results, the head of the operating room reviewed the methodology used and quickly understood that, in their requests, the auditors had not taken into account the total closure of a specialty for technical and medical reasons. The number of hours of actual occupancy of the operating rooms was related to the number of hours of shifts that had not been updated.

For Nicolas Belorgey, what characterizes these consulting firms is their status as independent professionals, which paradoxically puts them in a position of subordination and dependence on their principal. "In executing one contract, they would also aim to sell the next and would be guided by their firm's turnover" (Belorgey 2014). Caught in a competitive market, they therefore have every interest, in order to perpetuate their activity, in following the ways of thinking of their client as closely as possible. The author then denounces the tendency of firms "to consider the intentions of a project or an intervention as raw data, without questioning the relevance, honesty or validity of the request".

For example, we participated in the presentations of consultants to a call for tenders concerning the reorganization of surgical services. During this session, four out of five consultants questioned the management of the establishment about the volume of full-time equivalents to be eliminated, implicitly committing themselves to include this figure in the conclusions of the audit report. Above all, we note that most of the interventions we observed within the hospital remained little followed up in practice and were marked by a lack of responsibility on the part of these actors. This was deplored by the director of the university hospital mentioned above: "[...] We end up with these boxes that are not accountable to anyone, but which define the right number of beds. [...] and what bothers me is that the consultants end up defining public policy".

In addition to occasional but repeated interventions in health-care institutions, the major consulting firms are present at all levels of the health-care system and are at the heart of hospital reforms These reforms have led to a veritable frenzy of regulations and legislation, as if each new change legitimized the intervention of these firms. Faced with this, the "Fellinger-Boiron" report called for a "regulatory lull" in 2012, but in fact, this request has gone unheeded and we are witnessing a strategy of perpetual change justified by the "necessary adaptation" to an "evolving environment".

5.2.2. *The effects of permanent change*

For Danièle Linhart, these incessant evolutions go far beyond regulations alone:

> What we see are permanent restructurings of services and departments, incessant software changes, systematic mobility imposed on the local hierarchy, movements so that teams are not always side by side, outsourcing followed by re-internalization. (Linhart 2019)

The problem, she continues, is that in these unstable contexts, employees' know-how and skills quickly become obsolete. Deprived of their professional fundamentals, they lose their calm. A kind of feverishness sets in, caused by the fact that they no longer recognize and identify with their work environment.

Despite their deleterious effects, these changes are presented by management as opportunities for progress, the acquisition of new skills and self-development. The questioning of professionalism is thus accompanied by a questioning of employees themselves, who see themselves as unable to take advantage of the "great opportunities" offered by change. Fearing that they will be suspected of "resisting change", they try as best they can to find their place in the organization. They then deploy considerable energy to reduce the gap between what they are able to produce and what is expected, between what they know how to do and what they should do, between the way they do it and the method recommended. This vain effort to constantly reposition oneself in the institution weakens the employees and put them in a situation Danièle Linhart (2015, 2019) denounces as "subjective precariousness".

This expression covers the feeling of uneasiness, fragility and damage to the professional identity of employees, linked to the uncertainties and the questioning of their professionalism associated with a loss of control over their know-how. It was in the 2000s, following a survey conducted within France Telecom, that the sociologist developed this concept. She then demonstrated that this subjective precariousness is the result of a managerial strategy of transformation of the company:

> It is a matter of trying to weaken and destabilize employees in such a way that they are receptive to new ways of working methodologically, procedurally, in relation to the values that we want to impose on them. [...] This strategy of permanent change is officially deployed to get employees out of their routines, their habits, their networks of complacency with their colleagues or with their users. (Linhart 2019)

The aim is to make employees accept new ways of working, other values and another professional identity more in line with the company's new status. In this example, the destabilization and subjective insecurity of the employees are the result of a deliberate strategy based on continuous change at all structural levels of the institution.

As we have mentioned, the world of health-care is also undergoing ceaseless transformations, the main aim of which, however, is not to destabilize employees but to reduce costs. Restructuring, mergers, regroupings, closures and creations of services change in activity and orientation, which call into question skills and expertise (Juven et al. 2019). Innovative modes of care are appearing (fast-track recovery after surgery): they promote the early restoration of patients' abilities after surgery. They require the reorganization of care pathways and the rethinking of cooperation within multidisciplinary teams. The objective is to reduce costs by reducing the length of stay and the length of care. These new methods of patient care are causing a conflict of paradigms among caregivers. They find that they are providing less and less care, filling out more and more checklists, and following restrictive procedures. All of this gives them a strong feeling that they are moving away from their core business and losing the primary meaning of their work. Ultimately, hospital staff are faced with increasing uncertainty about their environment and doubts about their values, their missions, their practices and their ability to evolve and adapt. These upheavals lead to a destabilization of employees and a loss of confidence. In such a context, it is not surprising to see the development of "symptoms" of subjective insecurity which, when brought to a climax, lead to exhaustion, or even "a personal collapse" as underlined by Danièle Linhart.

The sociologist refers to planned perpetual change as the root cause of subjective insecurity because it aims to deprive employees of their experience and skills to force them to adhere to the new criteria of efficiency, quality and new methods desired by management. Our experience invites us to also mention the loss of meaning in the process of destabilization of professionals. In other words, employees react negatively to "a change" but mobilize and find secondary benefits in a change that they consider legitimate.

Indeed, COVID-19 requires radical reorganizations in a very short time. The management of this crisis led hospitals to reconfigure care units (transforming recovery rooms into intensive care units), reorganize technical and material resources (search for protective equipment), close entire sectors (programmed activities), devise new circuits (of people, information and decisions) and create new care units (COVID-19 units) and new support services (bed management units). Simultaneously, hospital staff were reassigned. Teams were reconfigured. New modes of cooperation came to light. New professional practices emerged (teleworking). In addition, yet, the staff were able to adapt, to the point of making a doctrine out of it, tinkering with the means at hand, using a "blend" (Desjours 1998), as a technician from La Pitié-Salpêtrière put it in *Le Monde* of April 22, 2020: "It was not tinkering, it was ingenuity!" The staff has rediscovered in their missions the fundamental values of their professions. We hypothesize that the meaning of work was clear enough, shared enough, to overcome the uncertainty linked to this health crisis. This experience and this common sense shared by the entire hospital community (directors, medical and paramedical staff, administrative staff, technical staff) led a nurse at the APHP (Parisian hospital and medical center group) to say, "Everything that was not possible before has become possible now, and this is the first time I have seen the director of my hospital". In fact, there was no reported opposition to these rapid, sometimes contradictory changes, but rather a momentum, an active and unsubdued movement.

5.3. Conclusion

After having tried to free themselves from Taylorism, the new work organizations, by placing the individual at the center, have induced a certain "schizophrenia" in employees. Incited to harness their capacity, intelligence, creativity, they are forced to use standardized methods, designed away from the field, erasing the particularities of the context, the specificities and the know-how of individuals. For the health and social sector:

> It appears that the importation of management methods from the private sector to the hospital has produced a paradoxical result: the reinforcement of centralization and bureaucratization, embodied by the multiplication of intermediary hierarchies that control each other, is eroding the autonomy of both field workers and managers. (Pierru 2012)

This trend is exacerbated by the arrival of consulting firms in ministries and institutions. The latter introduce working methods that are disconnected from the environments in which professionals, who have a perfect knowledge of them, are operating. We are then witnessing what Danièle Linhart describes as "a full-scale attack on professionalism", which results in a perpetual questioning of the knowledge, skills and experience of employees. There is therefore a loss of mastery of know-how that destabilizes the employee, provoking his "inoperationality". This inability to act, compounded by the loss of meaning, becomes a source of dissatisfaction at work and places employees in a subjective precariousness.

However, this loss of meaning is not inevitable. As the COVID-19 period showed, exceptional circumstances have made teams emerge and share a common meaning that was thought to be lost. In addition, the emergency allowed us to free ourselves from standardized procedures and to give back the possibility of acting efficiently to practitioners in the field. All in all, happiness and fulfillment in the workplace would no longer be a matter for chief happiness officers but would result from the trust afforded to professionals, the freedom to do their work, which they have been trained to do and they are paid for.

5.4. References

Belorgey, N. (2014). Machiavel aujourd'hui : des consultants au travail dans le secteur public. *La Nouvelle revue du travail* [Online]. Available at: http://journals.openedition.org/nrl/1604 [Accessed 6 November 2019].

Boiron, F. and Fellinger, F. (2012). Mission Hôpital public. Report, Ministère du Travail, de l'Emploi et de la Santé, Paris.

Boltanski, L. and Chiapello, E. (1999). *Le nouvel esprit du capitalisme*. Gallimard, Paris.

Dejours, C. (1998). *Souffrance en France. La banalisation de l'injustice sociale*. Le Seuil, Paris.

Dejours, C. (2015). *Le Choix. Souffrir au travail n'est pas une fatalité*. Bayard, Montrouge.

Dujarier, M.A. (2006). *L'idéal au travail*. Presses Universitaires de France, Paris.

Juven, P.A., Pierru, F., Vincent, F. (2019). *La casse du siècle. À propos des réformes de l'hôpital public*. Raisons d'Agir, Paris.

Laurent, S. (2020). À l'hôpital, le rôle controversé des consultants. *Le Monde*, June 6.

Linhart, D. (2015). *La comédie humaine du travail. De la déshumanisation taylorienne à la sur-humanisation managériale*. Erès, Toulouse.

Linhart, D. (2019). Retranscription de la conférence du 8 février 2019. Transcription, CHU Saint-Étienne.

Migaud, D. (2018). Le recours aux marchés publics de consultants par les établissements publics de santé. Report, La Cour des Comptes, Paris.

Pierru, F. (1994). Le mandarin, le gestionnaire et le consultant. Le tournant néolibéral de la politique hospitalière. *Actes de la recherche en sciences sociales*, 4, 32–51.

Tesson, S. (2020). Avec les "invisibles" de la Pitié-Salpêtrière : l'écrivain Sylvain Tesson raconte les coulisses de l'hôpital parisien. *Le Monde* [Online]. Available at: https://www.lemonde.fr/planete/article/2020/04/28/avec-les-invisibles-de-la-pitie-salpetriere-l-ecrivain-sylvain-tesson-raconte-les-coulisses-de-l-hopital-parisien_6037954_3244.html.

6

Implementation of an Innovative Project in a Nursing Home as a Catalyst for Managerial Innovation

How can new management practices be implemented within organizations? Success stories exist – Favi, Poult, Harley Davidson, Belgian Social Security – and are told through films, articles and books. However, there do not seem to be any "recipes" or "models to follow", but rather contexts, people and teams that initiate and implement managerial innovations within their organization. How do they proceed? What are their successes and what difficulties do they encounter?

In this chapter, we propose to look at an *Etablissement d'hébergement pour personnes âgées dépendantes* (EHPAD, a nursing home) and the experience of a nursing home director who wished to break with a traditional management model and implement a caring management approach. This model favors collaboration between actors and the empowerment of each person. In section 6.1, we briefly present the PYA nursing home[1] and our questioning, and define the key concepts. The study carried out has brought to light several levers that have favored a collaborative work model within the PYA nursing home. We will present them in section 6.2. It is then a matter of adopting a management style appropriate to this collaborative model. This mode of management explains the success of an innovative project, presented in section 6.3: the 4M project – "*Mixons Moins, Mangez Mieux*" ("Mix Less, Eat Better"). This project has also been a catalyst for new management practices. A final section, therefore, will provide a discussion about the implementation of innovative projects as a catalyst for managerial innovation.

Chapter written by Nelly MASSARD and Florence VICHI.

1 Fictitious name to respect anonymity.

Finally, we will discuss the management of the COVID-19 crisis by the PYA nursing home and reflect on caring management as a lever to manage this crisis.

6.1. Context, questions and conceptual framework

PYA is one of the four establishments of a non-profit charitable association (1901 law). This association has a board of directors, composed of a president, a vice president and 10 administrators.

In 2009, PYA was the second establishment opened by the association. Today, the nursing home offers three types of care, 72 beds in permanent care, eight beds in temporary care and eight places in day care. The multidisciplinary team is represented by a coordinating doctor, a health executive, nursing assistants (*aides-soignants* [AS]), nurses (*infirmiers* [IDE]), medical-psychological assistants (*aides-médico-psychologiques* [AMP]), educational-social assistants (*accompagnants-éducatifs-sociaux* [AES]), hotel agents, laundry room attendants, a maintenance technician, cooks, a receptionist secretary, an accountant, a management secretary, a social project coordinator, a coordinator, a physical activity teacher (*activités physiques adaptées* [APA]), a quality and training coordinator and a director. PYA has approximately 80 employees (or 49 full-time equivalents).

When the establishment opened, the director wanted to break away from a traditional management model. She received a degree in quality management in 1995 and implemented a quality approach in an EHPAD in 1998, a "new method" at the time for this type of organization. Then, with a Master's degree in Health Organization Management and with the strength of her past experience, the director was inspired by success stories (Belgian Social Security) to implement a different management model within PYA, one that is different from the one typically found in medico-social institutions.

How did they do it? What are the success stories? What are the difficulties to overcome when a leader or a manager wants to implement new management methods to break with the traditional models?

Before focusing on the EHPAD, let us return to several key concepts, such as managerial innovation, collaborative work and the role of the liberating leader.

6.1.1. *Managerial innovation*

Le Roy and Giuliani (2013) have studied the genesis of the notion of "managerial innovation" and show that the first works appeared after the 1980s.

They emphasize the new aspect, for the company, of practices, techniques, methods, structures and management (Kimberly 1981; Damanpour and Evan 1984; Damanpour 1988; Rogers 1995; David 1996). This bibliographic work leads them to consider that managerial innovation is "the adoption, by an organization, of management practices or methods new to it, with the objective of improving its performance". Autissier et al. (2016) take up the idea of initiating novelty to the classical management model to make it evolve. For the authors:

> The political model of the organization has never been questioned. They have a consensus to speak only of evolution and not of division. The hierarchical-functional management illustrated by the manager who commands-controls and the employee who executes is questioned. Societal demand is evolving towards collaboration: the trend is towards "co" (co-construction, co-development, etc.). (Autissier et al. 2016)

The authors thereby explain that managerial innovation "aims to create new ways of cooperation between people in such a way that the goals are achieved effectively and efficiently, taking into account the changes in the world" (Autissier et al. 2016). They add "that current managerial innovation places collaboration at the heart of people's concerns and performance issues of the company" (Autissier et al. 2016).

6.1.2. *From collaboration to collaborative work*

The notion of collaboration or cooperation etymologically means "working together". While these "two notions consider only action, the concept of collaborative or cooperative work designates both the mode of contribution of each member of a group and the final product resulting from this participation, thus simultaneously identifying action and realization" (Gangloff-Ziegler 2009). Collaborative or cooperative work is defined as working together to collectively realize a project. The author distinguishes cooperative work from collaborative work by going back to the etymology of these two terms: *operor* means to work, to carry out, in the sense of producing, and *laboro* means to work by making efforts. For the author, the collaboration reveals a stronger implication by the effort to which it refers. Collaborative work implies a mutual commitment of actors in a coordinated effort to solve a problem together. Blanquet (2007) distinguishes cooperative work from collaborative work through three characteristics:

– The relationship between the actors (obligation or freedom).

– The responsibility of the actors in relation to their actions (responsibility delegated to a cooperator or shared).

– The ability of the actor to influence the definition and sequencing of actions to achieve the goal assigned to the group (hierarchy or equality).

Collaboration is a situation of collective work in a company where the tasks and goals are common. These three distinctive characteristics show that collaborative work is based on a form of freedom of action for the participant, a commitment of their responsibility for the actions and their ability to take initiative.

To put the actors in such a position, the leader and the manager have a role to play.

6.1.3. *The role of the liberating leader*

Some business leaders have established freedom of initiative and responsibility as fundamental principles of their way of operating; these are liberating leaders (Getz and Carney 2016). For Getz, certain qualities are necessary for a leader to "liberate the company": first, they must control personal ambition, demonstrate objectivity by systematically referring to their vision and be at the service of their team.

Managerial innovation is based on the organization's ability to put its actors in a collaborative work mode. This collaborative work requires a break with the classic management model (action-control). How can we break with this model? What are the levers to be used? What role should the manager play? What positions should they adopt?

The case of the PYA nursing home allows us to identify the levers that enabled the establishment and the director to put the actors of the organization in a collaborative work mode to create new management practices.

6.2. Levers to put the actors in a collaborative working mode

To identify the levers, we conducted several semidirected interviews (4) with the director of the establishment, a health executive (*cadre de santé,* CS), a nurse (*infirmière*, IDE) and a care assistant (*aide-soignante*, AS) who is also a staff representative. We were then able to identify four levers for the implementation of new management practices in this establishment:

– a context conducive to solidarity: the organization is to be built;

– a director who is convinced and consistent in their vision and their actions;

– management based on trust and the principle of subsidiarity;

– numerous collaborative work situations.

In section 6.2, we revisit each of these levers to better understand them.

6.2.1. *An organization to be built*

In 2009, "everything had to be built: we were a team of 40 people, we didn't know each other, we were discovering each other and we had to welcome the residents and their families. We had the premises, but we had nothing: we therefore had to build procedures, reception contracts, supports, etc.". A collaborative effort was then put in place to design the organization of the EHPAD, led by the management. "We're all going to do it together, we're all in the same boat". A form of solidarity developed, and it is not unusual to hear employees in the establishment say "we are from 2009!" The team has been stable since the beginning. Team members have helped build their organization, and it is in the "PYA DNA". For example, the nursing and caregiving teams have written their job descriptions and are amending them as changes occur. Another more recent example is the reorganization of the nurses' schedules to improve the care of the residents. The five nurses "organized themselves" to work one weekend out of five. The nursing profession imposes specific life rhythms: morning-evening and weekend shifts. It is therefore rather pleasant to work one weekend out of five. On the other hand, they were alone on weekends to do the work. After facing many difficulties, they decided to rethink the management of the weekend schedule so that there would be two nurses: one on duty in the morning and the other in the evening, thus obliging them to work one weekend out of two, or even three. We note here that they refused a comfortable situation for their personal life to do a better job, to make the organization work and to take better care of the resident. The teams feel concerned about the operation and will therefore make it evolve according to the needs.

It is also common for working groups to be formed to solve problems identified by the team. For example, a working group was initiated, composed of nurses and care assistants, to reorganize the floor where the most dependent residents are housed. As the department was becoming too challenging to manage, the caregivers joined forces to identify the difficulties and propose areas for improvement: the need for lifting equipment, the distribution of the most dependent residents among the three departments on the second floor, etc. We notice that the teams take initiatives and feel free to do so. The teams feel concerned about their organization.

We can then ask ourselves about the levers that enable this initiative and commitment.

6.2.2. *A convinced director who is consistent in her vision and her actions*

In well-known success stories, the leader is often a "liberating leader". In this case, the implementation of managerial innovation is also "driven" by the director of the establishment and influenced by her profile, professional background, values and beliefs. A graduate in quality and a dietician by profession, she implemented quality certification in an EHPAD in 1998, which is the first experience of managerial innovation.

It is a personal journey that leads her today to have management practices based on one principle: "trust". This position is delicate because, where other managers would see risk-taking, the director sees it as a form of learning: "we learn from our mistakes". For some employees, this attitude is also criticized because they see it as a form of laxity on the part of the manager, who did not sanction the employee who made a mistake. It is therefore, from her point of view, essential to "stand firm" to be consistent in her vision and her actions. For the director, it is necessary to "manage for 90% of the employees who agree with this principle". In organizations, there will always be people who disagree with any management style. You have to "manage for the others". It is therefore important to be sincere and, above all, in agreement with oneself. Therefore, in every situation, she shows perseverance by systematically referring to her vision.

"Quality is my foundation" (Director). The director, trained in quality, puts this management discipline at the heart of her management. In fact, it is essential to ensure traceability and transparency to manage the establishment properly. In medical and social establishments, all actions are traced. This may be perceived, at first, as a burden for the teams. However, the indicators that are filled in can then be used to produce activity reports and thus enhance the work of teams both internally and externally. "Traceability is no longer seen as a burden, as long as the teams see the benefits". It is therefore also necessary to create meaningful indicators. For example, keeping track of the number of bedsores to monitor their development and measure the effects of actions taken to reduce them. Indicators allow employees to evaluate the impact of their efforts. The process of evaluation through indicators is a source of pride for the teams and a tool to objectively recognize the work accomplished. It puts the players in a situation that allows them to reflect on their work and the way they do it.

6.2.3. *Management based on trust and the principle of subsidiarity*

The management team is composed of a director and a health executive. Since the management team is not present seven days a week in the establishment, as the nurses are, the management principle is as follows: decisions are made by the competent people. The nurses therefore supervise the employees. This is a well-known phenomenon in EHPADs: the nurses "have power" over the nursing assistants and the residential service agents. However, this power is not hierarchical in the institution, since each nurse is in a managerial position. For example, the health-care manager assigns orderlies to the departments, but it is the nurses who make the decision to reassign them according to the department's workload, the employee's level of competence or the employees' requests.

The health executive shares the director's vision. "We have to trust the employees". The health executive is present at all meetings and listens to the teams. For example, the employees make requests to purchase equipment during the changeover. After validation by the team, as there may sometimes be people who disagree with the request, the equipment is purchased and made available. There is no abuse, as one care assistant confided: "We know our organization and its resources".

6.2.4. *Collaborative work situations*

6.2.4.1. *Through training*

Each nurse forms a pair with a caregiver to be a specialist in a field. They are therefore in a collaborative position. For example, a nurse's aide explains to us that she has been trained in "oral hygiene". Together with her nursing partner, they will be trained and will then pass on the training to their colleagues in the form of meetings and role playing. Their role as specialist leads them to check with the residents that their colleagues are applying the knowledge they have learned. The care assistant confided to us that she appreciated this training and transmission time. This role of specialist also leads her to be responsible, with her partner, for care within the establishment. This organization of training allows the nurse and the care assistant to be responsible in the same capacity and thus to put them in a situation of collaboration without any hierarchical link. It also allows the employees to be involved in a learning process. For the director of the establishment, it is necessary to "train to implement innovation in the establishment".

6.2.4.2. *Through project management*

The project is a vector of managerial innovation. Several projects are initiated within the establishment. Each profession is represented and contributes to the common objective of caring for the resident. The actions of the project and the results of the project are at the heart of everyone's work, which is to take care of the resident.

All the actions implemented are promoted through press articles, competitions and challenges. The objective is to promote collective work.

One project in particular has put the team in collaborative mode and has had an impact on the institution and the teams through its innovative nature. Florence Vichi presents this project in section 6.3.

6.3. An innovative project as a catalyst for managerial innovation: the 4M project, "Mixons Moins, Mangez Mieux"

The institution implemented an innovative, ambitious project that few people believed in. The project was a success. This success can be explained by the collaborative model deployed to carry it out, based on the four levers presented above. The implementation process generated new management practices.

The 4M project, "Mixons Moins, Mangez Mieux" ("Mix Less, Eat Better"), stems from an initial empathetic posture, driven by a quest for equity: to provide a quality service adapted to all, regardless of the level of dependency.

It all starts from the fact that no one wants to eat a totally smooth mixed diet. However, in EHPADs, between 20 and 40% of elderly individuals have a mixed texture that is supposed to be adapted to their swallowing problems. The observation is disturbing: the caregivers have to help people to eat a meal that they themselves would not like to eat, or even taste; the cooks are disappointed by the transition from their service to the blender; the elderly can only weakly express their dissatisfaction or weariness with these meals that can sometimes last several years; and the management strives to make this situation as qualitative as possible in order to be able to explain it to the families and relatives.

However, why choose this texture that takes away the pleasure of eating? Is it truly necessary? Is it a cultural situation? Can we do something different? Does it truly help to prevent false routes when we learn from studies that 61% of false routes have a mixed texture diet?

In April 2015, Sodexo, which provides on-site food service in the facility, raised the hypothesis that an alternative is possible to rediscover meaning in the food of dependent elderly people by stimulating through pleasure. The key is to bring together a multidisciplinary group of motivated experts to devise a completely different and innovative approach because there is no example to draw inspiration from.

PYA is seizing this incredible opportunity for an innovative approach. The establishment participates in the research project with experts and crossed competences to look for a solution to improve the existing practices. Through the initial position, the observation of the feeding practices for the residents within the nursing home and the ability of the teams to initiate change, PYA was selected to be part of the national pilot team, and the establishment embarked on an adventure lasting more than 18 months. It did not take long to convince part of the team, including the health executive, and to be able to rely on internal resources in search of a challenge.

Collective learning is necessary. Training provided by speech therapists introducing this subject to all the teams involved (doctor, direction, nurse, animator, assistant nurse, health executive, cooks, etc.) acts as a support in moving from the awareness phase to action.

This challenge has mobilized the teams, with a permanent evolution to convince even the most skeptical. There was no certainty at the beginning, but secure and tested trials allowed for progress, rectification and evaluation. The initial fears were overcome, and the risks evacuated, essentially one, that of the false route, which represents "*the*" great fear of the care and medical teams, a dynamic was found. As the months passed, the players became more confident, communication intensified, and the presence of Michel Bras, a Michelin-starred chef, brought an excellent and reassuring image to the project. Sodexo's R&D department provided the resources for deployment and supported the six French pilots in France.

After 18 months of relentless work on this topic, the results are very satisfying for PYA. The establishment has shown a decrease in the use of mixed texture and an increase in the satisfaction of residents (+12%), caregivers (+9.5%), families, cooks, etc.

The research project has made it possible to develop a new adaptation of the basic meal without using the blender, with specifications based on the size of the bites, their cohesion and the ability of the whole to slide down, without ever mixing solid and liquid.

All the complexity of the project and its richness rests on the triangular ABC approach (*autonomie*, *bouche*, *cuisine*, literally "autonomy, mouth, kitchen" in English). The challenge is to combine intersecting actions that interact with each other simultaneously for a common purpose. It was therefore necessary to work in parallel on the environment of the meals, the ambiance, the material, the conditions of service, the positions and the equipment, as well as all actions related to oral hygiene.

PYA has not served blended meals for more than 2 years. It is a great pride to be able to eat these adapted, tasty meals without any difficulty, where the food is recognizable, and for everyone to be able to rediscover the sense of pleasure at the table under the sign of conviviality; as Michel Bras says, “a food that connects them to their history”.

After some analysis of the project’s progress, it became clear that certain fundamental elements were necessary beforehand: relationships of trust with families, residents and employees, without which this project would not have been possible. In the same way, PYA’s values, based on fairness, transparency and trust, created the foundation, the *sine qua non* conditions.

As a result of my role as manager leader, initiator, facilitator and through an innovative project, the collaborative culture has changed to a culture of co-construction. We imagined and experimented together, which contributed to changing the managerial culture. A team that succeeds in such a challenge becomes strong and able to explore again, to dare to make change even if it has never been done before. I can also see the effects of such a collaborative experience: a shift in positions with more autonomy, more responsibility, more decisions made by the teams, more curiosity....

The most significant change was to modify the presentation of the organizational chart, which became circular, centered on residents and their families. It shows a level of equality of functions and professions, each one keeping its competences, its aims, its delegations in a cross-cutting and communicative vision in order to be reactive to satisfy and adapt to the situations, just like cogs in a machine, which are also connected to partners, suppliers and administrations, for a more open mind, more in line with the outside world, more connected, more on the lookout to build the retirement home of tomorrow.

PYA was nominated at the 2016 EAHSA (European Association of Homes and Services for the Ageing) Awards with the 4M project (English submission) in the “Best Facility in Europe” category.

6.4. Discussion, putting into perspective

PYA has not served blended meals since 2017. How can we explain this success when most EHPADs continue to “mix” meals for dependent residents? Indeed, the deployment of this practice is still far from unanimous. It calls into question the work practices of caregivers who have learned to give mixed meals to avoid “the wrong way”. Why did it work in this establishment, and why is it still difficult to institute it in others? What if the answer was to be found in management practices?

The project worked because the organization was prepared and had the conditions to welcome such a change. To use the allusion of the manager-gardener "who puts himself at the service of his plants" (1-min film on "a liberated company,[2] we would say that PYA had "the soil", the essential elements for "the plant to grow". The management practices and experiences, described in section 6.1: building the institution, trust, transparency, equity, the collaborative mode are constituent elements of the "compound", and the director harnessed her management and her vision in all objectivity and was not afraid of criticism. The 4M project, through its process and its results, has "anchored" and "generated" new management practices. In a way, "the plant feeds and grows, the soil is enriched and the plant grows". We believe that there is a virtuous circle, and we will try to explain it.

6.4.1. *Management promotes the implementation of novelty in the organization*

The 4M project required strong collaboration between the actors. The management method, based on transparency, trust and fairness, allows the organization to function in a collaborative mode. Each actor was able to advance the project regardless of their position and function in the organization. They could give their opinion, make proposals and express their doubts. The manager is in the position of "liberator": they are the guarantors of this "horizontal" mode of operation where everyone participates in the creation of knowledge about the project.

The innovative nature of the project has put the actors in a learning situation. They received training, but they were also led to reflect on what they had learned and to question their practices. It was a matter of questioning of everything (nursing assistants-nurses-cooks, etc.). Management practices often lead them to work together to train themselves (example: pairs train themselves and pass information on to their colleagues):

> Learning together on the 4M project was not difficult after agreeing to take on the challenge. (Director)

We also noted that the common goal of the project favors a positive dynamic: it is about improving the resident's quality of life. The team is committed to this project to change their work practices: no longer giving mixed meals because of the loss of taste and flavor. The team is driven by a desire to change to give more meaning to their work and thus obtain greater satisfaction. The actors are mobilized if they know the purpose of the project, if they can be proud of this purpose and if it corresponds to their personal values.

---

2 Available at: https://www.youtube.com/watch?v=ZrAFpPbz7O4.

The innovative nature also leads the team to take risks despite their doubts about the feasibility of such a practice, which clashes with their experience as caregivers. Managers must play their role: they must not allow themselves to be "taken on board" by the pessimists. They trust their co-workers. Cohen (2013) emphasizes that the caring leader "must trust his troops and show tolerance for failures. It is like giving them permission to try, and... to be wrong". Management therefore encourages taking initiative and risk-taking. Managers must then be in the position of facilitator. Their role is to work with the actors to identify the risks and the actions to guard against the risks. They provide reassurance of the feasibility of the project. Pass the doubts, risk taking is rewarded, and success has very positive effects on the actors. Success makes the team stronger, "getting there together" strengthens the team spirit and makes it grow.

6.4.2. *The innovative project as a catalyst for new management practices*

We note that the process and the result of the project generate new management practices. It is in this space that managerial innovation appears.

From a collaborative mode, the project led the actors to a logic of construction. The 4M project led internal actors to work with external experts and intersecting skills to think about and develop a new method for preparing and serving meals to residents.

The results of the project, the successes, lead the actors to "open up" to novelty, to be in "a process of not staying with what we know", to question dogmas and to "dare to experiment". Novelty is therefore possible in the medico-social sector and in EHPADs.

The novelty can come from ideas put forward by a member of the organization provided that management allows it. Indeed, anything that is not yet in place in the organization is new. It can also come from another facility. At PYA, a new practice is emerging: management is offering employees the opportunity to visit other facilities to see what is being done elsewhere. For example, several employees went to a local EHPAD that recycles all of the residents' incontinence protection. With a view to corporate social responsibility (CSR) and having knowledge of the consumption of protects in their residence, the employees discovered a new way of doing things that works. Based on their past successes, following this visit, the employees could draw inspiration from it and implement it within PYA. This dynamic can also improve the attractiveness of the professions within the EHPAD. Indeed, the complexity of recruiting personnel in EHPADs is well known.

Novelty can also come from institutions in other countries. Florence Vichi, together with several directors of the establishment, regularly goes on study trips[3] and then goes into "explorer" mode by visiting other establishments abroad. The study trips are a way to discover what other countries are doing to support the dependent elderly to stimulate their thinking and creativity. It is also the role of the liberating leader to provide an inspiring vision for their organization. This vision must, however, remain connected to the daily life of the employees who only identify with a meaningful mission vision (Cohen 2013).

It is also through this dynamic that employees and their management could think about "the EHPAD" of tomorrow.

Managerial innovation is based on the manager's ability to put employees in collaborative mode. This is based on several principles: the freedom of relations between the actors, the sharing of responsibility by the actors in relation to their action in the organization, and the ability of the actors to freely influence the definition and sequencing of actions to achieve the objectives assigned to the group. The manager must therefore adopt new methods that break with traditional methods (command-control). Rather, it is a matter of "embracing" a style or behavior appropriate to an organization in collaborative mode:

– trusting employees: the right to make mistakes allows the actor to take initiative;

– promoting transparency: management indicators must make it possible to evaluate and value the collective work accomplished and to highlight successes;

– ensuring fairness: actors are free to make decisions and to carry out actions in the context of their work. They are the best qualified to make decisions about their work.

The manager must also present a vision that makes sense for the employees, or more precisely, a vision connected to the daily life of the employees. Such behavior is not usual for a manager and requires much know-how. However, managers must stand firm and face their critics.

This "management" style favors innovative project approaches, and their implementation will institute new forms of collaborative organization. It is in this space that new management practices are born. In the case of PYA, employees "dare" to think about new practices and change to give more meaning to their work. They take risks to achieve this together and take pride in their work, so they can go

---

3 See the article "Des idées plein ses bagages", *Revue Directions* – December 2019.

further. Novelty is then allowed in their EHPAD. This novelty can come from an employee's idea or from the manager himself/herself.

It is important to emphasize the interest of institutions in engaging in innovation in the current context where the public image is sometimes not very flattering and where recruiting staff is complex. These innovation initiatives can improve the visibility and attractiveness of nursing homes.

6.5. The PYA nursing home and crisis management during COVID-19

The EHPAD nursing home managed, as all the establishments, two waves of the COVID-19 pandemic in March and September 2020. The establishment was not very affected during the first wave but was very strongly affected during the second wave in terms of residents and professionals infected by the COVID-19 virus.

In section 6.5.1, we will reflect on the management principles presented in this chapter. Are the collaborative mode, trust and transparency undermined in times of crisis or, on the contrary, are they levers to face them?

6.5.1. *A trained and "muscular", therefore resilient, team*

Collaboration between professionals in health-care institutions is one of the lessons to be learned from this crisis. A report on the hospital system during the crisis shows that the ability of teams to organize themselves and the ability of health professionals to coordinate their actions with others are two elements that should be kept in mind for managing future crises (Dumez and Minvielle 2020). The collaborative mode, already present before the pandemic, was rather accentuated within the PYA nursing home. Thus, unlike other establishments, teamwork and collaboration were not newly discovered during the crisis, and management did not wait for the crisis to see that professionals were capable of coordinating and sometimes even surpassing themselves.

Faced with this virus, all the PYA professionals had the same level of knowledge. They were also "equal" in their feelings. The cross-cutting and collaborative management style allowed the different professions and the management to find solutions on an ad hoc basis in a reactive and adapted manner while taking into account the fears and weaknesses of each person. In the institution, a decision is a compromise, and the solution is supported by all members. It can be re-evaluated if it does not work. Decisions had to be made quickly and implemented with government recommendations, a variable and evolving context over weeks and months.

The team discussions helped to allay fears and to constantly ask questions about the management of the pandemic and the best practices to adopt. The proximity of management to employees was an essential element in preventing the effects and collateral impacts of the crisis. For the director, it was a matter of "taking the pulse of the team" and "staying connected to them" by communicating to ensure that there was no breakdown during the crisis.

In addition, the professionals respect each other and are tolerant of each other's weaknesses. This way of working existed before the crisis. It has been accentuated and has prevented professionals from becoming exhausted. The management method allows the team to last over time and has enabled it to become resilient.

Here, we propose an analogy with the sports world: the team was trained; during the crisis, it made a greater effort, it experienced situations differently, it proved itself and continued its training, satisfied to have overcome difficult moments.

6.5.2. *Being in project mode despite the crisis: getting up and being ready*

During this pandemic year, PYA continued to seize opportunities to initiate new projects. For the director, this is a way to give employees a horizon and perspectives. "You have to seize opportunities even when the crisis is over. The project is the driving force of the establishment". The nursing home has responded to several calls for projects, despite the daily grind. The establishment has applied for funding for a music therapy project and has just initiated a project with a company that works according to a design thinking methodology to design furniture for the residents. Residents and professionals participate in the design as users and test the furniture using prototypes. This approach also allows new elements to be brought to light that were clearly identified during the periods of lockdown.

The management mode and this project approach gave employees the opportunity to propose new things to help the teams. For example, the psychologist proposed photolanguage sessions to the professionals to express the situations they had experienced. Then, a staff member, trained in sophrology, offered sessions to employees to help them take care of themselves to better take care of others. For the director, it is necessary to value these proposals and to accept that these initiatives are done during working time; "the team self-regulates and will do the work anyway".

6.5.3. *A director supported by her team and a stronger sense of work*

The regularity in the management mode of the management during the crisis is highlighted.

The director is convinced that it took everyone's expertise to cope. This crisis was managed and experienced collectively: "It fed the team, made it strengthen their bonds and the team continues".

Violence in the face of the death of residents is a trauma for all professionals: from management to nursing and hotel teams.

Management was transparent with residents, families, employees and administrators. The professionals, already tested by the deaths of residents, sometimes received harsh words from the families in connection with the sanitary measures that were sometimes considered too strict. The director managed the establishment with her emotions and vulnerabilities, and her team was also present to support her. This close-knit team was a necessity to absorb the shockwave of the crisis, and transparency also allowed for the development of a form of empathy from the administrators of the institution.

Convinced of the need to continue what was well done before, the director set up projects for her establishment and encouraged initiative to be taken. She is still very involved in the question of the EHPAD of the future and participates in seminars with researchers and professionals.

This crisis has proven to her that her management works, and she adds that she has never been so convinced of the meaning of her work.

6.6. Conclusion

The practices of caring and flexible management do not make it possible to contain the spread of the virus in an establishment, to erase the problems of absenteeism and recruitment of professionals, or to reduce the financial impact of the crisis, but they do contribute to favorable working conditions for managing current and future crises. They also lead to a consideration of the work carried out individually and collectively by the employees and their manager. Caring management would then create the right conditions to develop organizational resilience in times of crisis.

The crisis breaks codes, upsets reference points and habits, removes shackles and sometimes allows us to find other paths. If the organization is agile enough to take them with kindness, together, without judgment, without regret of the past, it is then possible to reinvent itself and innovate in ways the organization would perhaps never have considered because it is too often constrained to think outside the box; and paradoxically, all this is done in an environment with ultrademanding hygiene rules.

6.7. References

Autissier, D., Jonhson, K., Moutot, J.M. (2016). L'innovation managériale : rupture ou évolution du management. *Revue française de gestion*, 13, 25–33.

Blanquet, M.F. (2007). Web Collaboratif, Web Coopératif, Web 2/0 – Quelles interrogations pour l'enseignant documentaliste ? *Formation des personnes ressources en documentation tenue*, CRDP d'Aix-Marseille, Marseille.

Cohen, R.H. (2013). Plaidoyer pour un leadership bienveillant. *L'Expansion Management Review*, 148, 90–99.

Damanpour, F. (1988). Innovation type, radicalness, and the adoption process. *Communication Research*, 15(15), 545–565.

Damanpour, F. and Evan, W.M. (1984). Organizational innovation and performance: The problem of organizational lag. *Administrative Science Quarterly*, 29(3), 392–409.

David, A. (1996). Structure et dynamique des innovations managériales. *Cinquième Conférence de l'Association Internationale de Management Stratégique*, Lille.

Dumez, H. and Minvielle, E. (2020). Le système hospitalier français dans la crise Covid-19 : une contribution des Sciences de gestion. Report, Centre de recherche en Gestion, Palaiseau.

Gangloff-Ziegler, C. (2009). Les freins au travail collaboratif. *Marché et organisations*, 10(3), 95–112.

Getz, I. and Carney, B. (2016). *Liberté & Compagnie, quand la liberté des salaries fait le succès des entreprises*. Flammarion, Paris.

Kimberly, J.R. (1981). Managerial innovation. In *Handbook of Organizational Design*, Nystrom, P.C., Starbuck, W.H. (eds). Oxford University Press, New York.

Le Roy, R. and Giuliani, P. (2013). L'innovation managériale : généalogie, défis et perspectives. *Revue française de gestion*, 235, 77–90.

Rogers, E.M. (1995). *Diffusion of Innovations*. The Free Press, New York.

7

The Determinants of Happiness in the Workplace for Health-care Workers

Like other sectors of activity, the health and social sector is not exempt from the constraints of productivity (Gollac 2005), which impose organizations seeking efficiency, speed of execution or optimization of resources, among other things, or from the constraints of quality, traceability or safety, which generate a subjective intensification of work (Clot 2006). In the face of these profound changes, patients have become clients, and care is increasingly evaluated according to its costs and profitability. As Routelous (2018) points out, organizations, particularly public health organizations, tend to lose the purpose of their action in favor of more economic and financial dimensions. To use the classification of constraints proposed by Detchessahar (2011), this health sector is undergoing both:

– an "industrial" constraint linked to the need to respect quantitative and qualitative standards in the exercise of activities;

– a "market" constraint through the imperative of user satisfaction;

– a constraint known as "event-driven" (Zarifian 1995), which requires a rapid response to hazards and emergencies.

In addition to these constraints, the health and social care sector has also undergone numerous changes over the last 10 years due to changes in regulations. As Rivière et al. (2019) point out, these changes to the expected objectives, the work environments and the decision-making bodies have significant effects on the health of care workers. They are potentially at the origin of numerous "confusions" (Uhalde 2007) that weigh on the performance of organizations. They can have an impact on economic performance if they manifest themselves in absenteeism,

---

Chapter written by Vanessa FAZAL, Virginie MOISSON and Pascal MOULETTE.

turnover, work stoppages or even resignations. They can also affect social performance if they are the cause of subjective work-related problems (Detchessahar et al. 2012), such as stress, tension, burnout or exhaustion linked to the feeling of having to constantly adjust to the constraints of the organization (in terms of staffing, workload or resources, for example). At the same time, however, there is evidence from caregivers that despite all the professional difficulties in their health-care institutions, work can also contribute to their well-being and even to their happiness (Odoxa survey; Actusoins 2018). This notion of happiness remains quite ambitious and sometimes misleading for this socioprofessional category. The numerous demonstrations or strikes at the end of 2019 in France bear witness to increasingly degraded working conditions, ever more reduced resources or a health system increasingly decried.

It is in this context of hospitals on the verge of burnout that this chapter has the ambition to address the issue of happiness of happiness at work among health care personnel. What are the determinants of happiness at work as perceived by paramedics, nurses, orderlies, paramedics, hospital pharmacy technicians and physiotherapists? Today, happiness at work is indeed recognized as a prerequisite for the sustainable performance of the organization. For example, there is a growing interest in initiatives such as Great Place to Work (GPTW). This organization, which ranks and labels companies on the basis of the perception of their employees and their practices in terms of quality of life at work, enjoys significant media coverage, and the academic literature shows that the companies with the best GPTW ratings have significantly better financial performance (Edmans 2011). In some organizations, we are even witnessing the creation of new functions with the emergence of human resources responsible for happiness at work, referred to as chief happiness officers (Perroud 2017).

This chapter presents the results of research that focuses on the determinants of happiness at work in a population of 145 paramedics and on the capacity of managers to act on these determinants. Our interest was focused on this population because, as we have stated, they are subject to strong work constraints and evolve in an increasingly complex environment that threatens the quality of work life of health-care personnel and, consequently, the quality of care.

It will then be a question of questioning the elements that could contribute to their perceived happiness. To do this, we relied on a quantitative study carried out in various public and private health-care establishments in metropolitan France and in territories in the Indian Ocean zone (Reunion and Mayotte) in April 2019.

7.1. Presentation of the empirical study

There is no consensus on the definition of happiness, and its complexity is primarily due to the many factors that can influence it, such as genetic predisposition, the way we view life, or our own capacities for acceptance and resilience. Happiness is thus often synonymous with satisfaction or joy. Happiness is a question of individual perception and is a very personal matter. What about "happiness at work"? Is it possible to be happy within the framework of one's professional activity, when work can be synonymous with suffering? Or even be defined as an instrument of torture? Is not it utopian to think that some employees have professional experiences that can lead to happiness, even though companies and organizations very often stop at the notion of well-being? Is not happiness reserved exclusively for intimate experience, which can only be lived in the private sphere?

To answer these questions, a detour through psychology seemed to us very enlightening. Researchers in psychology differentiate between two approaches to happiness derived from the two main philosophical currents: hedonic and eudemonic. These two notions are similar to positive psychology, which scientifically studies the development and optimal functioning of people, organizations and associations, the subject of our work.

The hedonic concept of happiness is centered on affective elements and on satisfaction with one's life. From this approach, we speak of subjective well-being. This subjective well-being, which is difficult to perceive and process for a manager or service manager, will not be analyzed in this research.

The eudemonic vision of happiness, which speaks of psychological well-being, refers to self-realization, finding meaning and having a goal. In this context, the fundamental psychological needs that have an impact on happiness can be social belonging or the feeling of autonomy. Self-determination theorists (e.g. Deci and Ryan 2002), who study the intrinsic motivation of individuals, mobilize this concept of happiness in particular.

We have built our research model by identifying five main determinants of happiness at work. Our choice was guided by a central question: what are the levers on which the managerial function can act and which have both an individual and collective dimension? We chose autonomy, knowledge, professional relations, the feeling of a job well done and humor.

Most researchers agree that employee autonomy can be a factor of well-being at work and reduces psychosocial risks. The study by Baudelot and Gollac (2003), for example, highlights the link between happiness at work and autonomy. Indeed, the more autonomous a person is in their work, the happier they are at work, with this hypothesis being verified among executives in particular.

Similarly, it would seem that being recognized by one's hierarchy, colleagues or clients contributes to the perception of happiness at work (Dagenais-Desmarais and Privé 2010). According to Thévenet (2009), happiness at work is found in the team and its relationships. He establishes the four Vs of the team, namely, the verity of relationships, vigor of relationships, a common vision and voluntary participation. We are no longer talking about the individual and their personal contribution, but about an entity: the team. Teamwork induced by professional relationships would therefore potentially be a source of happiness at work.

Another element that could promote happiness at work according to Clot (2013): the importance of well-being at work when the work is well done. Indeed, the French would have difficulty in recognizing themselves in what they do at work, in "rediscovering themselves". The author focuses on the lack of quality at work. This problem would have consequences on happiness at work and is an important factor in the well-being of employees. The pleasure of "work well done" would be the best prevention against "stress": there is no "well-being" without "doing well". Thus, as Mellor et al. (2018) pointed out, "it is the presence of positive situations that most strongly influences subjective well-being. These positive situations reflect the presence of resources within the work environment, particularly social support".

Finally, Fortin and Méthot (2004) discuss the benefits of humor on the individual and its contribution to happiness at work because of its effect on feelings of self-control and personal effectiveness. Several virtues are attributed to humor: a reduction in depressive and anxious manifestations and better self-esteem (Deaner and McConatha 1993; Frecknall 1994), an increased sense of well-being (Kuiper et al. 1995) and even a greater capacity for resilience (Henman 2001) and an improved quality of life (Thorson et al. 1997). Humor and the laughter it provokes contribute to an emotional well-being that eases tensions and allows the release of endorphins and thus allows for happiness.

We have formulated several hypotheses based on our theoretical research model. These hypotheses, of which there are five, are formulated in the same way to test causal links of the "more..., then more..." type, for example, as follows: "the more autonomous an individual is in their work, the more likely they are to perceive happiness at work", "the more an individual is recognized in their work, the more likely they are to perceive happiness at work", etc.

We constructed a questionnaire using a five-point Likert scale ranging from "strongly agree" to "strongly disagree". It was pretested with five state-registered nurse respondents. Minor changes were made as a result of their feedback, such as rewording, adaptation of hospital vocabulary and adjusted translations from English.

The questionnaire was distributed by e-mail after requesting authorization from the management of the various targeted health-care institutions and through social networks (Facebook and WhatsApp, in particular). The data collection period lasted three weeks. We selected a usable sample of 145 respondents. This number is significant but remains low given the target population (Figure 7.1).

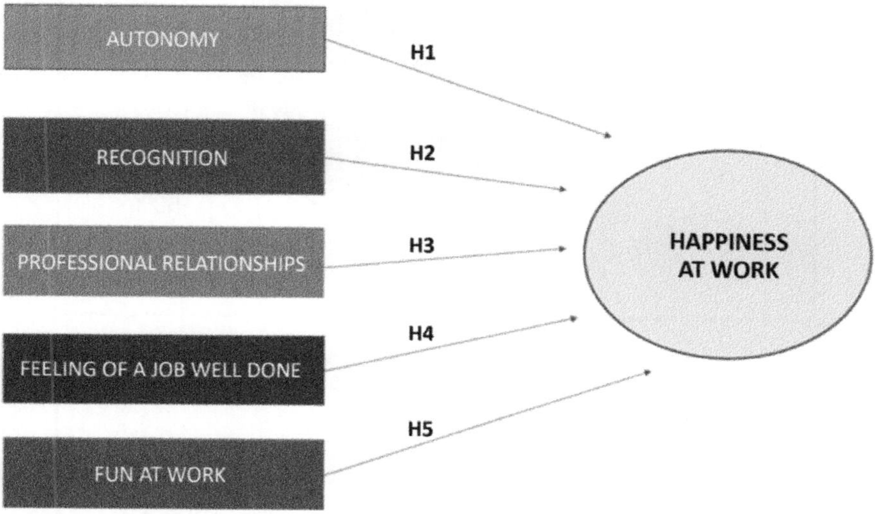

Figure 7.1. *Theoretical research model. For a color version of this figure, see www.iste.co.uk/bruyere/caringmanagement.zip*

7.2. Analysis of the results

Our sample is composed of a very large majority of women. They represent 81.4% of respondents. This can be explained by the fact that 87.7% of the nursing population in France is composed of women and 90.4% of the nursing assistants (Dares 2013). Some 51.7% of the respondents have less than 5 years of service.

Looking at the difference in respondents between the public and private sectors, the public sector is largely represented: 72.4% of the sample work in this sector. The percentage figures remain more telling for the different items of the happiness at work variable (Figure 7.2).

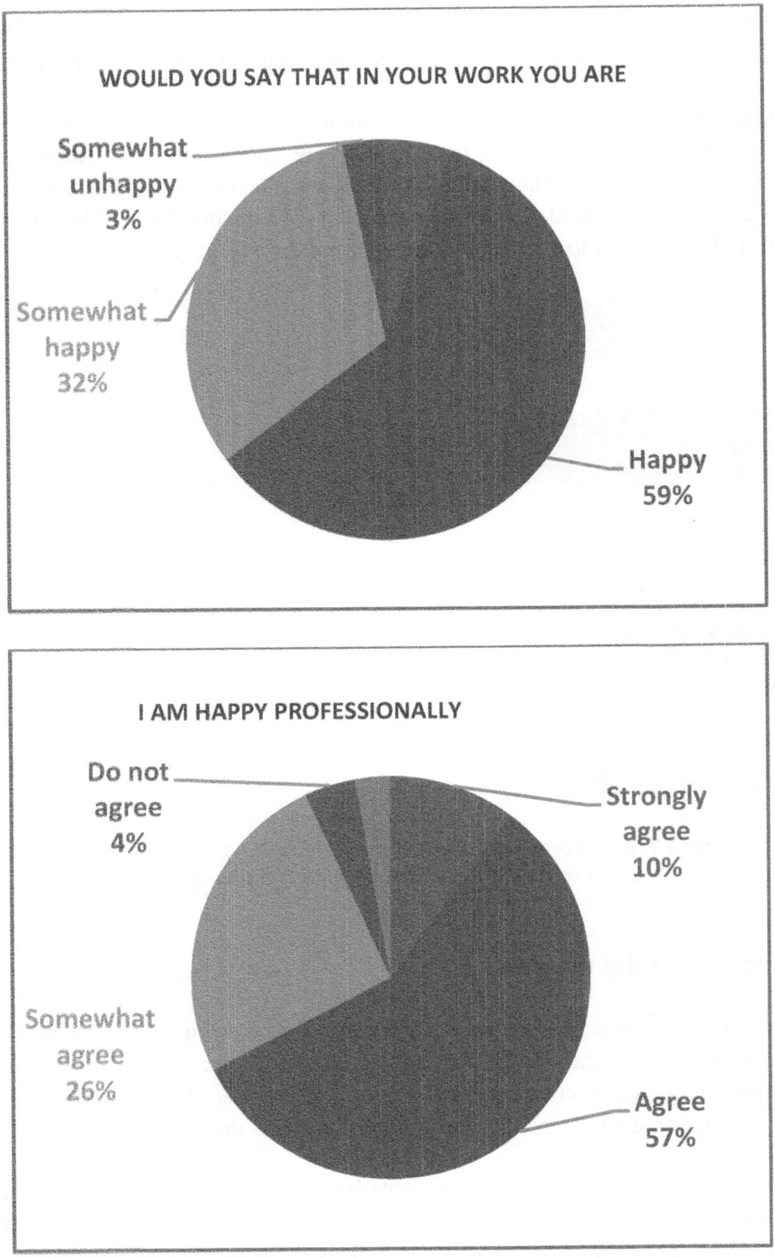

Figure 7.2. *The results for the "happiness at work" variable. For a color version of this figure, see www.iste.co.uk/bruyere/caringmanagement.zip*

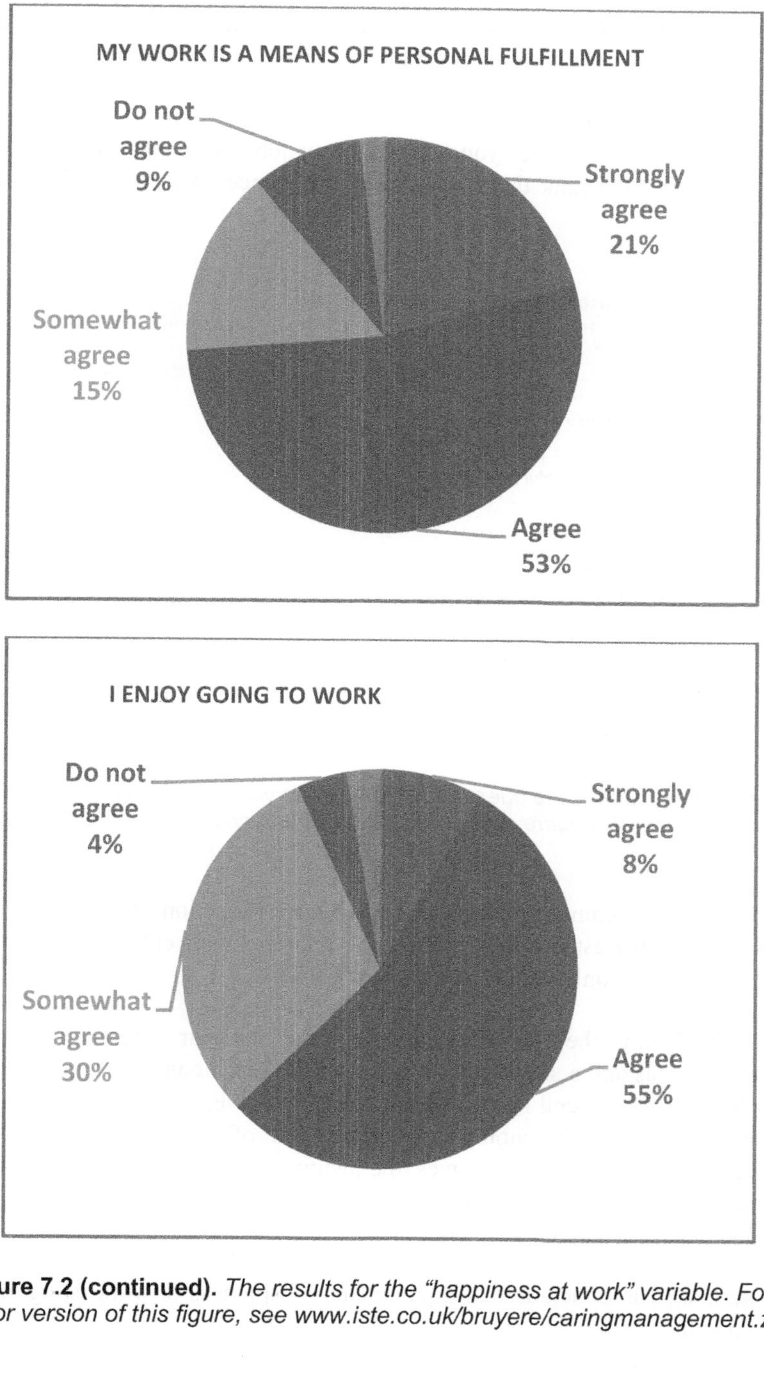

Figure 7.2 (continued). *The results for the "happiness at work" variable. For a color version of this figure, see www.iste.co.uk/bruyere/caringmanagement.zip*

We can therefore see from these initial results that the majority of the caregivers surveyed are happy at work and consider their work to be an important lever for personal fulfillment.

For the item "What makes you happy in your job?" respondents were asked to choose two items and rank them in order of preference. We present the results in Figure 7.3.

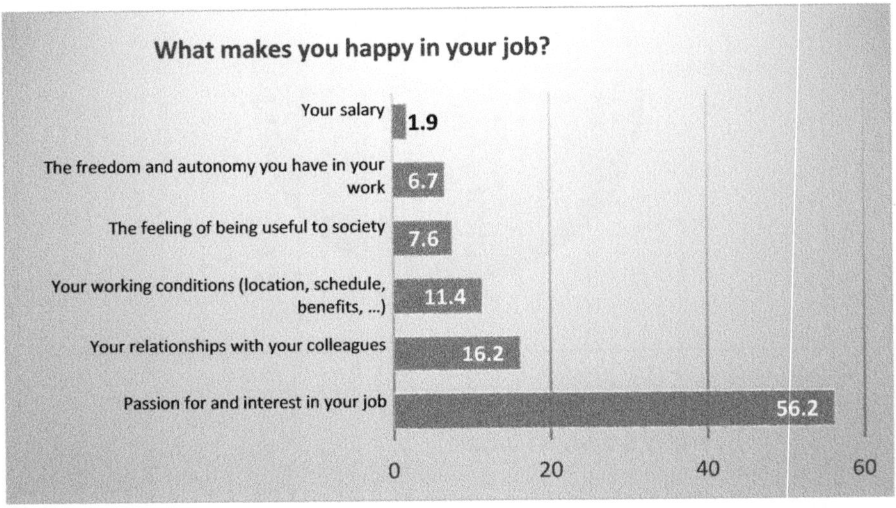

Figure 7.3. *Results to the question: "What makes you happy in your job?". For a color version of this figure, see www.iste.co.uk/bruyere/caringmanagement.zip*

By far, the most common answer and a real lever for action on happiness at work is "passion and interest in one's job", with "relations with colleagues" coming in second, and "salary" only very rarely chosen (1.9%).

After analyzing the reliability of our data and our results (by studying Cronbach's alphas and a simple linear regression for each construct) and testing our various hypotheses, several items appeared to be decisive in promoting happiness at work, particularly the autonomy and recognition of several actors or internal stakeholders (the hierarchy, colleagues, the institution and finally the patients). Thus, when the recognition of colleagues increases, happiness at work increases; when autonomy increases, happiness at work increases, etc.

Overall, we can conclude that a paramedic's happiness at work is significantly explained mainly by:

– relations with hierarchy;

– recognition from colleagues;

– degree of autonomy;

– the feeling of having done their job well.

7.3. Discussion of the results and impacts on the managerial function

The descriptive analysis of happiness at work has made it possible to highlight that, overall, the paramedics who responded to our questionnaire are happy in their work. Similarly, the first thing they say is that the passion and interest they have for their work and the good relationships they have with their colleagues or patients make them happy. The notion of salary is rarely mentioned as a primary criterion for happiness at work. We also found that age and seniority were not factors in the perception of happiness.

On the other hand, the added value provided by the managerial line takes on its full meaning. Having a relationship of trust with their line manager seems to be essential and justifies the qualification of "proximity" managers. Indeed, the teams expect their manager to provide both instrumental support (tangible help) and to listen and provide emotional support. This seems to be the most important factor and even the most important factor cited by paramedical staff in their responses to the questionnaire to create a climate conducive to happiness at work.

The implementation of work groups, discussion spaces and a certain flexibility in the organization give free rein to the expression of collective intelligence. These practices develop teamwork and promote well-being at work, a potential source of happiness.

Following the example of the work of Detchessahar, and in particular Detchessahar et al. (2012), who study the possible links between management modes and the occupational health of health-care workers, we consider that discussion spaces can be particularly suitable for developing the perception of happiness at work. Health at work being the result of a process of production of the employee's relationship with their work (Detchessahar et al. 2012), the creation of these spaces managed and facilitated by the management team, with the support of the management, is a source of performance. However, several conditions must be met to make them effective and to allow "work to be taken care of" (Clot 2006). These spaces must take the form of regular discussions (frequency to be defined between the actors according to the other constraints), relate to the real work (on the daily work, the tensions, the problems and the unforeseen), must be organized (definition of an agenda, facilitator appointed from among the members of the management, etc.)

and equipped (location close to the activity, use of service management tools, or decision support such as the transmission book for example, etc.).

They must be places for both psychological and political treatment of work-related issues. Psychological, because it is a question of dealing with the confusions, tensions and contradictions brought about by the organization and its constraints by creating lines of action and collective reaction. It is also psychological because the discussion requires everyone to state their representation of work and their difficulties in order to construct compromises of meaning and common perspectives of work. Detchessahar et al. (2012) speak of the creation of a "virtuous circle of visibility of work", a key element in the construction of health at work. Political, because the discussions can lead the players to define new methods of action and coordination and new local rules for carrying out the work, which could be defended to other internal stakeholders (HRM, quality department, management, etc.) and for which a request for human or material resources might be necessary.

The hospital or social structure must therefore find the means so that the local executives "organize the discussion" to find the right balance between the level of prescription of the work and the spaces of regulation, a source of construction of meaning, involvement, reappropriation of work, cooperation at work, attachment and ultimately health and happiness at work.

However, one of the conditions for the successful implementation of these spaces is that the departments must be able to give time to local managers. These managers are generally very busy feeding the information system (managing schedules, writing reports, managing steering indicators, updating procedures, etc.), participating more or less actively in various time-consuming meeting mechanisms and managing urgent situations on a daily basis.

Concerning the recognition of colleagues, several managerial recommendations can be proposed. The first, highlighted by Vinot et al. (2017), is to clarify the role of each person so that each member of the service can find meaning in their work and can be aware of the value each resource brings to the collective. This clarification of each person's role can also have the merit of clarifying expectations, updating job descriptions and thus regulating the delta between prescribed and actual work, often the cause of stressful situations. Second, it seems necessary to work on a real policy for the establishment, or at least for the department, allowing the implementation of a real recognition of work among colleagues and by colleagues. Our results have shown that the support given to colleagues encourages happiness at work. The implementation of recognition between colleagues can be achieved through a culture of challenges rather than a culture of competition or by setting team objectives rather than individual objectives.

It is also important to promote convivial moments between team members, facilitate their implementation and be attentive to the exclusion of a collaborator. In this context, the health-care manager has a real role to play as an initiator, federator and guarantor of respect for the rules of collective life in the service of the quality of care and patient safety. Our results thus corroborate the idea that recognition is achieved through the work group that supports the employee in the face of possible difficulties and by the organization or institution that rewards the quality of the work and allows the actors a certain freedom and capacity to act on their work and activities. The recognition of the "power to act" (Clot 2008) thus becomes central to the issues of health and happiness at work.

Regarding humor, the results of the questionnaire show how it is important to overcome difficult situations and to liven up the daily life of a department. Humor, and more generally laughter, appears to be a communication tool that promotes happiness in the workplace, creates social ties and helps to establish a friendly and pleasant work climate. Creating the conditions for a collective good mood can therefore be an objective for the managerial function to work on. Laughter is also an emotional release that calms tensions and allows the release of endorphins and therefore naturally brings happiness.

Finally, the analyses of the results of our questionnaire show that management based on benevolence, valuing the right to make mistakes, and trust are the keys to the quality of care and the medical service provided. It contributes to a calm social climate of trust and creates the conditions for employees to be happy to go to work. It is important, for example, that employees feel supported when a mistake happens and that this mistake can be analyzed collectively. The mistake-making culture is one of the pillars of the feeling of a job being well done. Quality management can encourage this mistake-making culture by introducing a habitual practice of reporting undesirable events, analyzing them and taking preventive action, thus reducing the risk of their recurrence. In the same spirit, the introduction of more collaborative decision-making methods, the co-construction of performance measurement tools, consultation mechanisms and so on are conducive to reducing the feeling of constraints imposed "from outside the service" felt by many health sector personnel. Following the example of Benallah and Domin (2017) and Virgili and Bornarel (2019), we believe that these collaborative or participatory approaches help to establish a climate of trust that limits the conflicts of value mentioned above and that contributes to collective performance.

We find these same recommendations in the current context linked to COVID-19. The feeling of a job well done, the relationship with colleagues, the relationship with the hierarchy and the degree of autonomy, in this context, appear more than ever to be the levers that allow staff to find meaning in their work and to be able to "get through" this health crisis. Given the psychological pressure and professional exhaustion felt by caregivers during this crisis, other needs are nevertheless emerging, as highlighted by Anton (2020): the collective creation of meaning through discursive practice, agility and the dissemination of knowledge through the implementation of mechanisms for the dissemination of new knowledge. All of these needs place the health executive at the center of the action and as a key player in the management of this crisis situation. The feeling of being abandoned by the political authorities, which is materialized, for example, by the suppression of beds or the reduction of staff, makes this managerial function all the more important. As Payre et al. (2020) point out, "we cannot continue to believe that the perpetual reduction, even if only of beds or of the attractiveness of professions, has no negative impact on the healthcare system" and, by extension, on staff.

It is important that the quest for happiness not be about organizational performance or performance or productivity. Management implies helping caregivers feel good about their work life, taking a holistic approach by developing autonomy and the ability to participate in the development of the department's objectives, without any ulterior economic or political motives. This management style also implies the development of staff skills, continuous training and, if possible, the enrichment and/or expansion of tasks. A team generally needs to feel heard, listened to and supported by its manager. Routelous (2018) reminds us, "managers must keep in mind that the social link includes all forms of social support, as well as the quality of interpersonal relationships", to create work contexts conducive to commitment. The term "proximity" manager thus takes on its full meaning. The health-care manager, because of their role in the organization of care, is therefore the main actor in fostering a feeling of happiness at work among health-care workers.

Faced with criticism of the "hospital-company" (Rivière 2019) or the "care factory" (Daidj and Pascal 2018), the difficulties of hospital governance still encountered by a bureaucratic model (Anton 2020) and the limits of a management that aims to minimize the costs of caring for its "patients" (Fall 2020), and taking into account all of these results and recommendations, it seems imperative to stop relying on commitment to public service and the involvement of carers and their duty of continuity of care and to stop confronting the carer with the disease and their responsibilities as a motivational factor. The levers of happiness at work for nursing staff are elsewhere and find their sources, in the vast majority of cases, in the mode of management and organization established by the manager and health executive.

7.4. References

Abord de Chatillon, E. (2003). L'audit de stress au travail : un audit de santé de l'organisation ? *Revue Performances*, 12, 2003/09-10, 29–36.

Actusoins (2018). L'importance du temps dans la relation patients-soignants. Enquête Odoxa pour la Mutuelle Nationale des Hospitaliers, Amilly.

Anton, P. (2020). Agilité organisationnelle et gestion de la pandémie Covid-19 : contribution d'une approche exploratoire réalisée auprès de managers hospitaliers français. *Question(s) de management*, 29, 45–59.

Baudelot, C. and Gollac, M. (2003). *Travailler pour être heureux ? Le bonheur et le travail en France.* Fayard, Paris.

Benallah, S. and Domin, J.-P. (2017). Réforme de l'hôpital, quels enjeux en termes de travail et de santé des personnels ? *La revue de l'IRES*, 91–92, 155–183.

Chanlat, J.F. (1990). *L'individu dans l'organisation : les dimensions oubliées.* Les Presses de l'Université Laval et les Éditions Eska, Quebec.

Clot, Y. (2013). L'aspiration au travail bien fait. *Le journal de l'école de Paris du management*, 99, 23–28.

Dagenais-Desmarais, V. and Prive, C. (2010). Comment améliorer le bien-être psychologique au travail ? *Gestion*, 35(3), 69–77.

Daidj, N. and Pascal, C. (2018). Des hôpitaux aux usines à soins. Un réel progrès ? *Management & Avenir Santé*, 3, 7–11.

Dares (2013). La répartition des hommes et des femmes par métiers. *Dares Analyses*, 79, 13.

Deaner, M.C. and Conatha, J.T. (1993). The relationship of humor to depression and personality. *Psychological Reports*, 72(3), 755–763.

Deci, E.L. and Ryan, R.M. (2002), Self-determination research: Reflections and future directions. In *Handbook of Self-determination Research*, Deci, E.L., Ryan, R.M. (eds). University of Rochester Press, Rochester.

Detchessahar, M. (2011). Quand le management n'est pas le problème, mais la solution. *Revue française de gestion*, 214, 89–105.

Detchessahar, M., Devigne, M., Grevin, A, Stimec, A. (2012). Contribution au débat sur les excès et les déficits du management : trois études de cas dans des établissements de santé. In *La souffrance au travail : quelle responsabilité de l'entreprise ?*, Bardelli, P., Allouche, J. (eds). Armand Colin, Paris.

Edmans, A. (2011). Does the stock market fully value intangibles ? Employee satisfaction and equity prices. *Journal of Financial Economics*, 101(3), 621–640.

Fall, A. (2015). Reconnaissance au travail : validation d'une échelle de mesure dans le contexte des entreprises. *Revue européenne de psychologie appliquée*, 65(4), 189–203.

Fall, I. (2020). Une crise peut en cacher une autre : comprendre la crise du management pour comprendre la crise sanitaire du coronavirus. Quelques pistes de refondation du management. *Question(s) de management*, 29, 61–69.

Frecknall, P. (1994). Good humour: A qualitative study of the uses of humour in everyday life. *Psychology: A Journal of Human Behavior*, 31(1), 12–21.

Gollac, M. (2005). L'intensité du travail : formes et effets. *Revue économique*, 2(56), 195–216.

Henman, L.D. (2001). Humor as a coping mechanism: Lessons from POWs. *Humor*, 14(1), 83–94.

Kuiper, N.A., McKenzie, S.D., Bélanger, K.A. (1995). Cognitive appraisals and individual differences in sense of humour: Motivational and affective implications. *Personality and Individual Differences*, 19, 359–372.

Mellor, N., Dufoix, F., Saunder, L., Albert, E., Collange, J. (2018). Le bien-être subjectif au travail et sa relation avec le soutien social perçu. *Archives des maladies professionnelles et de l'environnement*, 79(1), 23–33.

Payre, S., Tissioui, M., Joffre, C. (2020). Quels enseignements tirer de la crise du Covid-19 que rencontre le système de santé en termes d'organisation, de compétences et de métiers ? *Management & avenir santé*, 6, 7–13.

Perroud, M. (2017). Le bien-être au travail est-il une mode ou une réelle préoccupation des entreprises ? *Revue Challenges* [Online]. Available at: https://www.challenges.fr/emploi/management/le-bien-etre-au-travail-est-il-une-mode-ou-une-reelle-preoccupation-des-entreprises_482533.

Rivière, A. (2019). Tensions de rôle et stress professionnel chez les cadres de santé à l'hôpital public – L'effet modérateur des stratégies d'ajustement. *Revue française de gestion*, 282, 11–35.

Rivière, A., Commeiras, N., Loubes, A. (2019). Nouveau management public, tensions de rôle et stress professionnel chez les cadres de santé. *Revue de gestion des ressources humaines*, 112, 3–20.

Routelous, C. (2018). Les conditions de l'engagement au travail : leviers d'un management du bien-être au travail. In *Le management en santé*, Louazel, M., Mourier, A., Ollivier, E., Ollivier, R. (eds). Presses de l'EHESP, Rennes.

Thevenet, M. (2009). *Les équipes : le bonheur est dans l'équipe*. Eyrolles, Paris.

Thorson, J.A., Powell, F.C., Sarmany-Schuller, I., Hampes, W.P. (1997). Psychological health and sense of humor. *Journal of Clinical Psychology*, 53(6), 805–819.

Uhalde, M. (2007). Quand gestion rime avec confusion. *Sciences Humaines*, 179, 5.

Vinot, A. and Vinot, D. (2017). Le management au défi du stress des professionnels dans les établissements d'accueil des personnes âgées dépendantes. *Journal de gestion et d'économie médicales*, 35, 159–177.

Virgili, S. and Bornarel, F. (2019). Faire confiance pour échanger plus efficacement l'information dans l'équipe : le rôle du cadre de santé. In *Supply Chain Management de la santé*, Bentahar, O., Benzidia, S. (eds). Éditions EMS, Caen.

Zarifian, P. (1995). *Le travail et l'événement : essai sociologique sur le travail industriel à l'époque actuelle*. L'Harmattan, Paris.

8

Management and Benevolence: How Can Managerial Action in the Development of Health Teams be Supported?

Talking about caring management in a context where changes in the world of work are leading to an increase in employee health problems may seem provocative. However, in this chapter, we wish to demonstrate through field experimentation that management and benevolence can be combined if we change the paradigm and that managerial benevolence focuses on and around work. We support the hypothesis that this managerial benevolence allows us to develop the health of employees, work groups and organizations.

The profound changes in the world of work in recent decades have made the issue of the prevention of "psychosocial risks" central to the point of imposing itself in the public debate. Many authors speak of these changes in the world of work: increased competition, adaptability to the economic market, restructuring programs, intensification of work and new technologies (Volkoff 2005; Molinier 2006; Ughetto 2007; Castel 2009). These same authors, and others with them, have demonstrated their negative consequences on the physical, mental and social health of employees (Davezies 1993; Gollac and Volkoff 2000), as well as on work teams (Aubé et al. 2006; Caroly 2010; Lhuilier and Litim 2010) and the economic health of organizations (Chanlat 1990; Abord de Chatillon 2003; Askenazy et al. 2006). The link between psychosocial risks and health problems is well established.

In addition, many companies have focused their psychosocial risk prevention plans through training initiatives aimed at improving the skills of internal actors (human resources professionals, occupational health services and preventionists,

---

Chapter written by Annie DEBARD.

particularly managers). However, today, while the awareness-raising phase seems to have been achieved in most companies (Douillet 2013), questions remain as to the relevance of interventions to develop occupational health and, in particular, the role of management in these contexts of tension.

It was not until Lachman et al. (2010) reported that the representations of the manager's role in relation to psychosocial risks changed. In this report, managers are designated as "major players in the health of their teams", whereas the social trend, in a context where the term harassment and situations of suicide in the workplace were in the news, designates them as players in the deterioration of employees' health. The SORG survey (*santé, organisation et gestion des ressources humaines*; Health, Organization and Human Resources Management) conducted by Detchessahar and Grevin (2009) questioned this so-called "managerial pressure" among teams. It was a surprise when the results of this study showed that employees were not asking for less management but, on the contrary, were crying out: "give us back our managers"; the latter being monopolized by management tools such as multiple meetings, their own activity, activity reporting and so on.

This research and the numerous contributions of the activity clinic (Clot 2014) have led us to think about how to support the action of managers in relation to the health of teams (Debard 2015). Our interventions have been oriented toward the implementation of mechanisms to establish management of work through discussion (Detchessahar 2013), based on the controversy relating to work (Clot 2010). The term controversy refers to debates about real work between professionals involved in the same activity. In this paper, we examine the place and role of the local manager as a health actor and the processes supporting the action of occupational health managers. After showing the limits of a risk-based approach to work, we will present the theoretical orientations that underpin our work with organizations to develop occupational health. A large part will be devoted to the presentation of an intervention in a nursing home. We will discuss the potential of this type of intervention as well as its limits.

8.1. Limits of a risk-based approach to work: links between managerial action and team health

The question of developing the health at work of teams, employees and managers is not self-evident, even today. Indeed, we have to go back to the 1980s and 1990s to hear about psychological health at work. This arose following difficult situations encountered by employees in the course of their professional activity. It is the retail sector, the banking sector and urban transport that have been confronted with this problem, having to deal with robberies and various attacks. Today, we no longer measure the path taken to recognize these "invisible wounds" that the employees themselves sometimes had difficulty hiding (loss of self-confidence and in one's professional environment, disengagement akin to professional exhaustion, dissociation, phobias, etc.). The recognition and legal obligation to prevent physical and mental health from 2002 resulted in a focus on health, which was understood as individual health belonging to the employee.

Many questions have been asked (and are still being asked) about what belongs to the individual and what is the responsibility of the company. The notion of psychosocial risks, which appeared in the early 2000s, has not made it easier to recognize and deal with occupational health. In the interventions that have been developed, we have spent almost two decades trying to assess these risks, trying to set up action plans to curb them, or even making them disappear. The vocabulary has evolved: we have spoken of suffering at work, then psychosocial risks and then quality of life at work. However, regardless of the name, it is clear that the action plans put in place do not have the expected effects, either on health or psychosocial risk situations. In addition, the links between health and the performance of the organization are, most of the time, not mentioned in the agreements analyzed (Anact 2019).

We also observe in the field that the notion of psychosocial risks weakens the managerial position. The notion of "harassment" has particularly destabilized managers. We have met managers who, even today, worry about being accused of harassment when they are supervising professionals who behave inappropriately (e.g. recurrent lateness, professional misconduct). The manager's regulatory function is destabilized, giving free rein to an increase in work-related tensions. Moreover, when psychosocial risks are assessed in their departments, managers feel responsible for the deterioration of employees' health. We then very often observe a strong sense of guilt, which can result in a loss of interest in the manager's job and sometimes a crystallization of their position. However, paradoxically, it is they who are asked to implement action plans (from which they have often been excluded in their development). In 2013, Philippe Douillet alerted us to the impacts of interventions vis-à-vis managers:

> A particular point must be made about the management, whose position is also questioned on the subject. Having a major role in the processes of construction of psychological health via the modes of management, managers are very concerned by the subject. For both management and trade unions, the issue is a delicate one. Quite often, in fact, they are the target of criticism at the time of the first expressions of employees embarrassing the managements supposed to defend the system of hierarchical authority and the trade unions supposed to defend all the employees. (Douillet 2013)

In addition, it seems that interventions developed from suffering at work or from psychosocial risk situations at work or from psychosocial risk situations may tend to "psychologize" interventions with individuals, forgetting the work, its collective dimension and the conflicts inherent in the work.

Today, we maintain that approaching work through risk itself carries risks and has little potential for transformative action toward the "great health" of which Nietzsche spoke. In particular, we question psychosocial risk diagnoses that focus on risk and that have difficulty engaging the company's actors in actions to transform work to develop health for individuals, work groups and organizations. Talking about health at work requires us to specify what we mean by health. Roche (2014) calls on philosophers to help us understand the concept of health, never won, always to be conquered in constrained environments and to be developed in confrontation with the reality of work. "A conception in which health is not opposed to illness, but includes it in a positive way by transforming it into an opportunity to experiment with new values and standards of action" (Roche 2014, p. 4). All is said. If well-being depends on doing one's job well, as Clot (2010) reminds us, and if this well-doing must constantly be discussed with others at work (colleagues, supervisors, management, even clients), then controversy and professional disputes contain the potential for development as much for health as for the performance and innovation of our organizations. In addition, "it is a question of better understanding how work, which always includes a dimension of pain and suffering to the point of sometimes leading to wear and tear, or even to a premature death, can also, in many cases, constitute a powerful operator of health construction" (Davezies 1993).

We therefore propose that the action of managers to develop the health of their teams involves the facilitation of controversies and professional disputes. However, moving toward the management of work is not self-evident. A process of individual, collective and organizational learning must be supported.

8.2. Engineering spaces for discussion and decision-making on work: the example of an intervention in a nursing home undergoing restructuring

We have tested this theoretical position to link managerial action and the development of occupational health in different sectors of activity. The one we have chosen to present concerns a nursing home of a hospital center of the public hospital service.

This nursing home of 403 beds is divided into 11 units. On our arrival, the management team consisted of seven managers and one senior health manager. Our intervention included the biocleaning service (one manager and two local managers).

In total, 237 professionals (including the management and five doctors) participated in the activity.

In recent years, health-care institutions have undergone numerous transformations linked to ministerial reforms (2002, decree on working hours; 2007, hospital reform with activity-based pricing (T2A); 2009, the Hospital, Patient, Health and Territories Act). These different reforms require hospitals to control the resources used by health-care institutions in a more general context of strong public expenditure restraint. This expenditure reduction target is regularly monitored by the supervisory authorities, the Regional Health Agencies (*Agences régionales de santé* [ARS]), among other so-called "guardians". Contracts for a return to equilibrium are regularly negotiated between these supervisory bodies and health-care institutions in difficulty.

In this context, the gerontological sector of a hospital had to respond to the instructions of the ARS by implementing a plan to return to a budgetary balance. This resulted in several measures:

– A 10% decrease in the number of employees had an impact on the work (non-renewal of fixed-term contracts).

– A reorganization of work and professions was carried out in consultation with management and working groups with the teams.

– All professions have been affected: tasks have been redefined, service agents have been redeployed to the biocleaning department or to new positions as hotel agents, and the coordination activity of nurses has been strongly encouraged.

Our intervention began at the time of the implementation of this new organization in a particularly tense social context: articles in newspapers, distribution of leaflets to the local population and tense internal social dialog.

In this context, we drew on the work of Detchessahar (2013) and built an "ecosystem" of the discussion on work. Indeed, the discussion on work can have a political function in the sense that it introduces, in the decision chain, elements of wisdom, know-how and "common sense" (Morin 2010). It induces collective searches for solutions that produce rules at a local (team level), global (corporate strategy) and meso-level (intermediate discussion forums between teams and managers, as well as between managers and their management).

The ecosystem of the discussion and decision on work[1] requires an intervention process that aims to overcome the resistance to discussing work and to establish such

1 In French, the acronym is EDDT (*écosystème de la discussion et de la décision sur le travail*). We will retain the French acronym here.

discussions in organizations for the long-term. To meet these challenges, we have sought, on the one hand, to involve all actors in the process and, on the other hand, to build spaces for discussion at different political levels of the organization (Sarnin et al. 2012).

The launch of the approach was an important issue, and we took the time to communicate with the various actors. Our intentions and operational objectives were to develop individual, collective and organizational skills in discussion and decision-making about work. Additionally, in this phase of framing the approach, we built the governance of the intervention. Our steering committee brought together representatives of all the actors in this organizational system: the highest level of management was represented by the director of the hospital, the director of human resources and the director of care; they attended all the steering committee meetings. The staff of the whole establishment was represented by the members of the CHSCT (*Comité d'hygiène et sécurité sur les conditions de travail*; French Health and Safety Committee on Working Conditions) and therefore all the trade unions. We also wanted all the staff and a representative of each profession in the gerontological sector to be present. This steering committee functioned as a space for discussion and decision-making on the work (the work being the intervention itself). When we talk about the functioning of an EDDT, we include facilitation techniques that aim to foster collective intelligence. For example, we use mediation techniques based on photos that allow people to go beyond their own representations. Activities based on positive psychology are based on successful experiences to build new communications dynamics. It seems essential to us to allow these major players to experiment with this approach to work-related discussion and decision-making, which is not self-evident, and to acquire individual, collective and organizational skills in professional disputes.

This steering committee, in the engineering of the approach, has a real political function. Indeed, to support the discussion and decision-making on work, it is necessary to connect three levels of discussion and decision-making (Detchessahar 2013; Anact 2015):

– A global level concerns the discussion and decision-making forums that define the institution's strategy; the steering committee represents this first level.

– A meso-level that is a space for discussion between management and its teams; this concerns the work activity and its organization.

– A local level centered on job-related discussions and the sharing of rules between professionals to carry out the work.

The articulation of these three levels of discussion was part of the intervention process. First, we chose to discuss the work between professionals in the same profession, without any hierarchical link, to allow free expression of what constitutes “good work”, a source of satisfaction and health at work, the tensions encountered and the resources, as well as the “tips and tricks” to be shared between professionals. These exchanges can be partly emotional; we remember the discussion of these care assistants who shared “how to realize” that an elderly person does not like this or that food when verbal communication is impossible. This first stage of the process allows us to bring out the “objects” in tension (in the industrial sector, we use the term “irritants”).

From the perspective of establishing the sustainability of spaces for discussion and decision-making on work, we choose to position managers as the major actors in the deliberation on work. They have an important role to play in keeping these EDDTs alive after this learning process. Above all, as actors in the health of their teams, they need to acquire the skills to lead them (putting work under discussion by giving professionals a voice in their concerns and how they envisage resolutions).

For us, the question of the decision about work is central to the sustainability of EDDTs. Indeed, as Mathieu Detchessahar (2015 colloquium at the Hôpital du Gier) said, the EDDTs are not places “where you make noise with your mouth”. However, deciding on work is not so simple. For managers, this skill requires a change in position: one decides “with” and not “for” one’s team. This also means that not everything can be discussed (which would be demagogy). The theme of the discussion must come from the concerns of the teams, and the question they are asked must be related to the perimeter of their potential action on their work. Managers must also be ready to discuss with their superiors the courses of action that belong to the global level (e.g. what relates to an investment may not be in the manager’s perimeter). Another skill for a manager to acquire is the ability to follow up on validated actions and to implement them.

In addition, the third phase of the approach concerns the development of managers’ skills in EDDT engineering. After a training period in groups of managers, we accompanied each manager individually over two sessions to prepare a “relevant” discussion and decision-making space to be facilitated with their team. The pitfalls were mainly related to the choice of the theme to be addressed. Indeed, during the discussion of the job, we found that some topics were a source of tension and some were discussed outside our intervention between the teams and the managers. In the next step, we chose cross-cutting topics to be discussed between different professions. The themes were varied: mutual aid and cooperation between the professions, management of violent residents, replacement in the services and so on.

We can only advise managers, in this learning phase, to discuss with their teams what we call “emotionally competent objects” (ECOs). This term was used by

Damasio (2003) to designate "objects" that will provoke neuronal excitement and trigger thought. We use this term to designate themes that will allow a team to debate, even if they have communication difficulties. These ECOs belong to the real world of professional activity and may seem emotionless to those outside the profession. For example, an ECO detected among care professionals in a nursing home is the question of how to cut the toenails of residents. This professional act leads to many emotional questions. How not to hurt? How to do for people who are diabetic? On what criteria should the podiatrist be called? And how to make sure that the cut nail does not injure the professional's eye? And so on. We see by these examples of objects put under discussion that they are as close as possible to the reality of the work and not outside the ground.

Our fourth step in the intervention process brought together the managers and their teams. In this phase, we co-facilitated with the managers in a supportive position, ensuring the quality of the discussion. The methods of organization were prepared beforehand in consultation with the managers. The participatory techniques that encourage collective intelligence, the commitment of employees and, as we have seen, the manager's pleasure in seeing of the manager in seeing solutions emerge to the questions asked.

We tend to repeat that the EDDT is a meeting like no other (it requires a different position, only one theme is dealt with, it ends with decisions and a follow-up) and it is also a meeting like any other; indeed, a record of decisions must be transmitted to the teams. We share the words of the director of care in the steering committee:

> I've heard that there are a lot of meetings and not a lot of availability of managers. If you want to capture the attention of the teams, you have to act on concrete things and this is what will make them want to continue to be with the health-care manager. If the teams realize that this is just talk and that we've wasted time discussing it, we won't keep them in the working groups for long. Starting with practical things and on the main concerns is essential.

8.3. Evaluation of the process and discussion

To support the sustainability of the approach, we evaluated the approach with the teams and managers. A questionnaire was given to the professionals at the beginning and after 18 months of intervention. A quantitative evaluation was carried out by individual interviews with a representative sample of the steering committee. We will present the results of this intervention.

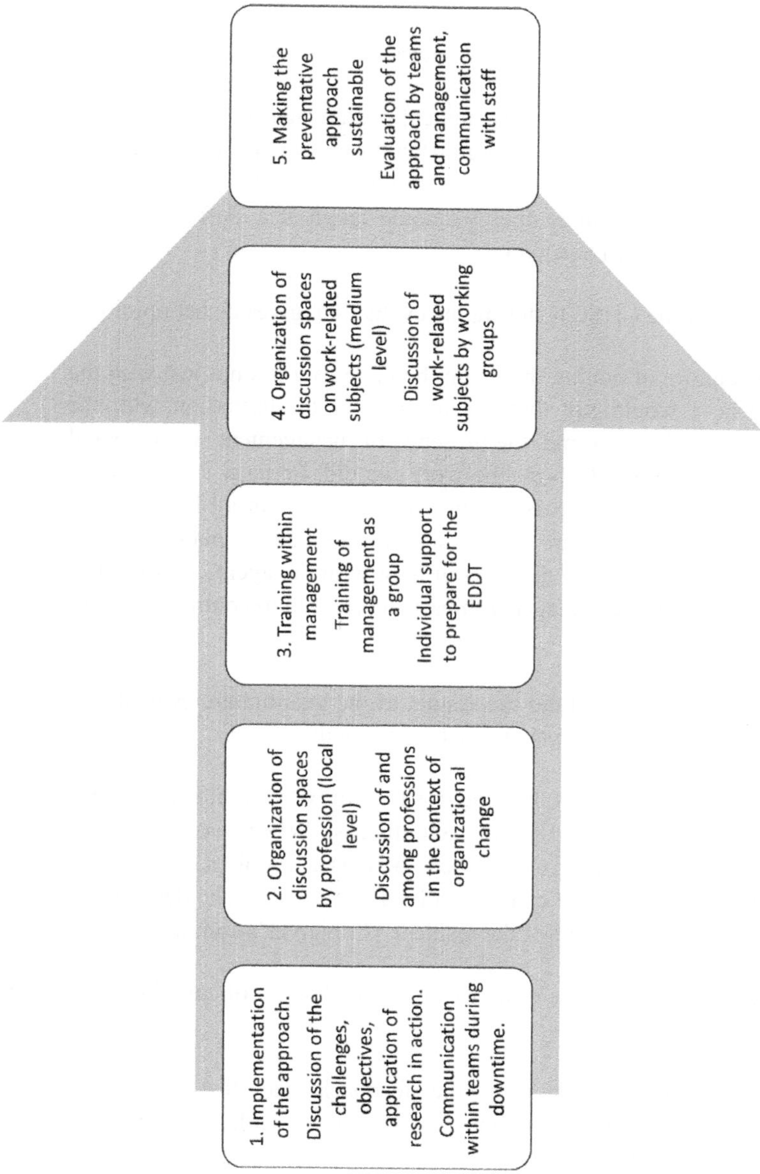

Figure 8.1. *Process of engineering the discussion spaces by level. For a color version of this figure, see www.iste.co.uk/bruyere/caringmanagement.zip*

It is interesting to note that beyond the concrete solutions that were found by the professionals and their commitment, the quality of the relationships between the various actors changed notably during the intervention.

An executive, following an EDDT on succession, conveys:

> In my opinion, it was a really authentic exchange because everyone was able to say what was causing difficulties for them. And, indeed, to say it in a very positive way. That's how it happened: we were able to tell each other that sometimes we could laugh at a shift change but that it wasn't against a person.

The secretary of the CHSCT, during the evaluation, gives us her opinion:

> It's the culture of putting things on the table. But it's not just with the managers. I would say that it's the culture of discussion with the whole institution. For me, the presence of management was essential in everything we did, in all the work we did. Perhaps I would keep this, yes, we put in discussion but it must be kept at all levels of the institution when there are critical situations, when we plan important projects. Because it is a question of trust with the agents. It's not just about trust with the manager. I think that we need to continue like this at all levels.

We were able to observe (and the results of the quantitative evaluation confirm this) that the position of the manager was transformed:

> The executive, she takes the time to sit down with us. She doesn't put the schedule down and leave. She listens. Whenever we have a problem, she tries to fix it. When there is a problem, she calls a meeting and asks how it can be resolved. Afterwards, she decides and it's based on the comfort of the resident. (Caregiver's comment)

In terms of learning, we report the words of the director of care during a steering committee meeting:

> What I found interesting in the feedback was that the agents mentioned the need to communicate, to exchange with each other, so I said to myself that this reorganization, the project outlined the main lines and directions. Inevitably, there were points that were going to clash and malfunction, and the idea is to make the professionals actors, and this is also our main concern. Finally, these points of

> dysfunction are the tool to be used to make them talk about their concerns, but about the daily life, what really causes them a problem, situations where they had difficulties. OK, that happened like that. We're going to see how to solve it around the table and it's done in different jobs. That's what this project is all about. What I've heard is that the agents want to talk to each other. There are tensions and things to be reviewed. And it seems to me that this is a real management tool for managers. (Extract from the steering committee)

From the beginning, we planned to evaluate the action in terms of its impact on health. Therefore, we proposed a quality-of-life questionnaire to the 240 professionals of this nursing home at the beginning of the intervention. We proposed the same questionnaire 18 months later with a similar return rate of approximately 60%. The results in Table 8.1 show the evolution of the professionals' satisfaction with the items measuring health.

	Before intervention	**After intervention**
The ability to make decisions on my own initiative within the scope of my duties	36%	47%
The creativity in the realization of my work	16%	37%
The way my work is respected	16%	32%
The work atmosphere in my department	47%	67%
My relationships with the people I work with	56%	70%
Time to discuss work with my colleagues	29%	40%
The way in which my hierarchy takes into account the team's proposals	21%	44%
The way my manager leads and motivates and motivates their team	18%	40%
The daily support I received from my hierarchy in case of difficulty	21%	40%
My supervisor takes my opinion into account	11%	30%
The help I can give to patients	38%	51%

Table 8.1. *Results of the satisfaction questionnaire*

These results show that discussion and decision-making spaces support managerial action to develop the health of teams, work groups and organizations. However, we have observed that discussion requires a learning process that is based on experimentation. It can take time. Moreover, discussion is not self-evident in some environments. While our interventions are based on the existing culture, the implementation of EDDT has an effect on the organizational culture. Indeed, despite a particular focus on the tools for discussion, we have been confronted with "cultural" difficulties in venturing into discussion. For example, in this nursing home, agents with fewer diplomas than others will refrain from speaking, imagining (or experiencing) that the colleague with a higher diploma will retort: "You only have to get the diploma if you know better than me". Additionally, it is important to consider the time of the intervention to establish management by discussing work in a sustainable way.

Another stumbling block concerning the sustainability of these interventions is the turnover of managers in the hospital public service, particularly in the nursing home. Less than 2 years after our intervention, only two managers we supported are still present with the teams. What did they pass on to their colleagues? How did care management and senior managers transmit this culture of debate to new health managers? Were these new skills sought after and supported in recruitment? These are all questions that remain unanswered and could be the subject of a new evaluation. Nonetheless, this experience enabled us to reinforce the prescription of an internal system connecting the discussion forums and the decision-making forums when we act to establish management by discussing the work.

8.4. Conclusion

The evaluation of our intervention shows that "managing through discussion" produces positive effects on health. However, we must agree that managers need to acquire skills that are based on essential knowledge:

– Knowledge of processes: talking about one's job and work requires learning to discuss for the work teams as well as for oneself. The manager and their management must take into account the timeframe required for any learning process. It varies according to the vitality of the work group.

– Knowledge of tools to question the job: although the objective of the discussion is to make decisions or to produce concrete solutions, it is the manager's ability to question the obvious aspects of the job of their teams that allows the work to be transformed. To transform (or improve) the work, it is essential that the quality of relationships within the team is secure. Acquiring facilitation techniques, enforcing a relational framework and arbitrating are necessary tools to question the job in safety.

– There is the knowledge of... the rest. We would like to quote this scene between two supervisors, one experienced and the other a novice. The first was teaching the second how to make schedules when he/she pushed the sheet toward his/her new colleague and told him/her, "and the rest is up to you". The rest is the unspeakable part of the job. To know this "rest", he/she has to take an interest in his/her teams, to know the rituals and to grasp the subtleties of relationships.

It is the "art of questioning the job" that must be built with the managers in a caring way based around the work. Taking care of work means taking care of your teams, their health and your own health.

8.5. References

Anact (2019). Un cap à tenir. Analyze de la dynamique de l'Accord national interprofessionnel. Qualité de vie au travail – Égalité professionnelle du 19 juin 2013 [Online]. Available at: https://www.anact.fr/sites/anact/files/20190221_anact_dynamique_ani_qvt.pdf.

Askenazy, P., Cartron, D., de Coninck, F., Gollac, M. (2006). *Organisation et intensité du Travail*. Octarès, Toulouse.

Aubé, C., Rousseau, V., Savoie, A. (2006). Les interventions régulatrices groupales et le rendement des équipes de travail : un modèle théorique. *Le travail humain*, 3(69), 269–294.

Caroly, S. (2010). Activité collective et réélaboration des règles : des enjeux pour la santé au travail. PhD Thesis, Université Victor Segalen, Bordeaux.

Castel, R. (2009). *La montée des incertitudes*. Le Seuil, Paris.

Clot, Y. (2008). *Travail et pouvoir d'agir*. Presses Universitaires de France, Paris.

Clot, Y. (2010). *Le travail à cœur : pour en finir avec les risques psychosociaux*. La Découverte, Paris.

Clot, Y. (2014). Réhabiliter la dispute professionnelle. *Le journal de l'école de Paris du management*, 1(105), 9–16.

Damasio, A.R. (2003). *Spinoza avait raison. Joie et tristesse, le cerveau des émotions*. Odile Jacob, Paris.

Davezies, P. (1993). Éléments de psychodynamique du travail. *Éducation permanente*, 116, 33–46.

Davezies, P. (2012). Enjeux, difficultés et modalités de l'expression sur le travail : point de vue de la clinique médicale du travail. *Pistes*, 14(2) [Online]. Available at: http://pistes.revues.org/2566.

Debard, A. (2013). La prise en compte des risques psychosociaux par les encadrants : le métier comme repère des ressources psychosociales. *Les cahiers des RPS*, 21, 28–33.

Debard, A. (2015). La prise en compte des risques psychosociaux par les encadrants. PhD Thesis, Université Lumière, Lyon.

Detchessahar, M. (2013). Faire face aux risques psycho-sociaux : quelques éléments d'un management par la discussion. *Négociations*, 1(19), 57–80.

Detchessahar, M. and Grevin, A. (2009). Faire face aux risques psychosociaux : quelques éléments d'un management par la discussion. *Négociations*, 19, 57–80.

Douillet, P. (2013). *Prévenir les risques psychosociaux*. Anact, Lyon.

Gollac, M. and Volkoff, S. (2000). La santé au travail et ses masques. *Actes de la recherche en sciences sociales*, 163, 4–17.

Lachmann, H., Larose, C., Penicaud, M. (2010). Bien-être et efficacité au travail : 10 propositions pour améliorer la santé psychologique au travail. Report, Inspection Générale des Affaires Sociales [Online]. Available at: http:// www.travailler-mieux.gouv.fr/IMG/pdf/RapportHenri_LACHMANN_-Bien-etre_et_efficacite_au_travail-.pdf.

Lhuilier, D. and Litim, M. (2010). "Crise du collectif" et déficit d'histoire : apports de travaux sur le groupe et le collectif de travail. *Connexions*, 2(94), 149–173.

Molinier, P. (2006). *Les enjeux psychiques du travail*. Petite Bibliothèque de Payot, Paris.

Morin, E. (2010). La santé mentale au travail : une question de gros bon sens. *Gestion*, 3(35), 34–40.

Roche, P. (2014). Normativité, grande santé et persévérance en son être. *Pistes*, 16(1) [Online]. Available at: http://pistes.revues.org/3469.

Sarnin, P. (2008). *Psychologie du travail et des organisations*. De Boeck, Brussels.

Sarnin, P. and Debard, A. (2008). Sensibilisation et formation des encadrants. In *Risques psychosociaux au travail : vraies questions et bonnes réponses*, Grasset, Y., Debout, M. (eds). Liaisons, Paris.

Sarnin, P., Bobillier-Chaumon, M.E., Cuvillier, B., Grosjean, M. (2012). Intervenir sur les souffrances au travail : acteurs et enjeux dans la durée. *Bulletin de psychologie*, 65(3), 251–262.

Ughetto, P. (2007). *Faire face aux exigences du travail contemporain. Conditions du travail et management*. Anact, Lyon.

Volkoff, S. (2005). *L'ergonomie et les chiffres de la santé au travail : ressources, tensions et pièges*. Octarès, Toulouse.

PART 3

Let Us Take a Look Elsewhere: What Do Other Sectors of Activity Say?

Introduction to Part 3

In this final part of the book on caring management, it seems appropriate and enriching to consider other sectors of activity beyond the health sector alone. Are the constraints inherent to the health and medico-social sector specific, or can they be found in other professional spheres? To do this, we will look at several examples from the Auvergne-Rhône-Alpes region. The objective is, indeed, beyond a certain chauvinism to demonstrate that there is no need to cross the border to find organizations committed to a management that combines the search for results and the consideration of the individual.

Chapter 9 is based on the testimony of a project manager at the Regional Association for the Improvement of Working Conditions. Each section of this chapter begins with a description of one or more company cases, which are then analyzed and put into perspective.

Chapter 10 offers an illustration of caring management in a school context. The authors study the case of a middle school in Saint-Etienne that has experimented with a "Well-being for better learning" system. The concept of a "health-promoting school" inspired by the health promotion strategy of Canadian schools is then developed to demonstrate that good school results are closely linked to good student health (in the sense of well-being), which is itself correlated with caring management of the teaching team.

Finally, Chapter 11 describes the deployment of a general "caring management" within an international retail group. This large organization was the first in France, and probably in the world, to initiate such an approach. However, is it a happy marriage?

9

Caring Management: What are the Experiments in the Auvergne-Rhône-Alpes Region?

The objective of this chapter is to broaden the questioning around "caring management" to any sector of activity. Are the approaches initiated and the obstacles encountered in the health and medico-social sector specific to it, or do they exist in other professional spheres? Our discussion will be supported by the field experience of one of the authors of this chapter, who is a project manager at the regional association for the improvement of working conditions in Auvergne-Rhône-Alpes (Aract AURA[1]). The companies cited as examples in this chapter are part of two specific public schemes:

– The first is dedicated to support for social relations (AReSo[2]), jointly supported by the Ministry of Labor and the Anact-Aract network. The system examines 30 requests from companies of all sizes and sectors of activity in the AURA region on an annual basis.

– The second program (Élence[3]), financed by the French government and the AURA region, aims to "place people at the heart of the overall performance of companies" by mobilizing companies, academics and consultants.

The authors of this chapter (Aract and academics from the Coactis laboratory) were brought together on one of the Elence project sites involving 20 companies

---

Chapter written by Manel ABDELJALIL-DINÉ, Sébastien DINÉ and François JUTRAS.

1 Available at: https://auvergnerhonealpes.aract.fr/laract.

2 Available at: http://www.anact.fr/areso.

3 Available at: https://elence.fr.

with the common objective of working on the link between the health and quality of life at work of their employees and the company's "economic performance" (hereafter referred to as S/QLW-performance).

It should be emphasized from a semantic point of view that the organizations whose example is cited in this chapter do not all find themselves in the terms of "caring management" but that, on the other hand, in common, they share a search for improvement in the quality of their management. The questions that arise are therefore how do they intend to undertake this evolution? Is the acculturation of middle management to so-called "caring" management a sufficient lever? If so, do their results meet expectations?

The cases of companies involved have been selected, or even gathered, according to the problems encountered. These will be presented in a progression of thought. Section 9.1 shows how certain preconceived ideas of the actors in the dialog can be detrimental to the quality of their exchanges, both in terms of content and form. However, overcoming these preconceptions does not guarantee the success of the S/QLW-performance approach. The methodological framework, which is the subject of section 9.2, is also an essential success factor. Finally, section 9.3 addresses another key element in the final outcome of the process, that of the decision-making processes. In terms of form, each of the three sections of this chapter begins with the description of one or more company cases, which are then analyzed and put into perspective.

9.1. The quality of the dialog

9.1.1. *An attempt at dialog on the notion of performance to overcome sterile representations*

In this company, which manufactures non-alcoholic drinks and syrups and has 300 employees on one main site, social dialog is marked by a sense of defiance. The takeover of the family business by an Anglo-Saxon group is no stranger to this. Staff representatives are perplexed by the lack of industrial investment in aging production equipment.

Contrary to what management thinks, especially at English headquarters, employee representatives are concerned about the company's performance. They are confident in the quality of their products and their place in the market, but they are not without concerns. They are well aware that the preservation of this position depends on their competitiveness.

For local management, the sustainability of the company is a subject that can be shared through the Industrial Master Plan (IMP) and, more generally, the company's strategy. Management feels that it communicates sufficiently on this subject, but the employee representatives think they do not have the right information. As a result, employees are worried about the future of the production tool. This concern is fuelling caution in the face of management's discourse.

During a dialog support seminar led by Aract, using facilitation-mediation techniques, both parties became aware that misunderstandings remained due to a lack of a shared definition of what an IMP covers and how the strategy could be communicated. The parties identify another blocking point to a constructive dialog: the subject is interfered with by a trial of intent by the staff representatives to the members of the management, whom they imagine to be opportunistic in their professional careers and therefore less concerned by the fate of the site. While management recognizes that the company's managers are more subject to mobility than other categories of employees, they are less likely to reiterate the sincerity of their commitment to the company as long as they are in office.

This speech did not convince all the staff representatives, but the exchange made it possible to shift the dialog that had been going on up to that point. Management is now aware of the concerns of employees and their representatives about the lack of visibility on the company's investment strategy for their site. For their part, the staff representatives know that their persistent feeling about the commitment of managers to the future of the site cannot be generalized, or even that it is likely to strain relations with the main people concerned, who see it as an unfounded judgment. In addition, management has expressed its willingness to share through the IMP the notion of performance for the company. The staff representatives explained their need to have access to the right information to prepare the discussions.

The work of the seminar highlights an additional difficulty. Management struggles, for its part, to overcome a paternalistic discourse based on confidence (the unalterable "trust us"). The collective memory of employees reasonably suggests to their representatives that they have reasons not to trust blindly. During an exchange on this subject, a union delegate said to the CEO, "To trust is to be ready to put your hand on the chopping block in front of the person holding the machete". The parties will agree that the term "transparency" is better suited to social dialog between individuals who do not have the ability to choose each other mutually as one chooses a friendship, for example. The staff representatives find it difficult to go beyond the managerial/non-managerial divide or the opposition between "those in the office and those in the factory".

Despite these obstacles, the seminar promises to continue a discussion without taboos on the notion of "performance" through the prism of industrial investments and complementary operational actions. Among the latter, a promising avenue will be identified concerning preventive maintenance in the factory. Unfortunately, this approach was not pursued during Aract's support, as it was affected by the company's current social situation: a disagreement during the mandatory annual negotiation between the HR department and the union representatives once again undermined the desire to work together.

9.1.2. *Performance: a common concern?*

The case underscores a number of features of challenging social dialog. There is "what is said" and "what is not said". Figure 9.1 illustrates this two-level (implicit–explicit) interaction between employee representatives and management.

As we can see, prejudices of intent or unspoken words hinder a meaningful dialog. The takeover of the company by a foreign group and the lack of investment in its production tools are fueling the concerns of employees.

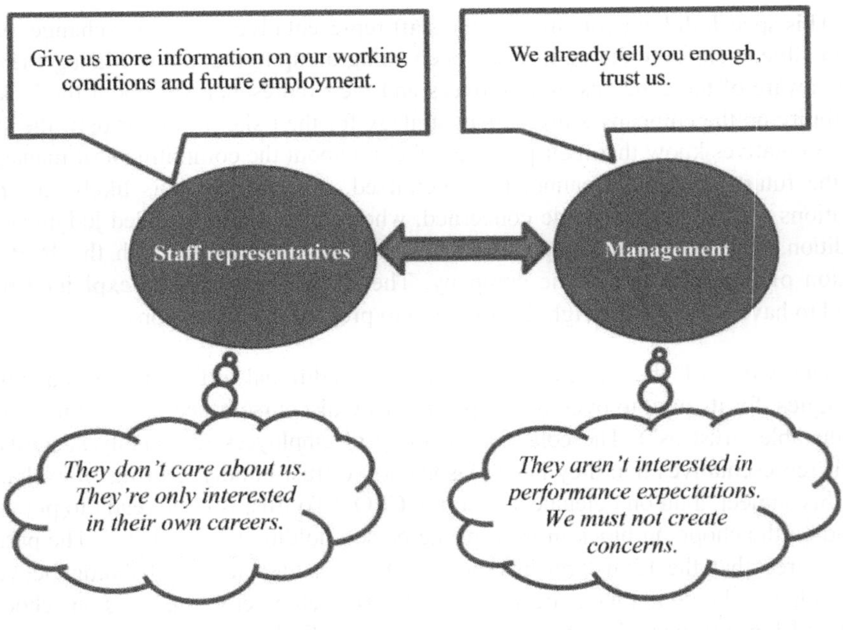

Figure 9.1. *Diagram of the double level of interaction between staff representatives and management. For a color version of this figure, see www.iste.co.uk/bruyere/caringmanagement.zip*

The information given by the management is not enough to fill these gaps. It is then quite typical that the lack of meaning is "mechanically" filled by speculation. The reasons for what is considered a "lack of information" by management could be found in context-related causes (e.g. "management cannot give us information because they do not know any more than we do, but they cannot admit it openly"). However, this concerns causes related to the individual (e.g. "the members of the management are more concerned about their own career development than about the development of the site"). This tendency to adopt an interpretation based on causes involving individual rather than contextual characteristics has already been highlighted in social psychology under the term "fundamental attribution error" (Ross 1977). The disadvantage is that this cognitive bias contributes more to bogging down the actors in the problem than to helping them to get out of it.

On the management side, its caring intention is to try to reassure the employees. It is not in its interest to maintain a climate of anxiety. However, the message it sends ("trust us") does not achieve this objective. We can even argue that it is counterproductive, since, beyond the injunction, the staff representatives base themselves above all on their perceptions of past exchanges with management to assess the "level of trust" that they can grant it. This injunction is paradoxical in nature when it omits the fact that trust is a representation built up over time and cannot be decreed. Another point deserves our attention at greater length. This is the presupposition that performance ("future investment decisions", for example) is of interest only to management. This assumption may lead management to withhold certain information. However, the absence of such information is precisely what fuels employee concerns. Why should we consider that employees are not interested in the performance of their company? Conversely, the work psychologist Yves Clot (2008) defends the idea that performance should be at the heart of discussions between management and employees. To do this, he starts from the premise that every individual needs to feel a minimum of pride in the work they do. They need to recognize themselves in their work. "Working" is not just about solving problems. "Working" also consists of creating problems along the way and thus of having to solve the problems that one creates oneself "while working". This part of professional creativity allows the individual to produce work that will be defensible in their eyes. According to Clot, this capacity to act on one's environment by one's own initiative creates health at work, unlike work in which one does not recognize oneself and which has harmful consequences on health.

It is important to consider that individuals judge a job "well done" or "poorly done" according to their own criteria. However, these criteria of quality (or performance) are not necessarily the same as those of their colleagues, their hierarchy or, in core, those established by the organization. Clot refers to the meeting of these differences in perception as a "conflict of criteria" concerning the quality of work. For this researcher, the fact that this "professional dispute" can take place is fundamental because otherwise its absence risks creating a gap between "those who prescribe" the performance criteria to be followed and "those who concretely carry out" the work in the field, or, to use the expression used in the case under study, "those in the offices and those in the factory". When an organization defines rules impersonally and its employees are faced with "real work" situations, posing problems that are difficult to anticipate, a "vicious circle of transgression" is created. The employee transgresses the rule to adapt to the particularities of the situation, the organization responds with more rules to reduce the gaps, and so on. Each party operates on its own and does not have the opportunity to discuss its own assessment criteria.

The link between Clot's statement and the case thus cited lies in the observation that when employees seek to do work in which they can recognize themselves (to preserve their health), they are in fact looking for performance. To what extent are their criteria for assessing performance close to or distant from those established by the organization? This question should be the subject of dialog between the parties concerned. Clot thus defends the thesis that it is essential to install a permanent debate on work and its quality through, for example, the quality of products, processes, groups or even the organization itself. In this context, we understand that a "caring manager" cannot limit themself to "passing on information" from management and trying to "give meaning" to the activity. They must also do the same in the opposite direction by going to their colleagues to determine the constraints inherent to their work activity. At the interface between management and employees, they are a "translator manager" (Desmarais 2010) who enables a debate on the quality of work to take place. This managerial posture must not neglect essential aspects of the method, as we will see in section 9.2.

9.2. The methodological deficit

9.2.1. *Untapped opportunities to link S/QLW and performance*

Our experience in contact with companies is recurrent. While their initial request may vary – the QLW approach, PSR diagnosis, staff satisfaction survey, conflict management, change management, etc. – the difficulty remains the same, that is, an inability to share the different issues due to the lack of a methodical approach that would facilitate the exercise. It is striking to note that while companies are convinced that S/QLW and performance are linked, without one taking precedence over the other, according to the management and staff representatives we met, it is still difficult to understand this linkage in a useful and lasting way, even though the search for it is not a matter of debate in itself.

What do a spare parts logistics center for a car manufacturer, a supermarket in the retail sector, an airport fuel supply company, a company that manages water and sanitation services for a community of municipalities or a social and cultural center with associative status all have in common? Quite simply, the same challenge of developing or consolidating their activity is prevented by a more or less unhealthy social climate. In short, an S/QLW-performance that does not materialize.

The director of a car parts logistics center entrusts the contributor from the Aract, solicited following a PSR alert from the occupational physician:

> Behind the warehouse where we are located, hundreds of square meters of land are waiting to be exploited to expand our storage capacity and develop our business. But this requires investment by the Group. In this respect, we are in direct competition with other of our logistics centers in Europe. Our social climate is too unstable to secure such an investment in the eyes of the head office management.

In the context of support for dialog suggested by the labor inspectorate to support the revival of staff representative bodies, whose meetings have not been held for several months, the facilitators of the AReSo program questioned the manager of a large food store: "How can you explain that your sales are among the best in France within the Group, when your productivity ranks your store among the lowest?" The manager's answer is laconic: "It is impossible to discuss this subject with the staff representatives because it would raise the taboo question of performance".

The same is true for refueling or water management companies. If the Aract workers perceive a number of organizational irritants there that could be areas for improvement for a better H/QLW-performance articulation, the actors are unable to grasp them. If it is rare that they are able to understand the subject, it is extremely rare, if necessary, that they share a common vision of the problem and even less of the path to take to implement this vision. The speech gets bogged down in ineffective generalities: "the problem is communication" launches a union delegate in an exploratory interview with a view to supporting the negotiation of an S/QLW agreement performance in the presence of his/her fellow staff representatives. An elected CSE (*Comité social et économique,* Social and Economic Committee) adds: "People should already learn to say hello in the morning!" Then, another elected CSE continues the round table: "Okay, but you can never change people...". No one will be surprised that at the end of such an exchange, the only avenue for improvement is limited to the drafting of a charter of good conduct.

However, no charter could have, or will ever be able to, stem the relational breakdowns observed in this association, whose missions include managing day care centers for young children. The breakdown, as is often the case in associations where the commitment of staff is also militant, is fueled by a recurring feeling of inequity. An employee points out: "Why was one person entitled to training, while another was refused?" There are many examples: compensation coefficients, internal mobility, working hours or vacations, assignments and so on.

These are all subjects that could be discussed in a concrete way rather than as wishful thinking following a diagnosis and an abstruse action plan to improve management, communication and trust, notions that are difficult to know and measure.

9.2.2. *The need for dialog engineering*

In our opinion, the cases cited refer to a large extent to the absence of a methodical approach to discuss the difficulties encountered. This lack of method is detrimental to the quality of the relationship and a source of inertia on each subject.

Dialog often suffers from the preconceived notion that it is an easy and natural activity. Therefore, dialog does not require any particular formalism; it would be enough to "solve problems informally". However, when we take a closer look at it, dialog entails many risks for its protagonists: the risk of losing face, entering into an escalation of conflict that is no longer under control, regretting sharing certain information and so on. Indeed, dialog about work implies exposing one's personal opinion so that it can be critically argued by others, which may require courage in certain situations. Detchessahar (2001) defends the thesis that the creation of spaces for dialog for discussion about work requires real engineering:

– The first reflection is necessary on the identification of the protagonists of the dialog between peers, between different levels of the hierarchy, etc. This is what Clot describes as the need to bring together and conduct debate between "those who prescribe" and "those who carry out" the work.

– The second reflection concerns the frequency of dialog on work (which can be called "setting the social agenda") to be adapted to the needs of the actors to exchange on work.

– Finally, the last reflection concerns the content addressed by these discussion spaces. Abord de Chatillon and Desmarais (2017) tell us that the formal and informal discussion spaces they were able to study are often diverted from a real discussion about work. It is therefore necessary to ensure that the focus is truly on work. This may require certain group facilitation skills that cannot be improvised. In addition, it must be emphasized that a lack of method and skills in mediation-negotiation often constitutes a hindrance in the situations that we have observed. Seeking to mediate implies a change of perspective by listening to the interests of the other party to find a mutually satisfactory solution. This is a creative process, called "integrative negotiation", as opposed to a posture in which the protagonists camp on their positions considering that "what one wins, the other loses". A win–lose vision locks the negotiation into a so-called "distributive" logic (Fisher 1982).

We would like to further explore this last point on spaces for institutionalized dialog. When you ask representatives of management and staff what they think of social negotiations in their company, the former almost systematically reply: "we would like to see more openness, constructive people who are not dogmatic, so that we can discuss all subjects, including performance" while the latter think: "today, we come to the table with the objective of limiting social regressions, there is nothing left to negotiate, it's take it or leave it". It appears that even before the discussion begins, expectations and preconceived notions are strongly oriented toward transforming these expectations into "self-fulfilling predictions" (Merton 1948). Management may then tend to lock in negotiations for fear that they will ultimately be fruitless. For their part, union negotiators adopt a defensive strategy that is perceived by the defensive strategy, which is perceived by management as an ironclad and hardline attitude.

Even though stakeholders intend to work on the S/QLW-performance linkage, they sometimes have difficulty grasping the issues that are relevant to the nature of their business. This is the case for two companies that we cite as examples: an organization that employs 650 people in the service of a public mission and that is dependent on a national fund and an industrial chemical company with a head office and six French production sites employing more than 1,200 people. Each having recently experienced an unsatisfactory mandatory annual negotiation, notably from a relational point of view, they both have the ambition to use negotiations as a lever to improve social dialog. Until now, their negotiations have been limited to traditional topics such as professional equality, job retention, working hours and compensation.

During the seminars led by Aract, where the theme of negotiation played an important role in the discussions, a key question was asked: "What does negotiation mean to you? The answers helped to change representations and attempt to rebuild the social dialog of the future dialog of tomorrow:

– In this case, it is no longer a question of a power struggle aimed at imposing one's own vision on the other, but rather the search for compromises that are not seen as compromises.

– "Negotiating means putting difficulties on the table and seeking solutions together"; methodically identifying the issues that make sense in common, and therefore the negotiation topics to be prioritized in the months or years to come, which will constitute a shared social agenda.

– "Negotiating means giving yourself time"; time to take ownership of the information exchanged, to share the issues at stake, to gather the expectations of the constituents,[4] to imagine and evaluate solutions, to adjust the text that formalizes the implementation of the solutions adopted, to monitor the application of the negotiated agreement, etc.

– "Negotiation means being clear with the employees who benefit from an agreement or with the management in charge of applying it". This implies making the mandate of the negotiation explicit by specifying the scope of the discussion and the decision.

– "This is a break with all the little treatises on negotiation that advocate the art of persuasion, thus reinforcing distributive negotiation rather than encouraging integrative negotiation.

Whether in a family allowance fund or in a multisite industrial company, the question of the resources allocated to collective bargaining arises. These seem insufficient today in the face of the stated ambition to make social dialog a lever for overall performance. The spaces for dialog exist and function more or less, but while all negotiation is dialog, not all dialog is negotiation (Thuderoz 2006). In this respect, it is important to qualify the statement:

– the different *levels of dialog* (ranging from information to consultation through cooperation);

– as well as the *stages of dialog* (problematization, solution finding, decision-making);

– and the *actors in the dialog* involved in the system of social relations (ARAVIS 2008).

To rehabilitate negotiation as a space for debate (discussion according to Detchessahar, dispute according to Clot), which is balanced between the parties, useful and constructive, our observations in companies suggest that practices must change significantly. A company agreement cannot be concluded in two 3 h sessions. These should no longer be induced by a PDF text prepared by only one of the parties, usually management. The proposals submitted by both sides deserve better than a "take it or leave it" approach. Without being restrictive, these prerequisites of time, means, methodology and skills crucial to company negotiation seem to us to be indispensable in the search for a sustainable S/QLW performance that we would like to see.

4 The constituents for the employee representatives are their fellow employees who elected them. The constituents for the management can be a central management, a board of directors or a middle management called to apply a negotiated agreement on a daily basis.

9.3. The decision to change

9.3.1. *The case of exemplary change management, or almost...*

As part of the regional multipartner project Élence, this private hospital with 220 employees identified an action to be carried out – the redesign of the scheduling system – at the crossroads of S/QLW and performance issues.

On the one hand, there is a need to be more responsive and flexible so that the management of schedules is not a perpetual organizational headache, time-consuming for the coordinator in charge and synonymous with hidden costs related to replacements, affecting the profitability of the hospital. On the other hand, there is a challenge to create favorable conditions for mobility so that it is experienced by the nursing staff as an opportunity to enrich their professional practice rather than a constraint imposed, potentially in an unfair manner. In short, double challenges are:

– to allow for the flexibility of personnel between departments to deal with vacations, absenteeism, and variations in activity and thus to ensure that medical demand is met all year round, wherever it occurs;

– to preserve the quality of care by not weakening the caregiving staff who speak of a stressful experience associated with mobility outside of the usual assignment service.

Under the impetus of the speakers from Aract and the Coactis laboratory who support the hospital on this subject, the work is structured in project mode. Management gives itself the means to achieve its ambitions by allocating the necessary material and human resources. A participatory working group is formed in a sufficiently broad way to guarantee an interbusiness, interdepartment and interhierarchical composition. The replacement in their position of the members of the group during the meetings is ensured, allowing them to participate fully in two full-day working sessions, plus a time to present their work to the general management. The only downside is the unavailability of the care coordinator recently appointed to this function and who is nevertheless responsible for establishing the schedules of the nursing staff.

Another favorable condition for the proper conduct of the project is observed, namely, the explanation of the participatory modality according to which the group contributes. A "consultation" type framework is thus specified from the outset to preside over the development of possible solutions to a problem submitted by management, solutions to which the latter remains the decision maker for the final choices implemented. This is not neutral on the mobilization of the participatory group. On the one hand, this clarification limits the differences in representations of the expected roles, a source of disappointment; on the other hand, the participants in the group are thus safeguarded in the face of possible reproaches from their colleagues, who are not participants in the exercise, as to the responsibility for the choices of organizational changes made by the management.

Finally, the group conducts its work according to a methodology that is the subject of prior formative input. This problem-solving methodology, based on interests rather than positions, is modeled on the integrative negotiation method mentioned in section 9.2.2. This is not innovative in itself, but it is innovative in this hospital because these structuring elements are unprecedented.

Discussion based on interests (integrative approach) rather than positions (distributive approach) allows for a more constructive outcome in the sense of "building together". In a position-based discussion, the problem of interdepartmental poly valence could be resolved as suggested in Figure 9.2.

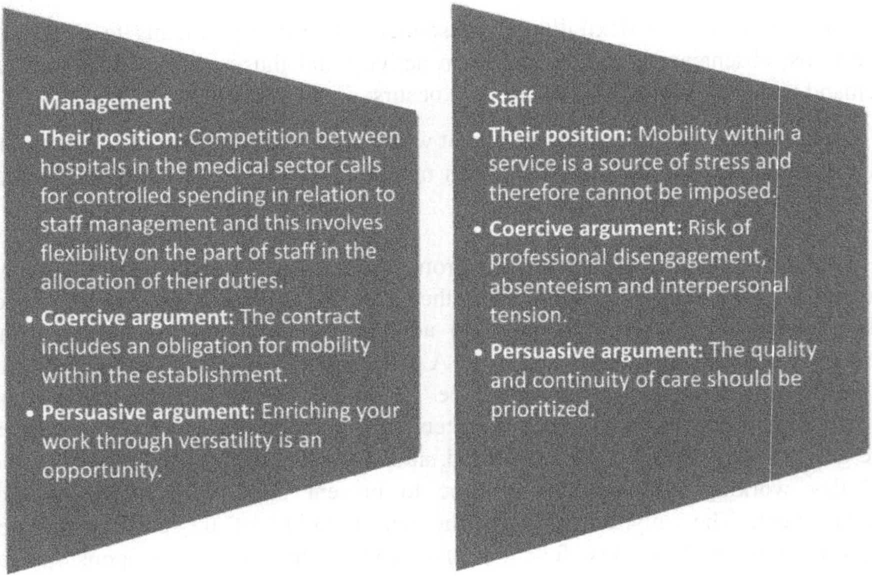

Figure 9.2. *Scenario of a discussion in a "distributive" approach. For a color version of this figure, see www.iste.co.uk/bruyere/caringmanagement.zip*

Thus, formulated, the arguments of each party would be opposable or inaudible for each other. Guided by the method, the exchanges take place in a logic that is more understanding of the respective constraints.

Management may express the idea that interdepartmental mobility is necessary to compensate for the inadequacy of human resources in the departments, assessed on a daily or weekly basis. In fact, a department may find itself understaffed due to a short-term absence or a one-off variation in activity. If recourse to temporary staffing is an option to compensate for such a situation, the response is not immediate and the temporary staff member called in does not necessarily have the same involvement in the work because of less knowledge of the establishment and the department to which they are assigned. This point of view was ultimately shared by all the participants in the working group.

The health-care staff can explain that if interdepartmental mobility affects their comfort zone, this should not be understood as a refusal of novelty but rather as a fear of failure, the fear of making a professional error, concern that they will be unable to fulfill their schedule owing to personal commitments and so on. It is primarily a source of stress because, notwithstanding the basic skills common to the profession, there are significant differences between departments in terms of the organization of care, protocols, practitioners' expectations, pathologies treated, working hours, equipment and facilities used and so on. One caregiver said, "I'm not a nurse, but I'm a nurse". Other caregiver said, "No one wants to be a burden to their colleagues". On this subject, the exchanges were also an opportunity for the nursing staff to recall that in the past, there had been experiences of changing departments that had not gone down well.

The clash of points of view allowed the group to formulate a common challenge: "How can the interdepartmental versatility of the nursing staff be developed while preserving individual and collective comfort zones?"

The group is responding to this challenge by developing a target scenario to elevate the debate beyond whether to grant a bonus to compensate for the stress of multiskilling. This target scenario, formalized in writing, includes four headings to specify an operational framework:

– conditions favorable to voluntary multiskilling;

– the practical organization of multiskilling;

– the procedures for informing and consulting employees, management and the staff representative bodies on the proposed development scenario;

– the timetable for completion.

An indicator of success for the implementation of the scenario is retained: the number of caregivers who would spontaneously offer their own internal mobility over a given period.

Despite the quality of the work carried out by the participative group and the support granted to it by the management, the scenario imagined was not followed up.

9.3.2. *When resistance to change comes from... management*

The first factor explaining this unfinished work is linked to an event outside the change project. The return of the target scenario to the CEO occurred at the same time as the takeover of the hospital by a major group in the medical sector. This leads to a tendency to freeze things in place, since purchasers generally seek to harmonize practices rather than to encourage local experiments.

Second, and without presuming a causal link with the previous point, the general manager does not demonstrate the necessary openness to the proposed change. The use of a list of volunteers for multiskilling, governed by criteria and rules, can potentially reduce management's right to manage and arouse the demand for financial compensation for this multiskilling. The cost/benefit ratio is not yet in its favor in the eyes of management. It prefers the *status quo*, reverting to the mobility obligation in the individual employment contracts, as well as to the universality of the skills supposedly guaranteed by the state diploma for nursing staff. The risk of tension, a source of psychosocial risks, is once again at its highest.

Rather than the central axis of the proposed target scenario, management adopted a propensity to develop "communication" tools (e.g. fact sheets and videos to "sell" the advantages of each department) while avoiding structural solutions (rules for managing a list of volunteers, budget for tutoring, interviews to monitor the quality of mobility, etc.). Communication then reverts to the "top-down information" mode, which is about "giving meaning" to multiskilling (the imperative need to change dictated by the "competitiveness challenge of the competitive market") to the detriment of a more pragmatic and immediate "meaning": what does the staff concerned gain or lose by accepting more interdepartmental mobility? It is the question of compensation, whether or not it is deemed mutually satisfactory, that is lost here. At the same time, the memory of past experience of unhappy mobility is also erased. In the final decision, there may be a form of denial of the feeling of uneasiness at work. Lasting changes to a "painful memory" could have been achieved by "working together" and by a change process that allowed for trial and error adjustment (Jutras 2020).

Finally, this case reminds us that a space for dialog about work must always be associated with a decision-making space. This is a fundamental characteristic of these places of exchange. Clot (2008) emphasizes that these spaces are not discussion groups or practice analysis groups where the collectives have to manage alone in the field. These forums serve to prepare a technical report so that it can be taken up in a space that is not usually accessible to employees: that of strategic choices. In the absence of management involvement, Detchessahar (2013) insists on the need for management to delegate explicit decisions to a stakeholder in these discussion forums, usually the middle manager. To be able to regulate the work through its discussion, the manager must have some leeway to do so. It is only by "bringing the organization down" as close as possible to the field that "prescribed work" can be brought closer to "real work". This link, thanks to an explicit delegation of decision, was missing in the case cited. Finally, let us add that the "translating manager" we mentioned in section 9.1 must also be able to practice the opposite path (bringing together the concerns of the field and the strategic vision of the organization).

9.4. Conclusion

Through the various experiments identified by Aract AURA, we have found that the difficulties in developing an approach linking S/QLW and performance are not specific to any one sector of activity. The obstacles that we have been able to highlight are numerous, and the successive presentation of the cases shows that the success of such an approach can sometimes be similar to a real "alignment of the planets". We saw in section 9.1 that taking up the issue of work is far from obvious, particularly in the mistaken belief that performance and its criteria are a subject that cannot be discussed openly with everyone. Once this taboo has been overcome, section 9.2 shows that a project, like any other project, is conducted methodically. It is not as simple as that to discuss the work; rigor, open-mindedness and creativity must be called upon, along with the framework that they imply. Finally, despite the intention and the method, section 9.3 shows that reconciling S/QLW and performance requires a rethinking of the organization of work and therefore involves decisions at a strategic level. The issues presented in these three sections also show that there can be multiple factors for adherence to a change project. Figure 9.3 illustrates a certain progression in the actions to be taken to achieve these factors. First, *informing* allows the actors to make sense of the change. In section 9.1, the absence of information that would allow the actors in the case cited to make sense of the change gave way to speculation. Beyond making sense, actors must find, at the very least, an interest in changing through the integration of their own issues. To do this, it is no longer enough to *inform* but to *discuss*, and to do so methodically, as we saw in section 9.2. Finally, the case studied in section 9.3 is close to triggering a third period, that of *acting*. Taking action initiated by a reflection co-constructed by the parties would have made it possible to change perceptions of a relationship damaged by past practices. Building (or rebuilding) trust necessarily requires action and time.

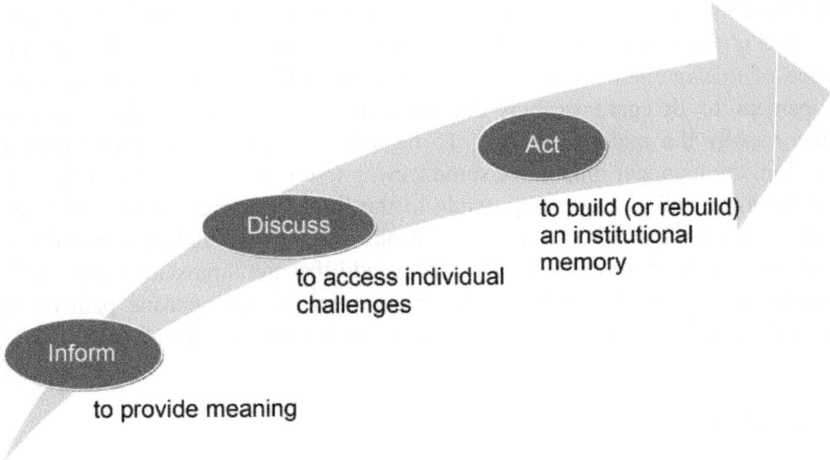

Figure 9.3. *Levers of action to be taken according to the desired adherence factor. For a color version of this figure, see www.iste.co.uk/bruyere/caringmanagement.zip*

This approach to change management is obviously in line with Lewin's (1947) work on the need to involve actors through dialog and action to "recrystallize" the outcome of a change.

Management is far from being just a few hours of training for managers in active listening techniques. To be sincere and viable, "caring" management should be based on a system of social relations that favors dialog, clarify the distinction between these spaces and the decision-making processes and find a balance between partial approaches to change and the negotiation of the latter with the interlocutors of the institutional social dialog. In short, everything that contributes to making change an opportunity to articulate S/QLW and performance, without the social issue being subordinated to the economic issue or vice versa. Making this concern a state of mind, a second nature in organizations, would thus relegate the Franco-French specificity of painful and unproductive dialog (known as cultural) to the rank of a simple structural shortcoming that any company can claim to remedy if it gives itself the means to achieve its ambitions.

As for the news of the health crisis linked to COVID-19, it constitutes a constrained context that shows the place of dialog in the implementation by company management of the required organizational adaptations. For Gilles et al. (2020), in the management of the crisis, some companies have opted to bypass staff representatives while others have intensified social dialog to promote exchange and alert mechanisms, as well as to define appropriate prevention organizations and systems (teleworking methods, application of leave and short-time work systems, prioritization of activities, protective measures, etc.). Moreover, it seems logical to think that companies able to count, before the health crisis, on a quality of dialog and controlled methodological and decision-making processes face this period of instability with more agility.

We could extrapolate the reasoning to any situation mobilizing an unusual organizational adaptability.

Finally, why does management need the adjective "caring"? Is it because, as discussed in section 9.2, management has not always been caring with all organizational stakeholders? Has it favored its shareholders, financiers and clients "too much"? Extending benevolence, or more simply taking into consideration all stakeholders, requires more than a communication effect by adding the adjective "caring". It requires at least "re-founding the company" to use the expression of Segrestin and Hatchuel (2012), this time putting the pursuit of objectives of wealth creation, social progress and preservation of the environment side by side.

9.5. References

Abord de Chatillon, E. and Desmarais, C. (2017). Espaces de discussion, management et épuisement professionnel. *GRH*, 2(23), 13–36.

ARAVIS (2008). Informer, consulter, se concerter, négocier. Report, ARAVIS/Réseau Anact Lyon.

Clot, Y. (2008). *Travail et pouvoir d'agir*. Presses universitaires de France, Paris.

Clot, Y. (2015). *Le travail à cœur : pour en finir avec les risques psychosociaux*. La Découverte, Paris.

Desmarais, C. and Abord de Chatillon, E. (2010). Le rôle de traduction du manager : entre allégeance et résistance. *Revue française de gestion*, 205(6), 71–88.

Detchessahar, M. (2001). Quand discuter c'est produire. *Revue française de gestion*, 132, 32–43.

Detchessahar, M. (2013). Faire face aux risques psycho-sociaux : quelques éléments d'un management par la discussion. *Négociations*, 1, 57–80.

Fisher, R. and Ury, W. (1982). *Comment réussir une négociation*. Le Seuil, Paris.

Gilles, M., Levrat-Pinatel, C., Rahou, N. (2020). Covid-19 – Renforcer le dialogue social pour faire face à la crise et préparer la reprise. *Semaine Sociale Lamy* [Online]. Available at: https://www.liaisons-sociales.fr/ssl/2020/04/03/renforcer-le-dialogue-social-pour-faire-face-a-la-crise-et-preparer-la-reprise.

Jutras, F. (2020). Pratiques informelles et formelles de négociation dans la conduite du changement organisationnel. *Négociations*, 33(1), 139–146.

Lewin, K. (1947). Frontiers in group dynamics : concept, method and reality in social science; social equilibria and social change. *Human Relations*, 1(1), 5–41.

Merton, R.K. (1948). The self-fulfilling prophecy. *Antioch Review*, (8), 193–210.

Ross, L. (1977). *The Intuitive Psychologist and His Shortcomings: Distortions in the Attribution Process*. Academic Press, New York.

Segrestin, B. and Hatchuel, A. (2012). *Refonder l'entreprise*. Le Seuil, Paris.

Thuderoz, C. (2006). Non au dialogue social. Oui à la négociation sociale ! In *Changement dans les organisations – Communication, négociation et interventions 2*, Crescenzo, J.-C. (ed.). L'Harmattan, Paris.

10

Caring Management: What is the Impact on Student Performance?

In this chapter, we will present an illustration of caring management in a school context based on the case of a middle school in Saint-Etienne. The entry point may be surprising: if the links between the management of a school and the management of a health establishment are not obvious at first sight, the connections are nonetheless numerous and enriching for the reflections to be carried out in terms of caring management.

Let us consider the student as a user as a resident or a patient, the teaching team as a management team, and the search for educational performance through well-being as the search for health performance through benevolence. The similarities are striking and a source of inspiration and innovation.

Evoking caring management in the school environment involves defining the concept of health promotion, which subsequently gives rise to the concept of "health-promoting schools". The story of one of these schools will be recounted and analyzed to open the debate on the possible transfers to health-care institutions.

10.1. The health-promoting school: what is it?

10.1.1. *Health and education are linked*

Health and education are linked because health creates the conditions for education, and education helps maintain health. Studies show that good school results

---

Chapter written by Sandrine BROUSSOULOUX and Christelle BRUYÈRE.

are closely linked to good health and that conversely, poor academic performance is more frequently linked to poor health conditions.

Taking into account the health of students is part of a context of reducing health inequalities of social and territorial origin, both because the school is able to reach all children, regardless of their social background and living conditions, and because education in itself constitutes one of the major determinants of health.

The concept of health to which we refer is the one defined by the World Health Organization (WHO) in 1946. The state of health of a person is thus not established on the basis of a continuum that would go from the absence to the presence of a disease, but it takes into account several dimensions that are linked to each other. These are the physical, psychological, social and environmental dimensions of health. We therefore consider a comprehensive, multidimensional approach to health, far from the biomedical approach to health reserved only for health specialists. The state of health of an individual is thus a subjective state appreciated by the person themself in reference to the representation of their own physical, mental, social and environmental well-being. As a consequence of the holistic approach to health, several factors are likely to influence it. In addition to personal, biological and genetic determinants, social, economic and environmental determinants are identified. All of these factors are linked and interact with each other.

In addition to this global definition of health, the WHO has specified the means to act to prevent disease and maintain or improve a satisfactory state of health. The reference text is the Ottawa Charter of 1986 (WHO 1986), which introduces for the first time the notion of "health promotion".

The Ottawa Charter advocates the simultaneous implementation of five strategic axes, which aim as much at modifying the social and political environment as at strengthening individual and collective skills.

The five strategic directions of the Ottawa Charter are as follows:

– build health public policy;

– create supportive environments;

– strengthen community action;

– develop personal skills;

– reorient health services.

10.1.2. *The health-promoting school*

The concept of health-promoting schools is based on this comprehensive approach to health and the deployment of the five axes of the Ottawa Charter in the living environment. The creation of health-promoting schools was largely supported by the WHO at a time when the organization was seeking to develop a living environment approach (Young 2005). Indeed, it was at the same time that the work that would lead to major networks, such as "healthy cities" or "health-promoting hospitals", was launched. As far as schools are concerned, the WHO European Office took the initiative in the early 1990s with the logistical and financial support of the European Commission and the Council of Europe. Then, the approach spread to the different WHO regional offices. It is therefore not surprising to see that initiatives have been taken around the world in this direction (Vince-Whitman and Aldinger 2009). However, the way in which health-promoting schools are developed in countries is largely dependent on (Rasmussen 2005):

– the education system and the enrollment rate;

– the socioeconomic and political situation;

– health characteristics;

– the involvement of policymakers and the quality of the partnership between the between the education and health sectors.

This explains why this approach takes different forms depending on the country and why it evolves over time for the same country.

Since the 1990s, the concept of the health-promoting school has developed considerably on all five continents. While it has taken on different names in different regions of the world, all of these approaches have commonalities that the International Union for Health Promotion and Education (IUHPE) has identified in a synthesis entitled "Towards Health Promoting Schools: Guidelines for School Health Promotion" (UIPES 2009).

The six criteria common to the different approaches are as follows:

– development of a health-promoting facility policy;

– consideration of the physical environment of the school;

– consideration of interpersonal relationships within the institution;

– the development of individual health skills and the ability to act (whether these skills are developed as part of the teaching programs or in the "hidden curriculum");

– the development of links with the school's social environment, that is, the school's partners but also the infrastructures outside the school (those who participate in the school's bodies and external resources);

– the involvement of health services.

These criteria demonstrate the conceptual proximity between the health-promoting school and the action strategies in the Ottawa Charter. Health-promoting school can be defined as a strategy through which the school takes into account and contributes to the health of the entire school community (students and staff).

In practice, a health-promoting school is first and foremost a school managed by a team that organizes its operations and organization around the preservation and improvement of the overall health of those who attend it. This includes physical health determinants related to the ergonomics of buildings and furniture but also to the quality of air, water and food, psychological health determinants related to the educational climate, the nature of interpersonal relationships, the development of individual skills, and social health determinants (related to the educational climate). The team working in a health-promoting school is aware that all these aspects influence health and that even a "non-decision" is not without consequences. The health-promoting school in its fullest form often remains a concept. Nevertheless, it is an ideal toward which to strive, which makes it possible to orient practices toward taking into account and improving the well-being of all.

10.1.3. *Presentation of the "wellness for better learning" system*

"*Aller bien pour mieux apprendre*" (ABMA, wellness for better learning) is a French school-based health promotion program that is part of the health-promoting school movement. Its objective is to enable a school to implement a health promotion approach. This concerns both students and staff. ABMA is based on a global conception of health and a systemic approach to the school. ABMA is not an addition to the school's preexisting measures, projects and actions. It is an integrating system that acts on the factors that determine health (Cloetta et al. 2007) and is intended to give coherence to the various actions already undertaken.

From this perspective, ABMA is organized around six domains and four intervention strategies. This organization contributes to the structuring of actions and projects and to the coherence of the different levels of action, as well as to the articulation of the different stakeholders within the institution, whether they are internal (e.g. nurse) or external (e.g. association).

Types of actions / Domains of intervention	Organization and operation of the establishment	Educational intervention	Link to the content of the teachings	Information activities
Time				
Places, spaces				
Interpersonal relationships				
Communication				
Development of psychosocial skills				
Partnership				

Table 10.1. *Summary of the general organization*

The "domains" refer to elements of institutional life that influence the factors that affect the determinants of health. These include time, space, interpersonal relations, communication, development of psychosocial skills and partnership. It is not possible to propose predefined actions because some of these areas depend on internal factors that the school team cannot change (e.g. the architecture of the building, the time of its construction, its geographical location, the way it is served, the size of the premises, the number of students, the number of staff, its classification as a priority education zone, etc.). The attention to be paid to the fields and the questions to be asked remain intangible. The approach and method used are invariant, unlike the actions and results.

To take into account the different areas, the institution is invited to organize its actions by adopting a project approach and by respecting its main stages, in particular the constitution of a team, the realization of an inventory and the prioritization of the actions to be carried out.

ABMA is also structured around a combination of interventions (those concerning the organization and operation of the establishment, those with an educational aim, those related to teaching, and one-off actions that are most often informative). The experimentation of the ABMA system started in seven voluntary establishments known to academic referents and whose head of establishment adhered to the approach.

10.2. Case study: implementation of ABMA in a school in Saint-Etienne

10.2.1. *Presentation of the case study*

The implementation of the ABMA scheme was accompanied by a process evaluation that took the form of interventional research from 2013 to 2015. Eleven schools were evaluated using a predominantly qualitative method that allowed for 24 semistructured interviews. The case study presented below is derived from this research.

The college under study was approached by the departmental referent in the first year of the experiment in 2012. The principal, who had just taken up his post, and the contractual senior school administrator (CPE) remained in the college for the duration of the experiment.

This is a small school located in a very poor commune on the outskirts of the department's capital. It has a population of disadvantaged students, the vast majority of whom are immigrants. The school is part of the various priority education systems[1]. The picture that the principal paints of the school's situation on his/her arrival is rather catastrophic: "Going well to learn better: they were not going well. There were 18 alarms[2] per day, there were fire extinguishers flying, there were kids running around, teachers who clearly told me that since the beginning of the year, they had not done one hour of class (...). I was in a school in crisis, a maximum emergency, there were 150 kids, 10% discipline boards". The buildings are poorly designed, and several landings isolated from each other on half-levels serve three classrooms. School life is slightly out of the way. This makes it difficult to supervise and secure the premises and multiplies the number of damaged fire extinguishers. The heating comes through the ceiling, the premises remain cold in winter. The teachers are often replacements and ask for their transfer at the end of their first year; the turnover of these staff is approximately 80% per year.

Three years later, the school climate is much calmer. While there were 18 fire alarms per day in 2012, there were only two in 2013 (whose perpetrators could be identified) and none in 2014. At the same time, the amount of incivility has decreased significantly, as have unexcused lateness and absences. The feeling of safety has been restored. "Well-being is first and foremost safety and a serene school climate. So today, that is settled". The feeling of belonging to the school has been strengthened, and the students' relationships of trust with the adults have been strengthened. The results of the National College Certificate (DNB) have improved.

1 "*École, collège, lycée pour l'ambition, l'innovation et la réussite*" (Éclair), then *Réseau d'éducation prioritaire renforcé* (REP+).

2 Triggering of fire alarms.

The teaching team has been stabilized, with teachers wishing to be assigned to the school. The school's enrollment is increasing, with some students returning to the school after having gone to private schools. There have been class openings. "And then we had some great successes, very great successes in terms of behavior, it's correlated. Behavior is improving, attitude is improving, grades are improving, well-being is improving, institutional awareness is improving, and the sense of belonging is improving". In short, this college has become a "classic" college with its strengths and weaknesses.

10.2.2. *Action levers activated by the college*

The school undertook numerous actions at the beginning of the 2012/2013 school year, following an assessment of the situation that began at the end of the previous year: "Based on a diagnosis agreed with the teaching teams, I reorganized the entire school". It would be tedious to describe each of the actions undertaken in detail, so only a limited number of actions will be presented as an illustration of the different areas of the ABMA approach.

Time management: the timetables have been modified to allow for 1 h common to all classes to organize a weekly homework assignment under the supervision of educational assistants. During this time, teachers have the opportunity to consult with each other. The duration of classes was reduced by 5 min, which made it possible to create two 30-min slots at the end of the morning and at the end of the afternoon devoted to homework done in the presence of a teacher. Recesses were organized around four locations and activities,[3] following a predetermined schedule that was posted for all to see. This was operational for the first 2 years and then evolved into 1 h of homework help at the end of the day on a voluntary basis.

Space management: school life has been reorganized so that supervisors can be present in each of the small units serving the classrooms. The circulation patterns in the school have been rethought, and an adult has been appointed as a reference point for each of the different areas. To exit the school, all students and staff must pass through a double door that is a sort of bottleneck. The CPE asked the person in charge of this area to systematically ensure that the doors were wide open before the end of classes to avoid the risk of jostling. It only took one oversight for an incident to occur. As the Dean half-jokingly told me, "ABMA hides in the details".

Interpersonal relations: for all the staff, the regular meetings and concerted decision-making, as well as their involvement in the various actions, have certainly helped them to get to know each other better and have contributed to improving

3 Kin ball, fast ball, 3C (previously school library), ping pong.

relations between them. As far as the students are concerned, the actions put in place have also contributed to the improvement of interpersonal relations (e.g. the organization of recreation time, which encourages exchanges between students and adults in a playful way, the reorganization of the school library, which encourages respect for others, etc.). The principal educational advisor makes a point of welcoming students in the morning at the school gate and often a little further down the street to encourage any latecomers. For the CPE, this morning "hello" is important, especially for this population of students who are easily "angry" at the school institution. It is a way of letting them know that the institution is interested in them. It is also a way to avoid slippage and dropouts based on small incidents that could be repeated and amplified.

> What happens in the classroom comes from what happens in the yard, often because what happened in the yard came from the street. In fact, you have to take the problem at the source, without being Superman because I don't stop everything. But you see, there are things that don't go away, because they know I'm there so they're not going to do it. So, it's not going to happen in the yard anymore, because there are the supervisors, and it's not going to come into class anymore, because in class, we work.

The development of psychosocial skills: the self-esteem of the majority of the students is rather low, particularly with regard to their academic potential. "We have a segment of the population in the commune that is very poor and very poorly served. So inevitably, I would almost say that there is already a statement of failure implicitly in the pocket. That is to say, we live here, we will never succeed, we will never do anything". Several actions explicitly concern the development of psychosocial skills, such as the "morale check" for the sixth-grade classes (children aged 11) and conflict management for the fifth-grade classes (children aged 12). The morale check is an action that aims to enable students to identify their emotions, name them and express them in words. For students in third grade (students aged 14), the development of PSR is linked to the search for a professional discovery internship to teach them to express themselves in this context, which is often new for the students (to prepare them to go out and approach companies, so that they do not say, "Yeah, you've got an internship, it's okay, you're taking me"). The college has set up improvisation work sessions. "At the beginning they are a bit reluctant because they don't like it very much, it's not swag,[4] they are seen from in front of everyone and everything, and then they don't know how to do it, and they have a voice complex, they don't know how to hold themselves with their big arms". However, when the cycle of

---

4 "Swag" designates people with a certain style in New York circles; it has been popularized and has become the new expression to designate "cool".

sessions ends, the students ask for more. In addition to the individual development of PSRs, these sessions also have an effect on the group dynamic by making the negative leaders aware of inappropriate behaviors.

Communication: the ABMA system has been presented to the staff of the institution. It is integrated into its contract of objectives and has been put on the agenda of a board of directors. In terms of communication, what is noteworthy about College C is its quality concerning the meaning and direction of the school project. The bodies for consultation between the personnel exist and meet very regularly.

Partnership: the school does not work much with external partners. "We work with the town hall, the schools of course, but that's not the outside world, it's the national education system. So I don't work much with the outside world." The various projects bring together the different categories of staff at the school, teachers and non-teachers. Parents are involved in the validation of projects through the various bodies that provide for their participation, but this is a small group of elected parents. "The involvement of parents is both strong and weak. That is to say, we have a group of parents who are extremely involved and with whom we work in full confidence, who are the elected parents, who are also the elected representatives of the commune". At the same time, the CPE is in regular contact with the families.

Finally, it is the participation and cooperation of the students and cooperation of the students in the various projects that concern them most. They are relatively critical of what can be put in place. Part of the explanation lies in the students' perception of the school institution. This is why projects have been initiated to try to mobilize students. We will return to one of them: the InterC cup, which mobilizes students, teachers and administrators.[5] "So we set up what we call the InterC cup to encourage links between students and develop trust between students and adults. We did a little bit of what's done in Harry Potter. We have four houses, each led by a captain, and each student from sixth grade to ninth grade enters a house, so when they arrive in sixth grade, they stay there for four years, and there are regular Olympiads that take place throughout the year, and the students earn points during these Olympiads, as well as throughout the year each time they participate in actions, in the validation of class councils, etc.".

This cross-cutting project is a summary of what a health-promoting project can be. It is based on actions that concern the functioning of the establishment as much as the transmission of information (during the different workshops, for example) and the educational and pedagogical dimensions. The different areas are mobilized:

5 The title of the project takes the name of the college.

– Time management, with a project that is both long-term (the entire duration of a student's schooling at the college) and iterative, since it is repeated each year and at several points during the same school year.

– The management of spaces, since the highlights of the Olympics take place in different places in the college.

– Interpersonal relationships are at the heart of the system, their improvement being its primary objective.

– The development of students' psychosocial skills, as they are placed in situations that are unusual for a school setting, allowing them to explore other facets of their personality.

– Communication because it is necessary to make the project well understood by the entire educational community, both in its operational development and in the goals pursued.

– Finally, the partnership since it is truly the whole college that is mobilized.

The effects of the InterC cup on the general atmosphere of the school were felt quite quickly. The collective dimension of the project is to be underlined because when a student carries out an action that allows them to win points, it is their "house" that benefits. This has helped to calm relations between students and to reinforce the students' confidence in the adults.

10.2.3. *Key success factors*

What are the conditions for success in this type of approach? Without being exhaustive, we will focus on the key success factors identified in this college, on the one hand, and in the six other schools that have experimented with the AMBA approach, on the other hand.

The posture of the head teacher: in this case, his investment was decisive; he was the one who carried out the complete reorganization of the school and who motivated and stabilized a team thanks to agreed objectives. "All my work is aimed at ensuring that I am involved in something that is participatory and that is a school project". This posture of the head teacher as a "leader who has the capacity to delegate and to encourage teamwork" is the element that was found in the evaluation as being a prerequisite for the implementation of ABMA.

Teamwork: the head teacher does not work alone; the various meetings that make up the functioning of the school all contribute at their level to the reflection on well-being. In this way, all the staff are involved at one time or another in the actions and their results.

The convergence of views between management and school life: although the reorganization carried out in the *college* (middle school) is largely based on the vision and will of the head teacher, the operationalization is greatly facilitated by the good understanding that the principal's advisor has been able to obtain. The latter readily compares the pairing he/she forms with the principal with an "old couple", which reflects the mutual trust they have in each other. This reflects the mutual trust they have in each other and their shared views on the school's mission.

The project approach: the reorganization of the school was done by adopting a "project mode". The principal first conducted a shared diagnosis and then defined priorities and actions. These are the subject of an annual assessment, which may lead to readjustment.

The ability to question oneself: the numerous actions carried out in the school are all the subject of concerted assessments and reflections on their effects and the possible changes to be made. This means that the actions are not repeated as they are from one year to the next. Each year, the lessons of the previous year are drawn, and the projects are modified accordingly.

The size of the school: it is a small school with approximately 150 students per year and approximately 30 staff. It is obvious that the size of the team facilitates consultation and communication with and among the staff. However, this argument must be moderated because a school that entered the program in the third year and that has also integrated ABMA into its operations and organization has a larger staff.

And afterwards what will you say to us? And then... well, everything remains to be done. Well-being is a constant concern that needs to be constantly questioned and re-evaluated: the students change every year, the parents change and the staff are transferred elsewhere and replaced. Second, benevolence does not have only allies; some may see it as a form of softness of laxity. It is therefore an eternal restart.

10.3. Discussion

We have defined a health-promoting school as a school managed by a team that organizes its operations and organization around the preservation and improvement of the overall health of those who attend. The parallel with health organizations is easy: cannot a health institution be defined in this way as well? It is made up of a team that contributes to the organization of work and the functioning of the structure and that watches over the overall health of the users and employees who make up the structure to guarantee the production of a quality service.

Thinking about the management of a health-care institution through the prism of health promotion means feeling responsible for the health of all (and not just the patient) in the name of a search for global and sustainable performance (economic, social and societal performance). This means being convinced that sustainable performance is no longer an option in an environment with limited resources. It also means being convinced that the health of all is not a sporadic concern, depending on the time we can devote to it, but a permanent state of mind necessary for the proper functioning of organizations.

The contributions of health promotion to caring management lie above all in the ideal that this concept constitutes its most accomplished form. The ideal, in the sense of Weber (1992), makes it possible to have a homogeneous picture of the thought of a complex phenomenon and to guide behavior. This is the very essence of an ideal: to try to achieve it and to do so, to give yourself the means. The concept of health promotion applied to management, in its ideal representation, can be structured around four inseparable pillars to have a solid foundation: integrating health promotion into its management means being concerned about the health of users, but not only them. It also means taking into account the health of employees, the establishment and more generally the territory. The four pillars of health promotion can thus be understood as a diagnostic tool aimed at first identifying the ideal functioning of a health-promoting establishment and second at analyzing the distortion with the existing functions, thus making it possible to situate its strengths and margins of progress.

More concretely, the management health promoter seeks sustainable performance by relying on the following:

– Users' health: this involves providing a response adapted to health needs (taking into account users' views, therapeutic education, etc.).

– Employee health (at all levels of the hierarchy): the challenge here is to develop a favorable work environment (through adapted work tools, discussion areas dedicated to work, etc.).

– The health of the institution: this involves instilling a dynamic of continuous improvement through federative projects that promote commitment (e.g. the 4M project mentioned earlier in section 6.3).

– The health of the territory: this lever consists of cooperating with local actors who are stakeholders in the organization (contribution to local employability, development of short circuits, etc.).

It is likely that each of us, at our own level, is already carrying out numerous actions that integrate one of the four pillars. Developing caring management through health promotion is not about adding yet another mechanism. It is a systemic and integrative approach that acts on the determinants of health and is intended to give coherence to the various actions undertaken.

If the concept is attractive, what are the limits or conditions for success? The experience of health-promoting schools has already made it possible to identify levers that can be transposed to health-care institutions. In its final form, such an approach is subject to the unavoidable support of management, whose task is to take the project to scale and make it the DNA of the organization. It is not a health-promoting action that we are talking about but rather a health-promoting establishment. We can therefore imagine a CPOM (*contrat pluriannuel d'objectifs et de moyens*, multiyear contract of objectives and resources), a facility project or a quality approach based on the pillars of health promotion, continually questioning the meaning of its practices to improve performance. Is not that the very purpose of these tools, whose original meaning is sometimes (often) lost?

However, what can we do if management is not involved? Do we have to deal with what exists without asserting our capacity to act? Fortunately, we can easily imagine a gradual increase in the use of caring management through health promotion within the perimeter of a team, a department or a division. Above all, it is an approach that reminds us that the search for performance of an organization can only be achieved in a sustainable manner by focusing its actions on the user, as well as on those who make up the organization.

10.4. References

Broussouloux, S. (2016). Évaluation du processus d'implantation d'un dispositif global de promotion de la santé en milieu scolaire, lien avec le climat scolaire et la réussite scolaire. PhD Thesis, Université Claude Bernard, Lyon.

Broussouloux, S., Morand, J., Cheviot, M., Berger, D. (2017). Aller bien pour mieux apprendre, un dispositif de promotion de la santé en milieu scolaire au service du bien-être. *Recherches & éducations* [Online]. Available at: http://journals.openedition.org/rechercheseducations/4609.

Cloetta, B., Spörri-Fahrni, A., Spencer, B., Ackerman, G., Broesskamp-Stone, U., Ruckstuhl, B. (2007). Outil de catégorisation des résultats de projets de promotion de la santé et de prévention [Online]. Available at: http://inpes.santepubliquefrance.fr/outils_methodo/categorisation/V6%20guide_fr.pdf.

Damasio, A.R. (2003). *Spinoza avait raison. Joie et tristesse, le cerveau des émotions*. Odile Jacob, Paris.

OMS (1946). Définition de la santé [Online]. Available at: http://www.who.int/about/definition/fr/print.html.

OMS (1986). Charte d'Ottawa [Online]. Available at: https://www.euro.who.int/__data/assets/pdf_file/0003/129675/Ottawa_Charter_F.pdf.

Potvin, L., DiRuggiero, E., Choveller, J.A. (2013). Pour une science des solutions : la recherche interventionnelle en santé des populations. *La Santé en action*, 425, 13–16.

Rasmussen, V. (2005). The European network of health promoting schools – From Iceland to Kyrgystan. *Promotion and Education, IUHPE*, 12(3/4), 169–172.

UIPES (2009). Vers des écoles promotrices de santé : lignes directrices pour la promotion de la santé à l'école. UIPES, Saint-Denis.

Weber, M. (1992). *Essais sur la théorie de la science*. Plon, Paris.

Young, I. (2005). La promotion de la santé à l'école – une perspective historique. *Promotion et éducation*, 13(3/4), 184–190.

11

Caring Management and Large-scale Distribution: A Happy Marriage?

This chapter is based on the case of a company, the Casino Group, which has undertaken a process of reflection and action around "caring management". The objective is to understand how managers concretely implement the notion of benevolence in their daily managerial practices and what levers can be used to contribute to developing benevolence at work.

Three university teacher-researchers have undertaken research-intervention since 2015. Individual and group time-in the form of interviews (59 interviews 1 h each), practice analysis sessions (five sessions of 5 h each year), roundtables (one "world café" of 3 h each year), training (112 h of coursework per year), expert interviews (six interviews of 1 h) and internal secondary data analysis informed this research.

Dr. Philippe Rodet, who has been working since the 1980s on the subjects of well-being, that is, health and self-fulfillment, particularly in the professional context, has contributed to the development of the management system within the Casino group. As such, he proposes in this chapter his vision of benevolence at work and the keys to action to irrigate management.

Chapter written by Christelle BRUYÈRE, Sébastien DINÉ, Frédéric PELLEGRIN ROMEGGIO and Philippe RODET.

11.1. Caring management in a French retail company

11.1.1. *Presentation of the case study*

Casino is a French group in the retail sector, present in several countries through numerous brands and employing several hundred thousand people. Since the beginning of the 1990s, the group has undertaken various social initiatives within its establishments, such as the fight against discrimination, the promotion of diversity and professional equality. More recently, starting in 2009, the group has been fighting against psychosocial risks (PSR). This PSR prevention policy has resulted in the creation of a network of some 2,000 "benevolence officers" and a specific training program involving 8,000 managers. Following this awareness of the impact of PSR on the health of employees and on the performance of the organization, Casino wanted to extend its approach beyond the sole prevention of PSR. Indeed, this first system highlighted the fact that stress and pressure are sometimes wrongly associated with performance by some managers. The Casino group then asked an expert in PSR to help them develop a program to better manage stress at work. The main idea is to promote the idea that it is a good management of the motivation of the employees that allows for reaching collective performance. This has led to a singular approach based on nine action keys for developing employee motivation (see section 11.2).

Since January 2014, these eight (then nine) courses of action have formed the basis of the group's new human resources policy, entitled "*management bienveillant*" (caring management). In addition, the human resources (HR) department wanted to make the caring management approach a fundamental element of the company's strategy, which has already been underway since 2010 with the creation of a CSR department within the HR department. Indeed, CSR is a more legible and unifying concept for all employees and stakeholders. Casino's general objective is to bring all employees to a change in managerial culture by renewing existing guidelines. The challenge is to develop motivation and well-being at work by acting on both managers and all employees through the implementation of a training and support system for caring management.

11.1.2. *The system implemented and its effects*

Since January 2014, nearly 3,000 managers (executives and supervisors) have been trained in "caring management" through a series of conferences led by Dr. Philippe Rodet, as a consultant, and by the Casino Group Training Department team. These conferences were followed by more than 130 round tables organized throughout France, with the aim of exchanging and sharing good managerial practices. A network of 800 “caring” internal listeners was set up at the end of 2015 for all of the group’s employees in stores, warehouses and support services.

These people, the majority of whom are employees, without the need for union membership, have the role of looking out for others, detecting people in distress and helping them by directing them to the right person (e.g. the occupational physician). These volunteers have been trained through two specific training modules and have the possibility of exchanging with each other through an intranet forum and with the consultant via a hotline (2 h of telephone calls per week).

In parallel to the conferences led by the consultant and the “caring” network, other tools were put in place to support the general system and to communicate continuously on the progress of the project:

– A simple and interactive mobile application aimed at supporting managers with numerous tips and an exchange of best practices, videos and quizzes to develop the motivation of his/her team.

– A website mainly dedicated to stress management and the development of personal well-being.

– Online training modules are proposed on the rules of life for the well-being of all in the company, based on videos extracted from the consultant’s seminar.

– A discussion forum has been created around a “caring management” community where everyone can share their managerial experiences.

– A “best practices” newsletter available on the Casino training center platform to help managers implement the keys to motivation.

– In addition, in 2017, to continue raising awareness among managers and appropriation of the keys to motivation, the group organized the first edition of the “*Trophées du management*”. The aim of this operation is to recognize and promote the caring managerial initiatives carried out on a daily basis by managers in all of the group’s subsidiaries.

– Still with the desire to support all managers in the process, a network of “ambassador managers” has been created. This is a sort of mentoring system where the most experienced managers help the new ones.

– A book on caring management within the Casino Group was published internally in May 2016 and distributed to all managers in the company. This book gathers the testimonies of 50 managers and employees on the implementation of the keys of motivation recommended by the consultant. It highlights the company’s strong commitment to this major change in managerial culture. A second book based on the testimonies of employees who participated in a training program oriented toward

"Caring Management" leading to a Master's degree and winners of the "*Trophées du management bienveillant*" will be published in 2021.

In addition, in terms of managerial practices, the Casino group had already established a common reference framework of the company's key values, LIDERS (*leadership, innovation, décision, engagement, responsabilité client, societal*; leadership, innovation, decision-making, commitment, customer responsibility, social responsibility), as well as the managerial attitudes and behaviors that arise from them.

What are the effects? Can we measure them today?

At the end of a 4-year process, a specialized survey institute measured the level of stress and motivation with a representative panel of Casino Group employees. It was found that the level of stress was lower than the estimate in identical structures and that the level of motivation was high, at 51% compared to 28% at the national level.

11.1.3. *The levers and obstacles perceived by field managers*

As a manager, how can you take ownership of the system that has been set up and make it work on a daily basis? Three avenues emerge from the intervention research conducted with the company's managers: a relational lever, a managerial lever and an organizational lever.

The relational lever is activated by managers who are convinced that it is possible to learn benevolence. We have grouped these "relational skills" (Faure and Cucchi 2020) into five themes:

– be alert ("open/listening/altruistic");

– be cheerful ("positive, humorous, relaxed, optimistic");

– to be reflective ("to distance oneself, to question oneself, to evaluate and self-evaluate, humility");

– be responsible ("exemplary", note that exemplarity is a recurring theme in the discourse of managers);

– be respectful of the company's values ("impartial, honest, fair, sincere, authentic, honest").

The second lever then questions the way of managing in a situation. The "caring management" described by the employees is based on participatory management or even the management of collective intelligence. Creating spaces for exchange and time for dialog are determining factors, as is trust, autonomy and recognition. It is also noted that managers can only manage with benevolence if they are "in touch with his or her system": benevolence at work presupposes knowledge of the work of each person and awareness of the repercussions of their actions in a systemic conception. "By taking into account the general context, and by proposing putting quality at the service of business, I have voluntarily chosen to set up a caring quality management system" (Damien[1]). "The implementation of caring management is therefore not linked to a single individual but also relies on a systemic environment that influences and has an impact on its proper application. We can also keep in mind that everyone can act, evolve, change, alert, raise awareness... and it is in these actions that everyone is responsible and an actor in caring management: collectively and in this spirit we can have a positive influence" (Clément).

Finally, the organizational lever consists of having a "caring" work organization. There are several elements that support this: having support from the hierarchy, having a network of resources, and having access to training to develop expertise. However, the managers point out the difficulties in fully using this lever. "Of course, the optimum approach would be to achieve well-being in the workplace, but does this objective rest solely on the individual? The organization of the group, whether technical or managerial, can thwart all the individual efforts made to achieve a caring management style. It is therefore essential to have a comprehensive approach" (Albert).

The levers activated to date within the Casino group are essentially centered on the individual: the group has chosen to initiate benevolence at work by focusing its efforts on training and managerial posture to cultivate the relational know-how of managers. Section 11.2 explains in detail the foundations of the approach developed by the consultant.

11.2. Benevolence at work and the subtle play of hormones

11.2.1. *A medical approach to benevolence*

With a medical background, the consultant working for Casino has naturally based his approach on scientific work in medicine. The objective of the demonstration is to initiate an awareness in the collaborator so that they reinforce their behaviors that tend toward "caring management".

The key to entry is positive emotions, and the work of Barbara Fredrickson (2009) shows that to flourish, human beings need 2.9–13.2 positive emotions for

1 Field managers employed at Casino, assumed name.

each negative emotion. Increasing positive emotions and decreasing negative emotions promote the release of two hormones: oxytocin and endorphins.

11.2.1.1. *Oxytocin*

The consultant for the group mobilizes, for example, a study conducted on dogs to show that if positive emotions are cultivated in this animal, for example, by petting it, its oxytocin level increases. The authors of this study refer to oxytocin as a biomarker of positive emotions. Moreover, in humans, the effects described as those of positive emotions correspond to those of oxytocin: better understanding of complexity, greater sociability, etc.

Furthermore, the work of Professor Paul J. Zak[2] explains that if we show someone that we trust them, we will promote the secretion of oxytocin in this person and thus make them more generous, empathetic and, in a way, happier. Trust is a vector of positive emotions.

11.2.1.2. *Endorphins*

In the same way, the increase in positive emotions and the decrease in negative emotions will promote the secretion of endorphins, which will enable the secretion of dopamine. In an article published in *Neuroscience & Biobehavioral Reviews*, the influence of positive emotions on dopamine secretion is clearly discussed.

> There is now a convergence of evidence to suggest that different regions of the limbic system, including especially ventral striatal dopamine systems, are implemented in an anticipatory (appetitive) positive effecting state (Burgdorf and Panksepp 2006).

The CASINO group consultant also notes that oxytocin will also promote the secretion of dopamine:

> It stimulates the secretion of other neurotransmitters, such as dopamine, which elicit pleasure and encourage the repetition of social behaviors[3].

He also points out that friendship promotes the secretion of oxytocin, a hormone that reduces stress levels. In fact, the higher the level of oxytocin in the blood, the lower

---

2 Paul J. Zak: American neuro-economist, he is currently working on the application of neuro sciences to improve human decision-making and performance.

3 Revue *Cerveau et Psycho*, no. 36, p. 68.

the level of cortisol. A study conducted by Katerina Johnson's team[4] at the University of Oxford and published in April 2016 shows that the power of friendship would go thus far as to promote the secretion of endorphins, our natural morphine (Johnson and Dunbar 2016). Endorphins have a significant ability to decrease pain, and this characteristic was used to measure the influence of endorphins. It was then realized that the more the participants were surrounded, the greater their ability to resist pain; concretely, the more they were surrounded, the more significant the secretions of endorphins were.

The fact that quality social ties promote the secretion of oxytocin and endorphins seems quite logical. When we have quality relationships, we will share our joys and sorrows, increasing positive emotions and decreasing negative emotions. Promoting the right social connections or behaviors is therefore essential to help increase positive emotions and decrease negative emotions.

11.2.1.3. *The effects of oxytocin in the human relationship*

Oxytocin has three interesting actions to highlight. First, it decreases the level of stress, which translates into a decrease in the level of cortisol in the blood. Second, it promotes trust, generosity and empathy, making team cohesion stronger. Finally, it promotes creativity.

11.2.1.4. *The effects of endorphins in the human relationship*

The endorphins will therefore allow the secretion of dopamine, the hormone of pleasure and motivation. The Casino Group consultant emphasizes that the role of dopamine in the pleasure circuits has long been recognized. Dopamine is one of the neuromediators that "arouse pleasure". In support of a study, he shows that pleasure decreases the level of stress hormones (cortisol by 40%, adrenaline by 70%) and increases the release of a protective hormone (growth hormone). Growth hormone protects against possible stress-induced consequences on immunity.

Regarding the influence of dopamine on motivation, it is recalled that blocking dopamine receptors in an animal stops feeding and hydrating itself because it no longer has the necessary motivation to do so.

These elements of argumentation must therefore demonstrate the interest of adopting a mode of caring management by decreasing the level of stress, increasing motivation and thereby strengthening cohesion and improving creativity. To help managers in a more concrete way and to get closer to the professional context, the Casino Group consultant then proposes action levers.

---

4 Katerina Johnson: psychologist, she carries out work at the crossroads of experimental psychology and neuroscience, particularly on social bonds.

11.2.2. *The nine keys to "caring management" proposed*

Each key will be accompanied by explanatory material to reinforce its adoption.

11.2.2.1. *Setting attainable goals with the right level of effort*

This key can be supported by the work of Mihaly Csikszentmihalyi[5]. If the objective is set just above the employee's capabilities, the employee enters a state of "flow", a state of optimal concentration. Since they are in a state of optimal concentration, they will be more successful. By becoming aware of their success, they perceive their usefulness for their department and their company and are therefore better protected from the effects of stress.

Professor Guy Cheron[6], professor of neurophysiology at the Université Libre de Bruxelles, tried to determine which brain waves were associated with success in high-level athletes and how to facilitate the emergence of these waves. It turns out that the presence of alpha waves goes hand in hand with success. For this professor, "the alpha rhythm is the basis of performance". In the professional field, the emission of alpha waves corresponds to the state of "flow". "The combination between the challenge and the ability to meet it can lead us to a state of flow that can generate the best performance" (Cheron 2016).

11.2.2.2. *Giving meaning to objectives, thus helping to feel useful*

Meaning is indeed a powerful way to reduce the effects of stress. Dr. Pierre Gagnon[7], a psychiatrist in Montreal, has shown that if we improve the meaning of life for a seriously ill person, we improve their quality of life because we reduce the effects of stress. Jean-Jacques Breton[8], a Canadian psychiatrist, explains that meaning is a "protective factor" at the psychological level. He is very clear: "If we promote these protective factors, people can improve their ability to cope with stressful events. We can equip them". In addition, meaning is a means to success.

An experiment in the United States is instructive. At universities, there are fundraisers who try to convince companies to donate to fund their students' scholarships. Year after year, the volume of funds raised dropped. When fundraisers

---

5 Mihaly Csikszentmihalyi: Hungarian psychologist who has done a lot of work in the field of positive psychology. He is the author of the successful book *Vivre*.

6 Guy Cheron: Doctor in neurophysiology at the Université Libre de Bruxelles; he has worked with athletes and astronauts to better understand the function of our brain's oscillations.

7 Pierre Gagnon: A psychiatrist specializing in psycho-oncology, psychosomatic medicine and geronto-psychiatry; he works primarily with cancer patients.

8 Jean-Jacques Breton: Psychiatrist and associate professor of clinical psychology; he works on mental disorders and suicidal behavior in young people.

were able to talk to students and see how important it was for them to have a scholarship, the number of phone calls increased by 140%, and the amount of money raised by 400%.

11.2.2.3. *Granting a fair level of freedom of action*

The absence of freedom of action is a source of stress. As Paul Ricœur wrote, "the amputation of the power to act is suffering". Conversely, the right level of autonomy translates into a confidence source of positive emotions. In a group that develops software in Australia, Daniel Pink[9] – an American lawyer who devotes his life to working on the influence of motivation on success – organized the annual Empowerment Day. The idea was to invite each employee to reflect on improvements to their workstation. The result was better relationships between people and more creativity in the design offices.

11.2.2.4. *Showing gratitude or expressing encouragement*

Gratitude, in any form, is a powerful source of positive emotions. It is not always easy to express and is often difficult to receive. On the other hand, there are thanks that mark a life.

As for encouragement, it has many interesting effects. By reinforcing the feeling of personal effectiveness, that is, the confidence that one has in one's abilities, it reduces stress and improves perseverance, self-confidence, optimism and creativity. If you are more optimistic, have more confidence and persevere, you can see the extent to which the encouragements promote success. Regarding the impact on stress, they reduce stress levels by 44% for women and 32% for men. Why this difference? When you encourage someone, you change the expression of one of their genes (OXTR), a gene that codes for an oxytocin (hormone of happiness). Oxytocin is more present in women than in men during a stress reaction.

11.2.2.5. *Ability to transform contempt into consideration*

Contempt is a source of negative emotions, frustration, stress and demotivation. Humans are so sensitive to contempt that sometimes they feel they are being despised when in fact they are not. The most powerful antidote to contempt is consideration. The writer Hervé Bazin expressed the importance of consideration perfectly: "People are thirstier for consideration than for merit". However, the sources of consideration are within reach: greeting a colleague by looking at them, checking up on them, especially when they are suffering, or taking an interest in the

9 Daniel Pink: a lawyer by training; he became a scriptwriter for U.S. Vice President Al Gore from 1995 to 1997, before becoming a journalist and author. He now works on atypical forms of motivation.

success of their children, explaining the keys to their success, and providing the conditions for their fulfillment.

11.2.2.6. *Avoiding inconsistency*

Inconsistency between the project and daily life, between the stated values and everyday behavior, between what is said and what is done. Inconsistency is a source of frustration, tension, disengagement and loss of meaning. On the other hand, the effort made to be consistent will lead to better team cohesion and efficiency. Benjamin Disraeli[10] summarizes in one sentence the influence of the consistency of objectives on success: "The secret of success is the consistency of objectives". Consistency is also a source of health by reducing frustration and therefore stress levels.

11.2.2.7. *Moving from lack of empathy to the ability to care*

The lack of empathy is a source of frustration. Can you imagine the level of frustration of an employee who is told bad news by an HR manager via SMS, without any empathy? Can we imagine the level of frustration of a mother who would be told bad news by a doctor over the phone, without any empathy? Frustrations that will generate demotivation, apathy...

It is important to remember that lack of empathy is accentuated by stress. An experiment conducted by Jeffrey Mogil[11], a professor in the Department of Psychology at McGill University, and his team showed that the more stress we feel, the less empathy we feel toward others. The scientists found that by blocking the main stress hormone, cortisol, participants were more likely to feel empathy toward strangers. Stress decreases the ability to feel empathy, and empathy decreases the effects of stress.

Empathy is a very effective lever to breakdown negative emotions to the point where it sometimes helps to reduce the worst suffering. To express empathy is perhaps to forget what the other person will think of you in order to be only interested in them; finally, it is a sign of love for the other person. In addition, if you "love" the other person, they feel it and that is when they commit themself.

---

10 Benjamin Disraeli: British politician and writer of the 19th century who was twice Prime Minister of the United Kingdom.

11 Jeffrey Mogil: Professor of psychology at McGill University; he is particularly interested in the mechanisms involved in fear, particularly at the level of the nervous system.

Psychiatrist Irvin Yalom[12] defines empathy as "the most powerful tool we have for relating to others".

11.2.2.8. *Transforming perceived injustice into a sense of justice*

Injustice creates frustration, negative emotions, stress and demotivation. In the United States, the cost of demotivation at work due to a lack of fairness is in the billions of dollars each year. Making the effort to be perceived as fair involves the ability to give more compliments than blame and to phrase blame well.

If we point out to a collaborator that what they do in such and such an area is excellent but what they do in another area is not at the same level, they will realize that we can see what they do well and will be more likely to consider us fair.

11.2.2.9. *Recognizing one's own behavioral blunders*

In difficult moments when you have to move quickly, a manager can be too firm with an employee. It is then essential, the next day, to go and see the employee and explain to them that the attitude one had is not good. It is necessary to take the time to discuss and analyze the causes of this incident to see how to prevent it from happening again.

To make it easier to reach out to the other person in a situation that is necessarily complicated, it may be important to think that the other person will be able to forgive.

Some of the behaviors discussed (setting ambitious and realistic goals, explaining the meaning, granting the right level of autonomy, expressing gratitude and encouragement) thereby increase positive emotions. Others (transforming the act of taking into consideration, turning inconsistency into consistency, making sure that lack of empathy gives way to care, cultivating a sense of justice, acknowledging behavioral blunders) are able to decrease negative emotions.

11.3. Discussion and perspective

To return to our original question "caring management and large-scale distribution: a happy marriage?", like any marriage, happiness is cultivated and comes up against the tensions inherent in human nature. The keys to benevolence at work seem easy to activate when considered in isolation. However, in practice, they

---

12 Irvin Yalom: American psychiatrist and author of numerous books. He received the Oscar Pfister Award from the American Psychiatric Association in 2002 for his article "Religion and Psychiatry".

come up against contradictory logics of action. In particular, we can identify three tensions that can hinder benevolence at work.

The first tension expresses the coexistence of contradictory representations of the organization's goals. It is a tension between the intensity of work and the intensification of work. The search for performance leads to work intensification (work overload), which does not respect the intensity of work (need to construct meaning). "Caring" managers are caught between a desire to do their work well by responding ever more quickly to increasing pressure to feed the "management machines" – to use Girin's expression (1983) – while at the same time needing to take time to respond to the demands of a caring position. How can we take the time to build meaning at work (intensity) when the economic and organizational context leaves less time for managers (intensification)? The most exhausting thing is not what we do but what we cannot do.

The second tension, of an identity order, is expressed between seemingly incompatible values, thus leading to a loss of meaning at work. Within the Casino group, as in many companies, two contradictory cultures collide: the culture of a finely assessable short-term financial result and the culture of benevolence whose medium-term to long-term effects on organization are more difficult to assess. Managers are immersed in a system of values based on the demonstration of the result, from dashboards and reporting. At the same time, a postulate of caring management as a vector of performance is disseminated: by managing in a caring way, the actors will be more motivated, and the results will follow. How can a sense of belonging to the culture of a company be developed in the face of instructions perceived as paradoxical by managers?

The third communicative level tension is reflected in the phrase "Be spontaneously caring!" Benevolence then takes the form of a prescription, which makes authentic and spontaneous positive intention impossible (Diné and Giordano 2012). How can I be authentic in my caring approach while responding to a hierarchical prescription (top-down approach)? All behaviors that attempt to respond will automatically be maladaptive: if I respond to the prescription, I am no longer in an "authentic" benevolence (in the sense of a natural or innate disposition). If I do not respond to the prescription, I am not responding to the request.

Caring management is thus similar to a search for a dynamic balance between authentic benevolence, motivated by the disinterested search for the well-being of others, and utilitarian benevolence, whose main objective is to ensure the well-being of workers in the context of their professional activities with a view to the performance. A project to change managerial culture is never free of tensions, as we have emphasized in this chapter. Following Gilbert et al. (2013), we show that "cultural learning is not only about the use of the tool; it is the experience of the tensions between systems of activity that, more than the use of the tool itself, leads to a transformation of the object and the aim of the system of activity". The double dimension of learning, both instrumental and cultural, explains its emergent and dialogical character. It occurs in debates, stories and experience-sharing and develops a situational learning character. To illustrate, many managers tell us that they use the "Caring Management" program when making collective decisions. When a debate leads to a decision that they consider too brutal, the reference to this new managerial culture gives them weight and allows them to bring certain decisions back to "the path of benevolence". If some managers could have had a "caring" management style before this cultural change program was put in place, the latter now offers them a framework to legitimize their "caring" actions. It is important to remember that it takes time for organizational routines to incorporate change.

As a result, if the reality of certain managerial activity systems may differ in certain places from the CASINO group's intention of cultural change, the "Caring Management" system put in place offers managers resources from which they can draw. However, the recent global health crisis was particularly stressful for many employees. Some of the group's employees were forced to telecommute, while another part was forced to stay on site to ensure the supply of stores. On the one hand, managers therefore had to "invent" remote management methods (giving more autonomy to their employees while taking more time to take an interest in their level of stress, in managing their life balance private-professional), and, on the other hand, the managers had to deal with the management of the anxiety-provoking nature of work on site and its risk of contamination by the virus. In this context, the implementation of a preexisting approach to stress and motivation management has found its full meaning, offering each manager a valuable resource. Although benevolence is often reduced to a naïve dimension to "humanize" management, we thus agree with Glaisner and Masclef (2018), who, when benevolence is nourished by a collective and organizational, "allows the worker to face the complexity of his work more effectively, to avoid the feeling of loneliness in the face of the objectives to be achieved and to generate a force of recognition".

11.4. References

Burgdorf, J. and Panksepp, J. (2006). The neurobiology of positive emotions. *Neuroscience & Bio-behavioral Reviews*, 30(2), 173–187.

Cheron, G. (2016). How to measure the psychological "flow"? A neuroscience perspective. *Frontiers in Psychology*, 7, 1823.

Csikszentmihalyi, M. (2006). *Vivre, la psychologie du bonheur*. Robert Laffont, Paris.

Diné, S. and Giordano, Y. (2012). Paul Watzlawick : un regard interactionniste et constructiviste sur les organisations ? In *Les grands inspirateurs de la théorie des organisations – Tome 1*, Germain, O. (ed.). Editions EMS, Caen.

Faure, F. and Cucchi, A. (2020). Quelle caractérisation du savoir-être ? Une revue de la littérature en deux temps. *Revue interdisciplinaire management, homme & entreprise*, 39(2), 3–25.

Fredrickson, B.L. (2009). *Positivity*. Crown, New York.

Gilbert, P., Raulet-Croset, N., Mourey, D., Triomphe, C. (2013). Pour une contribution de la théorie de l'activité au changement organisationnel. *@GRH*, 7(2), 67–88.

Girin, J. (1983). Les machines de gestion. In Le rôle des outils de gestion dans l'évolution des systèmes sociaux complexes, Berry, M. (ed.). Report, Centre de Recherche en Gestion, École polytechnique, Paris.

Glaisner, J. and Masclef, O. (2018). Du management bienveillant à la communauté de travail : le cas Yves Rocher. *@GRH*, 27(2), 13–35.

Johnson, K.A. and Dunbar, R. (2016). Pain tolerance predicts human social network size. *Scientific Reports*, 6, 25267.

Rodet, P. and Desjaques, Y. (2019). *Le management bienveillant. La bienveillance est l'indicateur d'un monde encore humain*. Eyrolles, Paris.

List of Authors

Manel ABDELJALIL-DINÉ
COACTIS
Université Jean Monnet
Saint-Étienne
France

Marc BERNAUD
IFCS
CHU de Saint-Étienne
France

Sandrine BROUSSOULOUX
Direction de la prévention
et de la promotion de la santé
Paris
France

Christelle BRUYÈRE
COACTIS
Université Jean Monnet
Saint-Étienne
France

Annie DEBARD
Côté Travail
Saint-Étienne
France

Sébastien DINÉ
COACTIS
Université Jean Monnet
Saint-Étienne
France

Vanessa FAZAL
CHU de La Réunion
Saint-Denis
France

Julia GUDEFIN
DanaeCare
Saint-Étienne
France

François JUTRAS
ARACT AURA
Lyon
France

Hervé LANOUZIÈRE
INTEFP
and
IGAS
Paris
France

Marie-Cécile LEGAY
IFCS
CHU de Saint-Étienne
France

Nelly MASSARD
COACTIS
Université Jean Monnet
Saint-Étienne
France

Virginie MOISSON
CEMOI
Université de La Réunion
Saint-Denis
France

Pascal MOULETTE
COACTIS
Université Lyon 2
France

Carole MURE
IFSI-IFAS-IFA
CHU de Saint-Étienne
France

Frédéric PELLEGRIN ROMEGGIO
COACTIS
Université Jean Monnet
Saint-Étienne
France

Philippe RODET
Bien-être et Entreprise
Paris
France

Cécile ROMEYER
COACTIS
Université Jean Monnet
Saint-Étienne
France

Martine SÉVILLE
COACTIS
Université Lyon 2
France

André SIMONNET
DanaeCare
Saint-Étienne
France

Florence VICHI
EHPAD
Saint-Victor-sur-Loire
France

Index

A, B, C

D, E, F

H, I, L

M, N

O, P

R, S, T

U, V, W

Other titles from

iSTE

in

Innovation, Entrepreneurship and Management

2022

AOUINAÏT Camille
Open Innovation Strategies (Smart Innovation Set – Volume 39)

BOUCHÉ Geneviève
Productive Economy, Contributory Economy: Governance Tools for the Third Millennium (Innovation and Technology Set – Volume 15)

HELLER David
Valuation of the Liability Structure by Real Options (Modern Finance, Management Innovation and Economic Growth Set – Volume 5)

MATHIEU Valérie
A Customer-oriented Manager for B2B Services: Principles and Implementation

NOËL Florent, SCHMIDT Géraldine
Employability and Industrial Mutations: Between Individual Trajectories and Organizational Strategic Planning (Technological Changes and Human Resources Set – Volume 4)

DE SAINT JULIEN Odile
The Innovation Ecosystem as a Source of Value Creation: A Value Creation Lever for Open Innovation (Diverse and Global Perspectives on Value Creation Set – Volume 4)

SALOFF-COSTE Michel
Innovation Ecosystems: The Future of Civilizations and the Civilization of the Future (Innovation and Technology Set – Volume 14)

VAYRE Emilie
Digitalization of Work: New Spaces and New Working Times (Technological Changes and Human Resources Set – Volume 5)

ZAFEIRIS Konstantinos N, SKIADIS Christos H, DIMOTIKALIS Yannis, KARAGRIGORIOU Alex, KARAGRIGORIOU-VONTA Christina
Data Analysis and Related Applications 1: Computational, Algorithmic and Applied Economic Data Analysis (Big Data, Artificial Intelligence and Data Analysis Set – Volume 9)
Data Analysis and Related Applications 2: Multivariate, Health and Demographic Data Analysis (Big Data, Artificial Intelligence and Data Analysis Set – Volume 10)

2021

ARCADE Jacques
Strategic Engineering (Innovation and Technology Set – Volume 11)

BÉRANGER Jérôme, RIZOULIÈRES Roland
The Digital Revolution in Health (Health and Innovation Set – Volume 2)

BOBILLIER CHAUMON Marc-Eric
Digital Transformations in the Challenge of Activity and Work: Understanding and Supporting Technological Changes (Technological Changes and Human Resources Set – Volume 3)

BUCLET Nicolas
Territorial Ecology and Socio-ecological Transition (Smart Innovation Set – Volume 34)

DIMOTIKALIS Yannis, KARAGRIGORIOU Alex, PARPOULA Christina, SKIADIS Christos H
Applied Modeling Techniques and Data Analysis 1: Computational Data Analysis Methods and Tools (Big Data, Artificial Intelligence and Data Analysis Set - Volume 7)
Applied Modeling Techniques and Data Analysis 2: Financial, Demographic, Stochastic and Statistical Models and Methods (Big Data, Artificial Intelligence and Data Analysis Set – Volume 8)

DISPAS Christophe, KAYANAKIS Georges, SERVEL Nicolas, STRIUKOVA Ludmila
Innovation and Financial Markets
(Innovation between Risk and Reward Set – Volume 7)

ENJOLRAS Manon
Innovation and Export: The Joint Challenge of the Small Company
(Smart Innovation Set – Volume 37)

FLEURY Sylvain, RICHIR Simon
Immersive Technologies to Accelerate Innovation: How Virtual and Augmented Reality Enables the Co-Creation of Concepts
(Smart Innovation Set – Volume 38)

GIORGINI Pierre
The Contributory Revolution (Innovation and Technology Set – Volume 13)

GOGLIN Christian
Emotions and Values in Equity Crowdfunding Investment Choices 2: Modeling and Empirical Study

GRENIER Corinne, OIRY Ewan
Altering Frontiers: Organizational Innovations in Healthcare (Health and Innovation Set – Volume 1)

GUERRIER Claudine
Security and Its Challenges in the 21st Century (Innovation and Technology Set – Volume 12)

HELLER David
Performance of Valuation Methods in Financial Transactions (Modern Finance, Management Innovation and Economic Growth Set – Volume 4)

LEHMANN Paul-Jacques
Liberalism and Capitalism Today

SOULÉ Bastien, HALLÉ Julie, VIGNAL Bénédicte, BOUTROY Éric, NIER Olivier
Innovation in Sport: Innovation Trajectories and Process Optimization (Smart Innovation Set – Volume 35)

UZUNIDIS Dimitri, KASMI Fedoua, ADATTO Laurent
Innovation Economics, Engineering and Management Handbook 1: Main Themes
Innovation Economics, Engineering and Management Handbook 2: Special Themes

VALLIER Estelle
Innovation in Clusters: Science–Industry Relationships in the Face of Forced Advancement (Smart Innovation Set – Volume 36)

2020

ACH Yves-Alain, RMADI-SAÏD Sandra
Financial Information and Brand Value: Reflections, Challenges and Limitations

ANDREOSSO-O'CALLAGHAN Bernadette, DZEVER Sam, JAUSSAUD Jacques, TAYLOR Robert
Sustainable Development and Energy Transition in Europe and Asia (Innovation and Technology Set – Volume 9)

BEN SLIMANE Sonia, M'HENNI Hatem
Entrepreneurship and Development: Realities and Future Prospects (Smart Innovation Set – Volume 30)

CHOUTEAU Marianne, FOREST Joëlle, NGUYEN Céline
Innovation for Society: The P.S.I. Approach (Smart Innovation Set – Volume 28)

CORON Clotilde
Quantifying Human Resources: Uses and Analysis
(Technological Changes and Human Resources Set – Volume 2)

CORON Clotilde, GILBERT Patrick
Technological Change
(Technological Changes and Human Resources Set – Volume 1)

CERDIN Jean-Luc, PERETTI Jean-Marie
The Success of Apprenticeships: Views of Stakeholders on Training and Learning (Human Resources Management Set – Volume 3)

DELCHET-COCHET Karen
Circular Economy: From Waste Reduction to Value Creation
(Economic Growth Set – Volume 2)

DIDAY Edwin, GUAN Rong, SAPORTA Gilbert, WANG Huiwen
Advances in Data Science
(Big Data, Artificial Intelligence and Data Analysis Set – Volume 4)

DOS SANTOS PAULINO Victor
Innovation Trends in the Space Industry
(Smart Innovation Set – Volume 25)

GASMI Nacer
Corporate Innovation Strategies: Corporate Social Responsibility and Shared Value Creation
(Smart Innovation Set – Volume 33)

GOGLIN Christian
Emotions and Values in Equity Crowdfunding Investment Choices 1: Transdisciplinary Theoretical Approach

GUILHON Bernard
Venture Capital and the Financing of Innovation
(Innovation Between Risk and Reward Set – Volume 6)

LATOUCHE Pascal
Open Innovation: Human Set-up
(Innovation and Technology Set – Volume 10)

LIMA Marcos
Entrepreneurship and Innovation Education: Frameworks and Tools (Smart Innovation Set – Volume 32)

MACHADO Carolina, DAVIM J. Paulo
Sustainable Management for Managers and Engineers

MAKRIDES Andreas, KARAGRIGORIOU Alex, SKIADAS Christos H.
Data Analysis and Applications 3: Computational, Classification, Financial, Statistical and Stochastic Methods
(Big Data, Artificial Intelligence and Data Analysis Set – Volume 5)
Data Analysis and Applications 4: Financial Data Analysis and Methods
(Big Data, Artificial Intelligence and Data Analysis Set – Volume 6)

MASSOTTE Pierre, CORSI Patrick
Complex Decision-Making in Economy and Finance

MEUNIER François-Xavier
Dual Innovation Systems: Concepts, Tools and Methods
(Smart Innovation Set – Volume 31)

MICHAUD Thomas
Science Fiction and Innovation Design (Innovation in Engineering and Technology Set – Volume 6)

MONINO Jean-Louis
Data Control: Major Challenge for the Digital Society
(Smart Innovation Set – Volume 29)

MORLAT Clément
Sustainable Productive System: Eco-development versus Sustainable Development (Smart Innovation Set – Volume 26)

SAULAIS Pierre, ERMINE Jean-Louis
Knowledge Management in Innovative Companies 2: Understanding and Deploying a KM Plan within a Learning Organization
(Smart Innovation Set – Volume 27)

2019

AMENDOLA Mario, GAFFARD Jean-Luc
Disorder and Public Concern Around Globalization

BARBAROUX Pierre
Disruptive Technology and Defence Innovation Ecosystems
(Innovation in Engineering and Technology Set – Volume 5)

DOU Henri, JUILLET Alain, CLERC Philippe
Strategic Intelligence for the Future 1: A New Strategic and Operational Approach
Strategic Intelligence for the Future 2: A New Information Function Approach

FRIKHA Azza
Measurement in Marketing: Operationalization of Latent Constructs

FRIMOUSSE Soufyane
Innovation and Agility in the Digital Age
(Human Resources Management Set – Volume 2)

GAY Claudine, SZOSTAK Bérangère L.
Innovation and Creativity in SMEs: Challenges, Evolutions and Prospects
(Smart Innovation Set – Volume 21)

GORIA Stéphane, HUMBERT Pierre, ROUSSEL Benoît
Information, Knowledge and Agile Creativity
(Smart Innovation Set – Volume 22)

HELLER David
Investment Decision-making Using Optional Models
(Economic Growth Set – Volume 2)

HELLER David, DE CHADIRAC Sylvain, HALAOUI Lana, JOUVET Camille
The Emergence of Start-ups
(Economic Growth Set – Volume 1)

HÉRAUD Jean-Alain, KERR Fiona, BURGER-HELMCHEN Thierry
Creative Management of Complex Systems
(Smart Innovation Set – Volume 19)

LATOUCHE Pascal
Open Innovation: Corporate Incubator
(Innovation and Technology Set – Volume 7)

LEHMANN Paul-Jacques
The Future of the Euro Currency

LEIGNEL Jean-Louis, MENAGER Emmanuel, YABLONSKY Serge
Sustainable Enterprise Performance: A Comprehensive Evaluation Method

LIÈVRE Pascal, AUBRY Monique, GAREL Gilles
Management of Extreme Situations: From Polar Expeditions to Exploration-Oriented Organizations

MILLOT Michel
Embarrassment of Product Choices 2: Towards a Society of Well-being

N'GOALA Gilles, PEZ-PÉRARD Virginie, PRIM-ALLAZ Isabelle
Augmented Customer Strategy: CRM in the Digital Age

NIKOLOVA Blagovesta
The RRI Challenge: Responsibilization in a State of Tension with Market Regulation
(Innovation and Responsibility Set – Volume 3)

PELLEGRIN-BOUCHER Estelle, ROY Pierre
Innovation in the Cultural and Creative Industries
(Innovation and Technology Set – Volume 8)

PRIOLON Joël
Financial Markets for Commodities

QUINIOU Matthieu
Blockchain: The Advent of Disintermediation

RAVIX Joël-Thomas, DESCHAMPS Marc
Innovation and Industrial Policies
(Innovation between Risk and Reward Set – Volume 5)

ROGER Alain, VINOT Didier
Skills Management: New Applications, New Questions
(Human Resources Management Set – Volume 1)

SAULAIS Pierre, ERMINE Jean-Louis
Knowledge Management in Innovative Companies 1: Understanding and Deploying a KM Plan within a Learning Organization
(Smart Innovation Set – Volume 23)

SERVAJEAN-HILST Romaric
Co-innovation Dynamics: The Management of Client-Supplier Interactions for Open Innovation
(Smart Innovation Set – Volume 20)

SKIADAS Christos H., BOZEMAN James R.
Data Analysis and Applications 1: Clustering and Regression, Modeling-estimating, Forecasting and Data Mining
(Big Data, Artificial Intelligence and Data Analysis Set – Volume 2)
Data Analysis and Applications 2: Utilization of Results in Europe and Other Topics
(Big Data, Artificial Intelligence and Data Analysis Set – Volume 3)

UZUNIDIS Dimitri
Systemic Innovation: Entrepreneurial Strategies and Market Dynamics

VIGEZZI Michel
World Industrialization: Shared Inventions, Competitive Innovations and Social Dynamics
(Smart Innovation Set – Volume 24)

2018

BURKHARDT Kirsten
Private Equity Firms: Their Role in the Formation of Strategic Alliances

CALLENS Stéphane
Creative Globalization
(Smart Innovation Set – Volume 16)

CASADELLA Vanessa
Innovation Systems in Emerging Economies: MINT – Mexico, Indonesia, Nigeria, Turkey
(Smart Innovation Set – Volume 18)

CHOUTEAU Marianne, FOREST Joëlle, NGUYEN Céline
Science, Technology and Innovation Culture
(Innovation in Engineering and Technology Set – Volume 3)

CORLOSQUET-HABART Marine, JANSSEN Jacques
Big Data for Insurance Companies
(Big Data, Artificial Intelligence and Data Analysis Set – Volume 1)

CROS Françoise
Innovation and Society
(Smart Innovation Set – Volume 15)

DEBREF Romain
Environmental Innovation and Ecodesign: Certainties and Controversies
(Smart Innovation Set – Volume 17)

DOMINGUEZ Noémie
SME Internationalization Strategies: Innovation to Conquer New Markets

ERMINE Jean-Louis
Knowledge Management: The Creative Loop
(Innovation and Technology Set – Volume 5)

GILBERT Patrick, BOBADILLA Natalia, GASTALDI Lise,
LE BOULAIRE Martine, LELEBINA Olga
Innovation, Research and Development Management

IBRAHIMI Mohammed
Mergers & Acquisitions: Theory, Strategy, Finance

LEMAÎTRE Denis
Training Engineers for Innovation

LÉVY Aldo, BEN BOUHENI Faten, AMMI Chantal
Financial Management: USGAAP and IFRS Standards
(Innovation and Technology Set – Volume 6)

MILLOT Michel
Embarrassment of Product Choices 1: How to Consume Differently

PANSERA Mario, OWEN Richard
Innovation and Development: The Politics at the Bottom of the Pyramid
(Innovation and Responsibility Set – Volume 2)

RICHEZ Yves
Corporate Talent Detection and Development

SACHETTI Philippe, ZUPPINGER Thibaud
New Technologies and Branding
(Innovation and Technology Set – Volume 4)

SAMIER Henri
Intuition, Creativity, Innovation

TEMPLE Ludovic, COMPAORÉ SAWADOGO Eveline M.F.W.
Innovation Processes in Agro-Ecological Transitions in Developing Countries
(Innovation in Engineering and Technology Set – Volume 2)

UZUNIDIS Dimitri
Collective Innovation Processes: Principles and Practices
(Innovation in Engineering and Technology Set – Volume 4)

VAN HOOREBEKE Delphine
The Management of Living Beings or Emo-management

2017

AÏT-EL-HADJ Smaïl
The Ongoing Technological System
(Smart Innovation Set – Volume 11)

BAUDRY Marc, DUMONT Béatrice
Patents: Prompting or Restricting Innovation?
(Smart Innovation Set – Volume 12)

BÉRARD Céline, TEYSSIER Christine
Risk Management: Lever for SME Development and Stakeholder Value Creation

CHALENÇON Ludivine
Location Strategies and Value Creation of International Mergers and Acquisitions

CHAUVEL Danièle, BORZILLO Stefano
The Innovative Company: An Ill-defined Object
(Innovation between Risk and Reward Set – Volume 1)

CORSI Patrick
Going Past Limits To Growth

D'ANDRIA Aude, GABARRET Inés
Building 21st Century Entrepreneurship
(Innovation and Technology Set – Volume 2)

DAIDJ Nabyla
Cooperation, Coopetition and Innovation
(Innovation and Technology Set – Volume 3)

FERNEZ-WALCH Sandrine
The Multiple Facets of Innovation Project Management
(Innovation between Risk and Reward Set – Volume 4)

FOREST Joëlle
Creative Rationality and Innovation
(Smart Innovation Set – Volume 14)

GUILHON Bernard
Innovation and Production Ecosystems
(Innovation between Risk and Reward Set – Volume 2)

HAMMOUDI Abdelhakim, DAIDJ Nabyla
Game Theory Approach to Managerial Strategies and Value Creation
(Diverse and Global Perspectives on Value Creation Set – Volume 3)

LALLEMENT Rémi
Intellectual Property and Innovation Protection: New Practices and New Policy Issues
(Innovation between Risk and Reward Set – Volume 3)

LAPERCHE Blandine
Enterprise Knowledge Capital
(Smart Innovation Set – Volume 13)

LEBERT Didier, EL YOUNSI Hafida
International Specialization Dynamics
(Smart Innovation Set – Volume 9)

MAESSCHALCK Marc
Reflexive Governance for Research and Innovative Knowledge
(Responsible Research and Innovation Set – Volume 6)

MASSOTTE Pierre
Ethics in Social Networking and Business 1: Theory, Practice and Current Recommendations
Ethics in Social Networking and Business 2: The Future and Changing Paradigms

MASSOTTE Pierre, CORSI Patrick
Smart Decisions in Complex Systems

MEDINA Mercedes, HERRERO Mónica, URGELLÉS Alicia
Current and Emerging Issues in the Audiovisual Industry
(Diverse and Global Perspectives on Value Creation Set – Volume 1)

MICHAUD Thomas
Innovation, Between Science and Science Fiction
(Smart Innovation Set – Volume 10)

PELLÉ Sophie
Business, Innovation and Responsibility
(Responsible Research and Innovation Set – Volume 7)

SAVIGNAC Emmanuelle
The Gamification of Work: The Use of Games in the Workplace

SUGAHARA Satoshi, DAIDJ Nabyla, USHIO Sumitaka
Value Creation in Management Accounting and Strategic Management: An Integrated Approach
(Diverse and Global Perspectives on Value Creation Set –Volume 2)

UZUNIDIS Dimitri, SAULAIS Pierre
Innovation Engines: Entrepreneurs and Enterprises in a Turbulent World (Innovation in Engineering and Technology Set – Volume 1)

2016

BARBAROUX Pierre, ATTOUR Amel, SCHENK Eric
Knowledge Management and Innovation (Smart Innovation Set – Volume 6)

BEN BOUHENI Faten, AMMI Chantal, LEVY Aldo
Banking Governance, Performance And Risk-Taking: Conventional Banks Vs Islamic Banks

BOUTILLIER Sophie, CARRÉ Denis, LEVRATTO Nadine
Entrepreneurial Ecosystems (Smart Innovation Set – Volume 2)

BOUTILLIER Sophie, UZUNIDIS Dimitri
The Entrepreneur (Smart Innovation Set – Volume 8)

BOUVARD Patricia, SUZANNE Hervé
Collective Intelligence Development in Business

GALLAUD Delphine, LAPERCHE Blandine
Circular Economy, Industrial Ecology and Short Supply Chains (Smart Innovation Set – Volume 4)

GUERRIER Claudine
Security and Privacy in the Digital Era (Innovation and Technology Set – Volume 1)

MEGHOUAR Hicham
Corporate Takeover Targets

MONINO Jean-Louis, SEDKAOUI Soraya
Big Data, Open Data and Data Development (Smart Innovation Set – Volume 3)

MOREL Laure, LE ROUX Serge
Fab Labs: Innovative User (Smart Innovation Set – Volume 5)

PICARD Fabienne, TANGUY Corinne
Innovations and Techno-ecological Transition
(Smart Innovation Set – Volume 7)

2015

CASADELLA Vanessa, LIU Zeting, DIMITRI Uzunidis
Innovation Capabilities and Economic Development in Open Economies
(Smart Innovation Set – Volume 1)

CORSI Patrick, MORIN Dominique
Sequencing Apple's DNA

CORSI Patrick, NEAU Erwan
Innovation Capability Maturity Model

FAIVRE-TAVIGNOT Bénédicte
Social Business and Base of the Pyramid

GODÉ Cécile
Team Coordination in Extreme Environments

MAILLARD Pierre
Competitive Quality and Innovation

MASSOTTE Pierre, CORSI Patrick
Operationalizing Sustainability

MASSOTTE Pierre, CORSI Patrick
Sustainability Calling

2014

DUBÉ Jean, LEGROS Diègo
Spatial Econometrics Using Microdata

LESCA Humbert, LESCA Nicolas
Strategic Decisions and Weak Signals

2013

HABART-CORLOSQUET Marine, JANSSEN Jacques, MANCA Raimondo
VaR Methodology for Non-Gaussian Finance

2012

DAL PONT Jean-Pierre
Process Engineering and Industrial Management

MAILLARD Pierre
Competitive Quality Strategies

POMEROL Jean-Charles
Decision-Making and Action

SZYLAR Christian
UCITS Handbook

2011

LESCA Nicolas
Environmental Scanning and Sustainable Development

LESCA Nicolas, LESCA Humbert
Weak Signals for Strategic Intelligence: Anticipation Tool for Managers

MERCIER-LAURENT Eunika
Innovation Ecosystems

2010

SZYLAR Christian
Risk Management under UCITS III/IV

2009

COHEN Corine
Business Intelligence

ZANINETTI Jean-Marc
Sustainable Development in the USA

2008

CORSI Patrick, DULIEU Mike
The Marketing of Technology Intensive Products and Services

DZEVER Sam, JAUSSAUD Jacques, ANDREOSSO Bernadette
Evolving Corporate Structures and Cultures in Asia: Impact of Globalization

2007

AMMI Chantal
Global Consumer Behavior

2006

BOUGHZALA Imed, ERMINE Jean-Louis
Trends in Enterprise Knowledge Management

CORSI Patrick *et al.*
Innovation Engineering: the Power of Intangible Networks

Printed and bound by CPI Group (UK) Ltd, Croydon, CR0 4YY
13/09/2026
14961041-0003